MYTHS AND LEGENDS
OF INDIA

D1048749

TO

A. E. M.

MYTHS AND LEGENDS
OF INDIA

AN INTRODUCTION TO THE STUDY OF HINDUISM

BY

J. M. MACFIE, M.A.

"WHATEVER the wise man thought and whatever in his philosophy was the instruction which he imparted to his peers, when he dealt with the world about him, he taught his intellectual inferiors a scarcely modified form of the creed of their fathers. . . . The elasticity of his philosophy admitted the whole world of gods, as a temporary reality, into his pantheistic scheme. . . . He himself believed in these spiritual powers, and in the usefulness of serving them. It is true that he believed in their eventual doom, but so far as man was concerned, they were practically real. . . . Hindu pantheism includes polytheism with its attendant patrolatry, demonology, and consequent ritualism."

HOPKINS' *The Religions of India.*

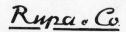

First published 1993
Third impression 1996

Published by
Rupa & Co
15 Bankim Chatterjee Street, Calcutta 700 073
135 South Malaka, Allahabad 211 001
P. G. Solanki Path, Lamington Road, Bombay 400 007
7/16, Ansari Road, Daryaganj, New Delhi 110 002

Printed in India by
Gopsons Papers Ltd
A-28, Sector IX
Noida 201 301

Rs 100

ISBN 81-7167-131-4

PREFACE.

THE literature from which these myths and legends have been chosen is of very great extent. The excellent translations of the Rāmāyana and the Mahābhārata, prepared under the editorship of Mr. M. N. Dutt, alone occupy five large volumes of more than eight thousand closely printed pages. And the present writer has to acknowledge, that in making his selection he has confined himself to what he considers the most interesting and characteristic narratives. In doing so, he has passed over much that is insipid, and also much that is unsuitable for reproduction. But it is hoped that what has been chosen will reveal the essential nature of Hinduism, in its strength as well as in its weakness. There are writers, who in their interpretation of Hinduism seem deliberately to ignore its lower elements : there are others, who in their readiness to criticise have failed to do justice to its merits : while it has also suffered at the hands of those who have offered to the public little more than its shell, in what are sometimes described as *translations* of India's epics, in slim volumes of less than two hundred pages, books which can afford no conception or understanding of what those great storehouses of Hindu thought and feeling really contain. This last defect is specially glaring in relation to the moral and philosophical teaching, which Hinduism has always sought to convey to its adherents. And in Part Two of this work, an effort has been made to correct that defect by the presentation of parables and legends which should enable the reader to appreciate what constitute the most vital, and in some respects, the most salutary influences of Hinduism.

Some of the legends described in the following pages have already appeared in *A Summary of the Mahābhārata* and *The Rāmāyana of Vālmīki*. I have to thank the publishers, The Christian Literature Society for India, Madras, for permission to reproduce them in this work.

J. M. MACFIE.

CONTENTS.

PART TWO.

INTRODUCTION.

THE literature of Hinduism is primarily contained in the two great epics of India, the *Rāmāyana* and the *Mahā-bhārata*, and in the *Purānas*. That statement does not ignore the fact that the roots of the tree of Hinduism are to be found in a still earlier literature, in the *Hymns of the Vedas*, the ritual of the *Brāhmanas* and the philosophic speculations of the *Upanishads*.[1] But it has too often been the case that those who sought to understand India's religions have been detained so long studying the foundations, that they have never got the length of examining the building itself. And it is the building itself which the succeeding pages seek to explain, not by means of analysis and exposition, but by setting forth in a series of stories taken from the literature itself, what men and women thought and said and did. The literature which is here employed is itself very ancient. It is true that the hymns of the *Rig-Veda* probably belong to a date not later than 1500 B.C. But both the epics, the *Rāmāyana* and the *Mahābhārata*, though neither of them may have been completed in their present form before the fifth century A.D., certainly began to be composed nearly a thousand years earlier, and some of the legends they contain are earlier still.

In a book such as this no purpose would be served by seeking to bridge the gulf which divides the teaching of the Vedas from the epics and the *Purānas*. In the

[1] See Note A on "The Sacred Books of India."

ix

notes some attempt is made to show how the germs of certain legends and the sources of certain theories and practices are to be found in the earlier literature.[1] Nor must it be forgotten that the more ancient portions of the epics are as old as some of the *Upanishads*. But while that is so, the student of both periods recognises that in passing from the Vedas to the epics he is passing to a new world, where new gods rule and where new ideas have taken root and flourish.

This is specially manifest with regard to the gods. " There are thirty-three gods," says the *Rig-Veda*; and the *Shatapatha Brāhmana*, which is some centuries later than the *Rig-Veda*, says: " There are thirty-three gods, and Prajāpati is the thirty-fourth." But in one of the oldest legends which the epics contain, while the thirty-three gods still receive lip-service, three new gods have already emerged to whom the whole future of Hinduism belongs. These are Brahmā the creator, who is the successor of Prajāpati, and Vishnu and Shiva, who were destined to. push even Brahmā aside in the estimate of later worshippers. It is true that Vishnu was one of the thirty-three gods, and so also was Shiva under the older name of Rudra, but their functions and attributes are entirely different. Along with Brahmā the creator, they go to form the Hindu triad, in which Vishnu plays the part of the preserver, and Shiva of the destroyer god. And as we proceed, we shall find that these three are reckoned as manifestations of Brahm the universal Spirit.

As he reads the earlier legends the reader may be disposed to doubt that statement. Brahmā, in particular, seems to play an important part. He appears constantly as the court of appeal to whom gods and men hasten in

---

[1] Two legends, "A Man Sacrifice" and "The Flood," are given at unusual length in the *Brāhmanas*. To show the contrast, they have been placed in the text alongside the same legends taken from the epics.

their difficulties and sorrows. This god is manifestly endowed with great powers, for do we not find him indulging in his fatal propensity of granting the most impossible and embarrassing boons. That is true. But it is still more true that once these boons have been granted, it is to Vishnu the other celestials and Brahmā himself are finally compelled to turn. And Vishnu never fails them. It is Vishnu who assumes the form of a boar, and raises the earth out of the waters in which it has been submerged. It is Vishnu who changes himself into a tortoise to enable the gods and demons to carry to a successful issue the churning of the ocean. And it is Vishnu who descends to the earth in the person of Rāma and slays the demon whom Brahmā's thoughtless promises have endowed with invincible strength. Indeed there are recorded no less than nine incarnations of Vishnu in his capacity of the preserver god, and each of them is represented as an act of the first importance.

It is the same with Shiva. The *Rāmāyana* has not much to say about that god. This poem is so peculiarly devoted to Vishnu that it presumably wishes to say as little as it can about a divinity who was to prove such a serious rival to its own special deity. But in the impartial pages of the *Mahābhārata*, though Vishnu for a large portion of the epic seems to be reckoned as the greater god, Shiva also is spoken of in language which claims for him a rank equally lofty. Indeed it is in the *Mahābhārata* that we find the beginnings of those later panegyrics which are to be found so frequently in the sectarian *Purānas*, where it is declared in turn that each of these two deities is the great and only god, and that he includes within himself all the attributes and powers belonging to every member of the Hindu pantheon, even identifying him with the Supreme Spirit, the soul of the universe, the eternal Brahm.

But to return for a moment to the lesser deities. Their frequent mention in the epics and the *Purānas* would seem to militate against the idea that their power has waned. This objection is specially true of Indra. He still ranks as king of heaven ; he takes a prominent place in the myths and legends which are recorded ; from time to time he goes on errands of importance to sages and others ; and he often leads the hosts of heaven against those who invade their rights. But the very fact that he and the other Vedic gods so often sustain defeat and have to be delivered by Vishnu, proves that their garlands are withered and that Brahmā, Vishnu and Shiva are the gods with whom the Hindu has learned to reckon. And as has been said, Brahmā also is past his best. The very fact that he is called the grandfather seems to show that his day is done. He has retired from active service. No doubt he created the worlds, and men and gods look to him as the source from which they derived their existence. But the time has come when more powerful beings must be conciliated or adored, and it is for that reason that Vishnu the preserver and Shiva the destroyer became the special objects of men's worship.

It is only in the later portions of the epics that their authors link the three gods together as creator, preserver and destroyer, in what some writers are pleased to call the Hindu Trinity. In the *Purānas*, however, which are in parts at least several centuries later, we find this phraseology in frequent use. In the *Vishnu Purāna*, for example, which, as its name implies, is devoted to the worship of the preserver god, the three are regularly united. But they are united with a purpose, and this purpose is to show that Vishnu is the eternal Spirit, who as Brahmā creates the worlds, as himself preserves them, and as Shiva destroys them. But the identification of these three great gods with the Supreme Spirit does not content

the author of the *Purāna*. The pantheism, which manifested itself in the later Vedas and which was pronounced
in the *Upanishads*, and is, of course, not absent from the
epics, declares that lesser gods and demons, animals
and men, indeed the whole universe from Brahmā to a
tree, are all parts of Vishnu.

Of these pantheistic ideas the reader will get a variety
of illustrations taken both from the *Mahābhārata* and the
Purānas, especially in the second part of this book. But
it is worth while observing, and observing with some
emphasis, that not even in a philosophic poem like the
Bhagavadgītā, which has been inserted in the sixth book
of the *Mahābhārata*, can we find a thorough-going pantheism. To use Mr. Hopkins' phrase, it is at best a poly-
theistic pantheism. That is to say, the existence of none
of the gods is ever denied. They are as real as men are,
as real as demons and animals are. It is true that none of
them are immortal, but they live for a very long time.
A day of Brahmā is equal to more than four thousand
million years, and Brahmā is to live for a hundred years,
each of which years is to be composed of such lengthy and
supernatural days. This is a real life, and so too with the
other gods. They live for one of Brahmā's days, that is,
for the duration of a universe. With the destruction of
the universe their life comes to an end, and when the work
of creation is resumed they are reborn, it may be as gods,
it may be as men. There is one being only who never dies,
and that is the eternal Brahm, with whom the followers of
Shiva and Vishnu identify their own particular god ; and
though the object of the *Bhagavadgītā* is to show that the
worship of Krishna the incarnation of Vishnu alone secures
the highest perfection and delivers those devoted to him
from the burden of rebirth, it quite as clearly recognises
that those who worship the gods, go to the gods and enjoy
in the celestial regions the celestial pleasures which these

divine beings are able to bestow (ix. 20). If this fact
were kept more firmly in mind, there would be less time
spent arguing about the amount of theism which is to be
found in the sacred books of India. There have been
many approaches thereto. In the fervour of their devotion
to their own particular god, many pious souls have for
the moment forgotten everything and everybody except
the object of their worship. But when the glow of their
ardour has somewhat cooled, the old thoughts reassert
themselves and the ancient gods are restored. Few poets
have written more beautifully than Tulsidās. He lived
in the time of Shakespeare. There have been few who
have manifested a deeper love for the god they adored
than Tulsidās shows for Rāma the incarnation of Vishnu.
"Rāma," he says, "is the holy God of supreme wisdom
and bliss, the bridge over the ocean of existence, the Lord
of the universe," and he cries out in touching words,
"They who never ask for anything but simply love you,
in their hearts abide for ever, for that is your very home."
But the Rāma of whom and to whom this is said is revealed
to us in another passage of the same book and in the same
section of the book as a worshipper of Shiva, and not only
so, but Rāma tells a penitent sage to repeat Shiva's
hundred names, and his soul will be relieved. He gives
as a reason for this advice the statement that there is no
one so dear to him as Shiva, "He on whom Shiva will not
show mercy shall never know true love to me. He who
loves not Shiva's lotus feet can never dream of pleasing
Rāma." As for the lesser gods, Tulsidās speaks with a
frankness which is never manifest in either the epics or
the *Purānas*. But he never doubts their real existence,
and in the many legends which he relates, allows himself
to return to an unabashed and primitive polytheism.

One often wonders why the development of Indian
thought should have been so fatally arrested. And

probably 'the explanation of that problem will be found
in the fact that the Hindu has always clung to a belief in
transmigration and its associated doctrine of *karma*. The
individual soul never dies. It passes from body to body,
from form to form, and each life that it lives is controlled
by the deeds that it performed in a former birth. These
accumulated deeds are the *karma* which account for what
any one is in his present existence. The soul may rise or
fall in the scale of being. The low caste man may rise if
his deeds have been of a high quality. He may eventually
become a Brāhmin, though the epic says that millions of
years must pass before such a lofty state can be achieved.
In course of time he may hope to become a god, but on
the other hand he may descend to a lower depth than
even that of an outcaste. He may be born as a beast,
as a demon or as a tree. In early Vedic times this terrible
belief had no place in Indian thought, and men believed
that when they died they went to live happily with the
gods : and the Hindu still believes that as a reward for
his sacrifices and piety he will be admitted to heaven.
But even in heaven he knows that he will not live for
ever. When his merit is exhausted he must return to
earth, once more to resume the weary round of birth and
death. The epics speak of the soul having to live through
countless ages. The modern Hindu has somewhat reduced
the number of these cycles, but even he acknowledges that
the burden of each soul is not less than eight million four
hundred thousand births. How to escape from that burden
is therefore his not unnatural cry, and as these pages will
reveal, the religious man has sought for and devised a variety
of methods by which to save his soul. The most ancient
method, and one which still holds the field for the more
prosaic worshipper, was to offer sacrifices to the gods, to
practise penance and asceticism, to become the father of
a son who would rescue his ancestors from hell, and to

fulfil the duties of the caste to which he belonged. These
and other similar rules constitute the way of works (*karma
mārga*), and were calculated to raise the worshipper to the
skies, securing for him the happiness of heaven. That he
would have eventually to return to earth, the worshipper
knew very well, and he was often content to think so. But
as time went on the weariness of life settled on his soul
and he found relief in two directions. One of these was
by the way of love and devotion to a particular deity, and
this was the *bhakti mārga*. We see it in the story of the
youth who was changed into a star. We see it in its
grosser form in the devotion of the milkmaids to Krishna,
and we see it in its highest form in the devotion of those
who looked to Rāma as their eternal friend and helper.
There was an element of pantheism even in this very
personal devotion, but it never satisfied those of a more
philosophic disposition, with the result that a third way
was evolved : the way of knowledge (*gyāna mārga*). The
advocate of devotion, no doubt, was convinced that the
deity he loved would receive him for ever; but the advocate
of knowledge had as his ideal the belief that it was only
by his method, when by virtue of this knowledge the soul
was able to say "there is no other than Vishnu; he is
I, he is thou ; he is all ; this universe is his form," that it
would secure absorption in the universal Spirit. The
legend entitled "The True Heaven" gives clear expression
to that belief : Mudgala was offered heaven and refused
to go. He had no desire for the society of the gods. He
would accept nothing which did not promise that he would
never require to be reborn. That condition we are told
is *nirvāna*. From several of the legends we can see that
for a long time this new teaching was looked upon with
suspicion and disapproval, and men declared that it was
no better than extinction. While those who lived by
sacrifice and penance, who put their trust in *works* and

hoped for a happy hereafter, were not filled with enthusiasm at the thought that, as far as their future was concerned, they could only be compared to rivers whose waters are merged in the sea.

That these three ways were followed in the days of the epics and *Purānas* is very manifest from a study of those books, and it is equally true to say that they are followed at the present hour. The majority continue to travel along the way of works. The sacrifice of animals has largely ceased except among the worshippers of Shiva and some of the more debased deities. But pilgrimages, penance and gifts, the worship of the gods and the spirits of the dead, with adherence to the duties of one's caste, are still reckoned as the way which will lead at least to a higher state and help to reduce the number of rebirths. The way of devotion has not failed, however, to retain its adherents, and though the followers of Krishna and Shiva have not unnaturally wandered into devious and unclean paths, those devoted to Rāma have often maintained a lofty form of piety which has not failed to show fruit in their lives. But it is equally true that there are others who believe that they have discovered a more excellent way, and though they bow their heads in the house of Rimmon and conform to the customs of their race and caste, they would accept the teaching of the *Laws of Manu* as the expression of their own thoughts. "The Self alone is the multitude of the gods ; the universe rests on the Self. . . . He who thus recognises the Self through the Self in all created beings, becomes equal minded towards all, and enters Brahm, the highest state " (xii. 119, 125).

If the reader asks in what further directions the Hindu has changed or modified his creed since the epics and the *Purānas* were written, attention may be called to the following points : Asceticism is of a much milder type.

Quite apart from the impossibility of seeking to emulate
the myriads of years through which the holy men of
ancient days continued to practise their austerities, we
find that it is the exception and not the rule for devotees
to live in retirement. The forests, which, if we are to
believe the ancient books, were once full of men and women
devoted to the study of the Vedas and the ascetic life,
are now empty. And it is only at the great festivals
that the Yogi and his confrères—and they are comparatively few in number—draw crowds of wondering spectators to watch them as they hang suspended head downwards from a tree, or sit between the five fires exposed
to the broiling heat of the midday sun. But asceticism
as manifested in fasts and vigils is still recognised as a
virtue calculated to obtain the object of one's desires.
The elaborate sacrifices, too, are a thing of the past.
The horse in certain parts of the country still receives at
certain periods of the year a modified amount of worship ;
but though the belief may still be accepted in theory
because it is to be found in their inspired writings, no
one would suggest that the sacrifice of that animal removes
all sin. The buffalo, perhaps as a substitute for the cow
whose sanctity is as great as ever, is still sometimes offered
up as a victim ; while the daily slaughter of goats, especially
in connection with the worship of Shiva and his consort
at the Durgā festival and elsewhere, is one of the most
objectionable features in the Hinduism of the present
day. That the gods were always worshipped by means
of idols and other emblems is manifest from the epics
and *Purānas*, but it is equally plain that that form of
worship was not specially obtrusive. Such is not now
the case. The whole country is crowded with temples
and idols. The revolting and obscene symbol of Shiva
meets the eye in every street, while there is no more
popular picture exposed for sale than that of this deity's

wife, wearing a necklace of human skulls and drinking blood. As for the celestials, so often spoken of as the thirty-three, they have gone on increasing by multiples of that figure and now stand at three hundred and thirty millions of gods and godlings.

The Brāhmin has not failed to keep his place at the head of the social system, and by his exceptional ability he continues to wield an influence out of all relation to his numbers. But his claim to be reckoned as equal or even superior to the gods, if it ever was acknowledged, is certainly ignored. On the other hand, the members of the fourth caste, and in particular the fifty million out-castes, one-fifth of the Hindu population, have suffered grievously in the interval. From several legends we can see how the Chandāla, that is, the offspring of a Brāhmin woman and a Shūdra, was held in great contempt. It was always reckoned as particularly obnoxious for a woman to associate with a man of lower caste. But in the days of the epics, members of the higher castes could marry wives from those beneath them and their children were sometimes considered to share their father's rank. All such ideas are now condemned, and the children of mixed marriages are outside the pale. That the hardening process had already begun, even in the *Rāmāyana*, is manifest when we compare two stories told in the life of Rāma. Rāma's father, when hunting in the forest, happened to wound an ascetic who was the child of a mixed marriage. The monarch was heartbroken and begged the holy man's forgiveness, which he graciously gave. But the point of the narrative is this : that a celestial car came for and carried off the ascetic to heaven. In strange contrast to this story we have another, mani- festly of later date, that tells of how, when it was dis- covered that a Shūdra was practising asceticism, Rāma went to his hermitage and cut off the presumptuous man's

head. The explanation for such drastic treatment, of
course, was that asceticism was only permissible to members
of the first three castes, and no doubt that *is* the teaching
of the epics and the *Purānas* taken as a whole. But it is
a teaching which, in those days at least, was not always
observed. It is a teaching, however, which is enforced
to-day, and nothing has done so much to hamper India's
progress as the treatment which is meted out to the
depressed classes. Prevented by social pressure from
sending their children to the government schools which
they help to maintain, forbidden to enter the temples
of the gods they are supposed to worship, or to make use
of the wells frequented by people of the higher castes,
debarred even in some places from travelling along certain
streets because not only their contact but their shadow
defiles : these are the descendants of the outcaste tribal
chieftain whom Rāma the incarnation of Vishnu folded
to his breast. Our use of the Portuguese word *caste*
obscures the fact that the Sanskrit equivalent *varna*
means colour, and that in consequence the people of India
have continued to insist on a colour bar, the most rigorous
and cruel that the world has ever known ; and it would
seem here also that the increasingly severe attitude
adopted towards the low caste and the outcaste is due
to the increasing hold which the doctrine of transmigration has taken upon the Indian people. Caste and transmigration, at least when associated with a belief in *karma*,
are inextricably mingled. If we believe that a man has
been born as an outcaste because of some evil that he did
in a former life—and the evil may have been of an entirely
ceremonial kind—we are tempted to think that we are
assisting the *eternal law* when we tighten the chains that
bind him. And if, on the other hand, a high caste man
believes that his superior position is due to the fact that
he is being rewarded for the good deeds and the good life

of a previous existence which he cannot recollect, he is not unwilling to assist heredity in seeing to it that his reward shall be complete.

With regard to the treatment of women the readers of the five legends beginning with *Shakuntalā* will be disposed to think that it has not improved with the passing of the centuries. And their opinion is in many respects justified. It is true that we are told over and over again that a woman's husband is her highest god, and that her chief object in life is to serve him. But the story of *Rāma and Sītā* goes to show to what heights a woman could attain more than two thousand years ago in India. Sītā is the best drawn character in the *Rāmāyana*. She is a much finer character than her husband, better even than her brother-in-law Lakshmana. She is twice most unjustly condemned, and her strong and noble nature is best revealed when, in response to the cruel suspicions of her husband and his subjects, she faces the test of the burning fire and seeks refuge in the earth which opens to receive her. There is no cloistered virtue in Sītā's life. She is far removed from the evils of the purda system and the degradations of polygamy. She lived a free life in the forest, the single wife of a husband who, despite his later foolishness, loved her and held her in reverence. The man who drew the character of Sītā had no low opinion of women. One would even venture to suggest that, when he makes Rāma and the people of Ayodhyā treat her so badly, he is showing us, not the fickleness of women but the ingratitude of man. But when we read these legends which set forth women at their best, and present, as the writer thinks, very beautiful pictures of married love, we must remember that there is another side to all this. To prevent misunderstanding, some illustrations of that other side are given in the notes. According to the *Laws of Manu*, women are devoid of all natural

affection, fickle in temper and essentially evil minded.
Love of dress, love of ease and sleep are the appointed
lot of the female sex. In the *Mahābhārata*, too, there are
many passages equally strong. No woman, we are told,
is fit for independence. She is only pure so long as she is
not tempted. Destruction, death and hell, the poison of
the snake, the sharpness of the razor, the vehemence of
fire, are all combined in the person of a woman. Once
in her toils no man can escape. They were created for
no other purpose than to deceive men. Happily we can
well believe that the love of a man for his wife often rose
superior to these lugubrious utterances, but so long as
polygamy is practised and women are kept in seclusion,
we must believe that the sentiments just quoted are more
or less operative.

In the preparation of this book it has been necessary
to give the larger place to myths and legends dealing with
gods and *rishis*, and for the simple reason that it is with
gods and *rishis* that the sources from which our stories
are drawn chiefly deal. But there are also tales of another
kind, and they are to be found in the second part of the
book. These stories have to do primarily with men and
women, and not with gods and supernatural men. They
tell us of their thoughts and fears, their joys and sorrows,
their speculations about this life and the hereafter. They
show us what was taught about meekness and temperance,
about kindness to man and beast, about patience and
self-control. They dwell on the dangers of anger and
pride ; on the beauty of truth and purity ; and much of
all this, though often somewhat negative in tone and too
ready to dwell on virtues of a passive kind, is teaching
that has seldom been surpassed outside the pages of the
New Testament. There is other teaching of the same
order in the volumes from which these legends have been
taken, but as far as it was possible all that is best has found

a place in this selection. And this has been done for two reasons. The Indian, even the well-educated Indian, is only too often ignorant of his own treasures. They lie hidden in a mass of puerile and sometimes repulsive rubbish, while the practice of treating everything as equally inspired leads him, as it has led people of other countries, to reckon the jewel and the paste, the false and the true, as of equal worth.

But the second reason has to do with Western students of Hinduism. Too many of the books written about India have dwelt at length on her philosophies and her religions, on her sectarian rivalries, on her fasts and festivals, and in their eagerness to discuss these things they have failed to consider as they should the life itself which is being lived, the opinions and actions common to men and women of good will. India has always been remarkable for the appositeness and worth of her *Nīti shlokas* or moral maxims, and we are indebted to writers like Muir and Monier Williams for making us acquainted with them. But when the outsider wonders how a people, bound hand and foot, as we reckon, to an unprofitable polytheism, can be so attractive in their daily lives, governed by principles of action which never seemed to influence their gods, he will find the explanation in the fact that the Hindu has lived a double life. When he returns to his home from the temple of Krishna, the god who played tricks on Indra and sported with the milkmaids, or from bowing before the phallic emblem of Shiva " the blessed god of curst attire," the Hindu has no intention, in most cases at least, of following the example of gods who, with the exception of Rāma, are possessed of lower moral qualities than his own. In fact, some of his holy books have already warned him of the danger of doing so. " Revere the actions of Krishna," says one of them, " but do not give your mind to the doing of them." Whatever the gods may do, whatever some of the specially distinguished *rishis* may have done, the householder knows that such deeds are not for him. He may give you a most illogical and unsatisfactory explanation and say, as he does say in one of their commonest proverbs, *Sāmarthi ko dosh nahin hai* (The powerful can do what they please and it is not reputed sin). But happily with man it is different. His moral instincts have told him that there is something better than that. He may not have risen to the conception of a God who is both righteous and pure. Those who care to criticise would probably assert that his pantheism, no less than his polytheism, renders that impossible. But God fulfils Himself in many ways, and India has heard God speaking to her soul, with the result that there has been expressed for her in living parable and legend that wonderful variety of moral teaching which has helped to make her people what they are.

MYTHS AND LEGENDS
OF INDIA.

PART ONE.

I.

THE CHURNING OF THE OCEAN.

"The demons were the older brothers of the gods, and were conquered by the trickery of their younger brothers."—*Mahābhārata*, iii. 33.
60.

In the golden age, when the world was young, neither
the gods nor their half-brothers, the demons, were immortal. Like other creatures, they were subject to old
age and death. This was a defect in their natures which
they were resolved to remove. A conference of the
interested parties was accordingly held on the slopes of
Mount Meru. It was presided over by their grandfather,
Brahmā, the creator god. After long consideration, they
came to the conclusion that if they churned the Sea of
Milk they would obtain a liquor called *amrita*, which
conferred immortality on every one who drank it. In
reaching this decision, gods and demons received great
assistance from their grandfather, who dwelt on the
necessity of their obtaining the co-operation of Vishnu.
Indeed, one narrative says it was that mighty deity who
first suggested that they should churn the ocean, and

I

promised that many other things in addition to *amrita*
would be secured as well.

Now in those days both gods and demons were equally
eminent for piety and virtue. They were the sons of the
same father, though by different mothers. Their father
was a very eminent *rishi*, and their mothers were sisters,
the daughters of an equally pious and eminent sage, who,
like their sire, was one of the god Brahmā's mind-born
sons. It was therefore very natural that, before they
set out upon their task, it should be agreed that each
should share equally in the product of their toil. It was
a long journey to the Sea of Milk. For that ocean is
the sixth of the seven oceans which in ever-widening
circles lie beyond our world. When they reached
their destination, they told the Sea of Milk what they
intended doing, and said they hoped their action would
not cause her any inconvenience. The Ocean replied that
she was strong enough to stand the agitation which their
activities would occasion to her, but her consent was
conditional on their agreeing to give her a share of the
amrita when it was produced.

Before operations could begin a churning pole was
necessary, and for that purpose gods and demons decided
to use a mountain called Mandara. It was 77,000 miles
high, with roots that went an equal distance into the .
earth. When they tried to uproot it, however, they
found that their united efforts were of no avail. They
therefore went to their grandfather and Vishnu who were
sitting together, and said they had been foiled at the
very beginning of their undertaking, and asked what they
were to do. Vishnu, however, told them they were not to
worry. The great snake Ananta would soon uproot the
mountain for them. And so indeed it proved. Ananta
uprooted the mountain with the greatest ease, for was
he not a manifestation of Vishnu ? and the brothers soon

placed it in position in the midst of the Sea. No difficulty was experienced in securing a churning cord. Another serpent, Vasuki, agreed to act in that capacity. For more than a thousand years, gods and demons worked at their task. The whirling mountain caused great havoc among the denizens of the ocean, many thousands of them being crushed to death, while the heat it engendered by its rapid movement consumed vast multitudes of the animals that dwelt on its sides. Indeed, the whole mountain, with all the beasts and birds that lived on it, would have been destroyed had Indra not come to the rescue and extinguished the flames with great torrents of rain. Nor was the snake, Vasuki, at all comfortable or pleased with his ignoble and painful task. The gods had hold of his tail and the demons of his head, and as they pulled him back and forward, back and forward for a thousand years, he poured forth streams of venom from his angry fangs. This poison swept along the ground and finally over the whole earth like a mighty river, threatening to engulf the entire universe and carry to destruction gods and demons, animals and men. In their distress the toilers once more called out for help. On this occasion they prayed to Shiva, the god of destruction. And when their plea was seconded by Vishnu, he heard their prayer and drank up the poison. Nor did this mighty draught do him the slightest harm. But it was noted ever after, that it left a blue mark on his throat, and to this day his worshippers call him the blue-throated god, in remembrance of the mighty service he rendered to creation so long ago. As Shiva drank the poison up, Vishnu laughingly remarked that as the oldest of the gods, it was only right that he should receive the first product of the ocean.

Having been saved from one danger, the gods and demons were soon exposed to another. The weight of the mountain, enhanced by the fact that it was always revolving, and at a very rapid rate, pierced a hole right through the bottom of the earth. For a moment they did not know what to do, but in their need they turned to Vishnu. He was, they said, the preserver and support of all creatures, of the gods in particular, and they looked to him to steady the mountain, and prevent it from sinking down to hell. Thus appealed to, Vishnu at once changed himself into a huge tortoise, stepped into the ocean, and placed the mountain on his back. Nor did he confine himself to this new task. So great is his power, and so many are the shapes he is able to assume, that while he supported the mountain on his back, he continued to help in the pulling of the churning rope, and also, seated on a hill top, imparted fresh vigour to his fellow-toilers.

We are not told how much longer demons and celestials laboured at their task. But they were very far spent when at long last certain objects began to emerge from the ocean. The first to appear was the wonderful cow, Surabhi, the nourisher and mother of every one that lives. She was followed by the goddess of wine, her eyes rolling in a drunken frenzy. The demons would have liked to secure her, but she said that she preferred the society of the gods. Yet another member of the female sex was the next to appear, Lakshmi, the goddess of prosperity, seated on a lotus and holding a water-lily in her hand. Her advent created a great sensation. The minstrels of heaven and the great sages began to sing her praises. The river Ganges and other sacred streams presented themselves before her and asked her to bathe in their waters. The four immortal elephants that hold up the world filled golden pitchers from the sacred streams and poured water over her, while the Sea of Milk asked her to accept a wreath of never-fading flowers. When she had been thus adorned, she seated herself on Vishnu's lap. The demons tried to gain her favour, but she turned her eyes away from them, an omen of impending doom. Dhanwantari, the physician of the gods, and the inventor of the Ayur-vedic system of medicine, a celestial tree, a horse, the moon, a wonderful gem which Vishnu took and placed upon his breast, and countless millions of beautiful women, were among the other products of the milky sea. These women offered themselves to both gods and demons, but as they refused to accept them, they have since been reckoned to be at the disposal of everybody. They live in heaven and are spoken of as the Apsarases, or heavenly nymphs.

The physician of the gods was the last to emerge with a cup in his hand. The vessel contained the *amrita*. Forgetful of their bargain that each side should share equally in the product of their toil, gods and demons began to fight for its possession. The battle raged for many days. Thousands and thousands of demons were slain. The earth was covered with dead. Vishnu played a great part in the contest. And yet for a moment the issue trembled in the balance ; because somehow or other the demons got a hold of the vessel containing the *amrita*, and were about to drink it. If they had succeeded in doing so, the demons would have been immortal and not the gods. But Vishnu once more came to the rescue. He was both too clever and too quick for his opponents. Transforming himself into a ravishingly beautiful woman, he began to flirt with the demons. Entranced by her beauty and overcome by infatuation, the deluded fiends placed the cup in the deceiver's hands, and thus lost their chance of immortality for evermore. Realising that all was over, they either plunged into the depths of the ocean or took refuge in the bowels of the earth.

With the *amrita* thus secured, the gods took the cup

from the hands of Vishnu and drank, obtaining, as they did so, the gift of immortal life. As they stood in rows, passing the vessel from one to the other, a demon named Rāhu managed to insinuate himself among them. The cup was in his hand, nay, the cup was at his lips, and some of the *amrita* was in his throat, when the Sun and Moon discovered the wolf in sheep's clothing. Quick as light, they told their fellow-deities what was happening, and it was the work of a moment for Vishnu to cut off the wretch's head with his discus. So strong was the blow that it sent the head spinning through the air, right up into the sky, while the headless trunk shook the earth in its fall. What would have happened if the demon had succeeded in swallowing the *amrita*, we are not told. In any case the loss of his head did not deprive him of life, and from that day to this Rāhu has never forgiven the Sun and Moon. Time after time he has persistently attempted to swallow them both, and that is the explanation of the eclipses from which these two bodies periodically suffer.

Greatly delighted with their success, the gods put Mount Mandara back in his place and set out for heaven, rending the air with their shouts. When they reached the upper-world they made the most careful arrangements for the guarding of the *amrita*. A great wheel, as sharp as a razor, and shining like the sun, revolves round it unceasingly, and two huge serpents, with winkless eyes, keep watch and ward night and day.

Mahābhārata, i. 17.
Rāmāyana, i. 45.

II.

THE CUNNING OF INDRA.

" Indra is like a dog in his ways. Though king of the gods, there is
no limit to his deceitfulness and villainy. He loves another's loss and
his own gain. He is crafty and disreputable, and has no faith in any
one."—*Rāmāyan of Tulsidās*, ii. 399–400.

WHEN Diti, the mother of the demons, heard that her
children had been slain, she vowed that she would have
revenge. She therefore approached her husband, and said
that she was resolved to give birth to a son who would be
strong enough to fight with and slay Indra, the king of the
gods. Her husband was full of sympathy with her in
her sorrow, and undertook to do what was expected of
him. But he pointed out that a son, capable of slaying
Indra, could only be procured if she kept herself absolutely
pure, and engaged in austerities for no less a period than
a thousand years. In fact, he said that the son born
under such conditions would not only be successful in
killing Indra, but would be able to destroy the three worlds.
Not long after, husband and wife went their own ways ;
he to resume the practice of austerities which his wife's
appeal had interrupted, she to engage in her millennial
toil.

We are not told what was the nature of the asceticism
in which Diti engaged, but it is manifest that she began
and carried it on with the utmost confidence as to the
result. Nor was she the least dismayed when her step-

son, Indra, came to help her in her labours. It was Indra's destruction that she sought ; the overthrow of his brother celestials that she most desired. But she allowed him, nevertheless, to gather wood for the sacred fire, to carry water, to supply her with roots and fruit, and to place in its proper position the sacred grass so necessary to the efficacy of her prayers. And when she was exhausted with her labours, she permitted him to massage her weary limbs.

When nine hundred and ninety years had passed away, Diti could restrain herself no longer. Without the least attempt at concealment she told her stepson what her object was. " In ten years," she said, " I shall give birth to a son. It is for this I have toiled and prayed, and when he is born he will relieve you of all the trouble that is involved in ruling over the three worlds. You will not need to worry any more, and the fever of your heart will be stilled."

Indra made no reply. But that very day when the sun was high in the heavens, Diti lay down to rest, and as she did so, apparently too exhausted to realise what she was doing, she made a frightful blunder. It was the first mistake of which she had been guilty throughout the centuries. She put her feet where her head should have been, and thereby made herself impure. Now her husband had told her that she must exercise the most scrupulous care, and avoid every possible taint of ceremonial impurity. When Indra saw his stepmother make this fatal error, he knew that his opportunity had come at last. Greatly delighted, he at once entered into her womb and divided the embryo which it contained into seven parts. The embryo raised a mighty shout, and Diti awoke. Strange to say, when Indra explained to her what had happened, and showed her how she herself was to blame, she meekly acknowledged her fault. Indeed

she said that her stepson was perfectly justified in what
he had done.   But she had one request to make, and it
was that the sundered embryo might become the seven
Maruts, or gods of the storm.   And so it came to pass.
The new deities were called Maruts, because Indra told
them *not to weep*, and ever since they have ranged about
the sky, armed with lightning, and riding on the winds.
Diti was apparently very satisfied with this arrangement,
and we are told that, accompanied by her stepson, she
went off to heaven.

It is recorded in the *Rāmāyana* that Rāma, prince of
Ayodhyā, visited the very place where Diti had her hermitage, and was so faithfully served by the great god Indra.

Rāmāyana, i. 46–47.

III.

A WONDERFUL COW.

"The man who threatens to strike a Brāhmin shall remain in hell for a hundred years. For every particle of dust that sucks up the blood of a Brāhmin, the man who caused that blood to flow must spend one thousand years in hell."—*Laws of Manu*, xi. 207–208, iv. 165–168.

THIS wonderful cow, otherwise known as the cow of plenty, was one of the many products which the gods secured at the churning of the ocean. It was called Surabhi, or Kāmdhenu, and became the property of the *rishi* Vasishtha. This cow was able to yield its fortunate possessor anything he happened to desire. It didn't matter what it was ; food of every kind, things to eat and things to drink, things to sup or things to suck, as well as clothes and precious gems. Whenever her fortunate owner uttered the word *give*, the cow was there to yield him an immediate answer. No wonder jealousy and greed were roused in the hearts of every one who saw or heard of the amazing creature. Now it so happened that the great king, Vishvāmitra, was on a hunting expedition which brought him, with many of his followers, to the hermitage of Vasishtha. The holy man not only greeted the monarch with every appropriate courtesy, but he called upon the cow to produce a most sumptuous feast for the entertainment of the king and his attendants. Food and drink of every sort and kind, clothes and gems, as they issued from the cow in what seemed an endless stream, filled the heart of the monarch with joy and gladness. But, alas ! baser feelings also stirred the royal breast, and he began to ask why a hermit in the forest should possess such an unending source of wealth. It would be much more reasonable, he thought, if the creature were in his hands to supply his many and constant needs. He therefore offered the *rishi* ten thousand cows in return for the cow of plenty. When the holy man refused to listen to the proposal, he offered his whole kingdom. But when he refused this magnificent offer, giving as his excuse that the cow not only supplied the necessary material for his own sacrifices, but served a like purpose for the gods and the spirits of the dead, the king replied : " Don't you remember that I am a king and a member of the warrior caste, and kings take what they want, take it by force." To this threat Vasishtha made a very meek reply. He acknowledged that he was only a Brāhmin whose life was devoted to asceticism and the study of the Vedas. Brāhmins did not profess to set themselves in opposition to the might and strength of armed men. And he supposed it was not for him to resist. Monarchs did what they liked, they took what they wanted and never gave the matter a moment's thought. The upshot of the conversation was that the king put a rope round the cow's neck and began to lead her away. The poor animal was very unwilling to go. She turned pathetic eyes in the direction of the *rishi* and refused to budge a single inch. The king struck her over the head several times with a stick. For some time the sage never said a word, but at last he spoke and said : " My dear and loving cow, I hear your cries, I don't wish to lose you. But what can I do ? A king is all-powerful. He is taking you away by force and I cannot prevent him. It is the duty of a Brāhmin to be patient and to forgive." When the cow heard these words she broke away from her captor and came running to the *rishi's* feet : " Do you wish me to go ? " she cried. " Have you lost all your affection for me ? Do you not care whether the king ill-treats me or not ? Have you abandoned

me entirely ? " To this the holy man with wonderful
patience and self-restraint made answer : " What can I
say ? A warrior's strength lies in the force he is able to
exert ; a Brāhmin's strength consists in the spirit of forgiveness which he displays. If you wish to go with him,
go. But I certainly do not abandon you." " Well
then," cried the cow, " if you say you don't abandon me,
that is enough. I won't be taken by force." As she said
this the whole appearance and aspect of the cow underwent an amazing change. Her eyes flashed fire. Her
head and neck grew to an enormous size, and she rushed
at the king and his followers. But what was still more
wonderful, great showers of burning coal began to issue
from her tail, and the burning coal was followed by troops
of soldiers who issued not only from her tail, but from
her udder and her sides, even from her urine and dung,
and the froth of her mouth. These countless hosts belonged
to many countries and races of men. There were Greeks,
Huns, Scythians, Parthians, Chinese, wild aborigines,
barbarians and outcastes among them, and they wore
the garments and carried the weapons peculiar to their
country and race. As they poured forth they attacked
the king and his attendants with the utmost fury. But
they were content with giving them a good fright. Because
we are told that though they chased Vishvāmitra and his
men for a distance of seventy-seven miles, they did not
slay any of them.

When Vishvāmitra had recovered breath, he was already
a changed man. He had boasted that kings could do
what they liked. But now he realised that kings were
very feeble persons compared with Brāhmins. As he
said, " Asceticism is the only true strength." He therefore
abandoned his kingdom and went to live in a forest. He
had resolved that he would compel the gods to make him
a Brāhmin. And in the end, after many years of the most

astounding austerities, he achieved his impossible task. The whole world was filled with his glory, and when he went to heaven he drank Soma with the god Indra.

That is how the *Mahābhārata* is content to leave the story. But the *Rāmāyana* tells us that before owning defeat, Vishvāmitra made another and more violent effort to overcome the sage's power. It also reports a great slaughter on both sides, and says that it required a great and special effort on the part of the cow before she secured the final victory. In the end, however, the victory was final and complete. Vasishtha had the satisfaction of seeing the king's followers, who had by this time swelled to a vast army, lying dead at his feet. The only exceptions were Vishvāmitra and his sole surviving son. In the heat of the combat no less than a hundred sons of that monarch had tried to slay the sage, but with his angry glance he reduced them all to ashes. Thirsting for revenge, Vishvāmitra handed over his kingdom to the son already mentioned and retired to the Himālayas, where he devoted himself for many years to securing the favour of the great god Shiva. When Shiva at last appeared and asked him what he wanted, he entreated the god to explain to him the use of every weapon that had ever been wielded by not only gods and *rishis*, but by every kind of spirit, whether kindly or malign. Shiva not only heard the monarch's prayer, but supplied him with a stock of celestial weapons. Their names are given in detail. They were endowed with miraculous power, and, being the property of so great a god, the king was confident that no one would be able to resist him. And so he hastened to Vasishtha's hermitage. The first thing he did was to set it on fire. The sage's pupils were panic-stricken, and urged their master to take refuge in flight. This he scornfully refused to do. Instead he bade them wait and see how he would punish the incendiary. But they would not stay. They fled in all directions. What happened to the cow we are not told, but it is said that the alarm spread to the beasts and birds that frequented the neighbouring woods, with the result that Vasishtha was left entirely alone. He was, however, not the least afraid. And so he advanced to meet the king. In his hand he carried his staff, the Brāhmin's staff, his only weapon. When he demanded to know what new folly the king was devising, Vishvāmitra replied by launching his weapons, one after another, at the sage. But each and all of them were robbed of their power by the mere raising of the Brāhmin's staff. They poured upon the saint like rain ; but one after the other the Brāhmin's staff consumed them. There remained one weapon only, which Vishvāmitra had not so far dared to employ. It was the dart of Brahmā, the most powerful of all. It is indeed a most terrible weapon. As the monarch raised it in his hand the gods were filled with fear. As he cast it forth the three worlds trembled. But it failed also. What could it do against the power of a Brāhmin ? At this particular moment a great change came over the appearance of the sage. He was something wonderful and awful to behold. Great sparks of fire flashed from every pore in his body, and he seemed to be surrounded by smoke and flame. His staff was equally wonderful. As it absorbed and overcame the dart of Brahmā, it shone like the sceptre of Yama, the god of the lower world, like the fire of Fate, which desolates the universe. It was then and then only that Vishvāmitra owned defeat. A Brāhmin's staff had vanquished every weapon that the great god Shiva possessed. A warrior's strength was as nothing compared with that of a Brāhmin. And so he resolved that by the might of his austerities he would achieve that lofty pinnacle.

Mahābhārata, i. 177.
Rāmāyana, i. 51-55.

IV.

THE KING WHO WAS MADE A BRĀHMIN.

" The gods are a mean-spirited crew ; though they dwell on high, their acts are low. They cannot endure to see another's prosperity."— *Rāmāyan of Tulsidās*, ii. 236.

THE foregoing legend has told us how the Brāhmin Vasishtha humiliated king Vishvāmitra, and of his consequent resolve to secure equality with the priest. When he sought to conciliate the god Shiva, he had gone to the Himālayas, but on this occasion he went to the south of India. He was accompanied by his wife. And there he lived for a thousand years, engaged in austerities of the most rigid kind, while roots and fruits were his only food. Such asceticism was bound to procure some response from heaven, and when the thousand years had passed away, Brahmā, the creator god, or grandfather, as he is called, appeared before the king, and said that his penitential toil had secured for him a place among these very eminent persons known as Rājarshis or royal sages. But the god said nothing about Brāhmin-hood, and without waiting to be questioned, disappeared from view. Presumably he saw that Vishvāmitra was not satisfied, for we are told that the monarch held down his head in shame and sorrow. And then he spoke. "What do I care for the rank of royal sage. Is this all the recognition they are prepared to give me after a thousand years of toil ? " But he would not own defeat, and resolved to redouble his efforts.

15

But owing to certain inconveniences which had arisen in Southern India, he resolved to return to the North. On this occasion he decided to go to Pushkar, where there is a pleasant lake, a spot that is to this day pre-eminently holy, in the eyes of all Hindus, for its cleansing power. And there he spent another thousand years ; his austerities were as rigid as before, while roots and fruits were, as formerly, his only food. When the second thousand years had expired, Brahmā once more appeared on the scene. He had come, he said, to congratulate the monarch on his praiseworthy efforts and to confer on him the honourable title of *Sage*. It will be noted that on this occasion the god dropped the invidious reference to the monarch's birth and caste. To this announcement Vishvāmitra did not deign to offer any reply. Of course he was not satisfied. He would not be content until the god had made him a Brāhmin, and addressed him by that name. He therefore resumed his austerities, as determined as he had ever been to bend the celestial to his will.

But, alas ! the gods had plotted his downfall. When many more years had passed, Menakā, the lovely nymph, came down from heaven to bathe in the sacred waters. Vishvāmitra saw her as she sported there. Smitten by her charms, he invited her to share his hermitage, and for ten years the two lived together. During all that time the king abandoned the practice of asceticism and listened to the voice of his passions alone. But at last his eyes were opened, and, overcome by shame and anger, he realised that the coming of the nymph was a conspiracy of the gods. Unable to break his purpose in any other way, they had ensnared him in the net of desire, and robbed him of all the merit he had so laboriously acquired.

He therefore told his temptress to depart, while for himself he fled from the scene of his downfall and took refuge among the Himālayas. There he added to his

austerities by taking the vow of chastity and bringing his
senses under control. In these he persevered for another
thousand years. By the end of that time the gods had
become positively alarmed, and at a conference which was
held in heaven it was decided to confer on him the rank
of *Mighty Saint*. It was Brahmā who once again approached him and conveyed the decision of his brother
celestials. But Vishvāmitra made the calm reply, " There
is only one title that will satisfy me. When you address
me by the name of Brāhmin, then and then only shall I
be content." " If that is what you want," said Brahmā,
" you will have to make a bigger effort than any you have
yet made."

The god went off to heaven ; and now we learn what
were the austerities to which the monarch bent his soul.
The text so far has been content to speak of Vishvāmitra's
asceticism in general terms. It now condescends to give
details. He stood on one foot for a thousand years.
He held his arms high above his head all that time. He
never moved, night or day. In the hot days of summer
he practised the penance of the five fires. In the rainy
season he was exposed to wind and rain, seeking no shelter.
If he ever lay down at all he made the mountain torrents
his bed. The air was his only food throughout the passing of the centuries. If the gods were afraid before, they
were now filled with consternation. It was manifest that
something must be done, and done quickly, to save the
gods from disaster, and crush for ever this ambitious
and relentless devotee. Indra was specially distressed,
and it was he who contrived the plot which seemed to
offer most hopes of a successful issue. We have seen how
they succeeded in the case of Menakā. Indra now
summoned another celestial nymph to his presence. Her
name was Rambhā. When told to go and tempt Vishvāmitra, as Menakā had tempted him, Rambhā was greatly

2

alarmed. She reminded the god that the ascetic was a
very powerful person, and would be certain to curse her.
She therefore entreated Indra not to send her on such a
dangerous task. But the god told her not to be afraid.
He himself would go with her in the form of a cuckoo.
It was the season of spring. The god of love would lend
his aid, and the three combined would beguile the hermit.
Her beauty, his music, and the power of love would lead
the monarch from the paths of virtue and rob him of all
that he had gained. Accordingly Indra and Rambhā,
accompanied by the god of love, went down to earth and
began to besiege the heart of the sage. Seated among
the branches of a neighbouring tree, the cuckoo sang his
sweetest notes. The nymph approached ever nearer and
nearer, displaying all her charms. The heart of the
saint was stirred. The music touched his heart. He
saw and confessed that the maiden was very beautiful.
But when the god prolonged his note, and the nymph
began to smile, Vishvāmitra recognised that the gods
were once more plotting his destruction. Poor Rambhā
was the chief object of his wrath. He cursed her to be
changed into a stone, and to remain on the place where
she then was for ten thousand years. As for Indra and
the god of love, they disappeared.

But though he had resisted this great temptation, the
monarch knew that by giving way to anger he had lost
a great deal of his ascetic merit, and that success would
only be possible when he had completely subdued his
wrath. He accordingly resolved to give himself up to
this one object. He would not speak to any one. He
would observe the vow of silence for a thousand years.
He would not permit anger to have any hold on him for
a thousand years. And so it was. He never opened
his mouth, he never spoke, he never ate, he even held
his breath for all that time. The result of this unparalleled

asceticism was that the body of the saint became as dry
as a log of wood, and never once did anger obtain possession of his heart.

When the thousand years were over, and Vishvāmitra
had completed his vow, he sat down to eat some boiled
rice. But the sleepless Indra was close at hand. Assuming
the guise of a Brāhmin beggar, he approached the king
and asked for the rice. Without the least hesitation
Vishvāmitra handed him the whole. He watched the
Brāhmin eat it and never said a word. Not only did he
remain silent, but he turned to his ascetic task, and for
another thousand years resumed the vow which he had
hoped to break with that solitary meal of rice. And so
for yet another thousand years he never breathed, he
never ate, he never spoke. But if the ascetic could stand
the strain of such austerities, Nature could not. The
saint was unmoved, but the three worlds were in a state
of bewilderment and terror. Gods and saints, demons
and serpents, gathered together in one motley throng
and told Brahmā that something must be done. They
had done their best to overthrow the saint. Lust, greed,
and anger, they had tempted him by all three. They
had failed completely, with the result that his powers
were greater than before. Immediate action was
necessary if the three worlds were to be saved from destruction. They had only to look around and see what
was already happening. Nature was in a state of con-
vulsion. The sun had ceased to shine, the hills had sunk
to the level of the plains, the waves of the sea refused to
retire, religion was imperilled and the gods would be
speedily dethroned. It was manifest that the monarch
was resolved to destroy everything, if he did not get an
answer to his prayer. They concluded by saying that
they thought the Grandsire should make Vishvāmitra a
Brāhmin. As far as they were concerned, they would

give him Indra's post and make him king of heaven, if
they thought that would pacify him.   The creator accepted
the advice of his brother celestials, and calling Vishvāmitra
Brāhmin saint, said that he and the other gods being
very pleased with the austerities in which he had so long
indulged, proposed to reward him with the rank of Brāhmin.
He added the hope that he would live long and be happy.
But Vishvāmitra, having been disappointed so often, was
determined that his new rank should be openly acknowledged by some member of the Brāhmin caste. He
therefore asked that his old enemy Vasishtha, the greatest
of all Brāhmins, be called on to confirm the boon which
the gods had granted. Some difficulty was experienced
in persuading Vasishtha to consent. But when he did
come at last, he declared in the presence of the assembled
gods, that Vishvāmitra's title was without a flaw. He
was a real *Brāhmarshi* ; that is, both a Brāhmin and a
saint. When this matter had been thus happily settled,
the celestials went off to heaven. As for Vishvāmitra,
he was immensely delighted. He even became the friend
of his old enemy, continuing to live through many generations and known to every age as the greatest of all ascetics,
asceticism incarnate.

Rāmāyana, i. 57–66.

V.

THE OUTCASTE WHO WAS RAISED TO THE SKIES.

" What man desirous of life would injure Brāhmins, to whose support the three worlds and the gods owe their existence. A Brāhmin, be he ignorant or learned, is a mighty god. They could create other worlds and other guardians of the world, and deprive the gods of their divine station."—*Laws of Manu*, ix. 314–317.

THERE once lived in the famous city of Ayodhyā a monarch of the solar race—his name was Trishanku—who formed a very strange resolve. It was that he would offer such a sacrifice as would compel the gods to admit him to heaven in his bodily form. He accordingly summoned to his presence his minister of state, the sage Vasishtha, and invited his assistance. Now there was no greater Brāhmin anywhere than Vasishtha. But he replied that the monarch was asking the impossible, and such a sacrifice was quite beyond his power. Nothing daunted by this firm refusal, Trishanku approached Vasishtha's hundred sons. These young men were at the time engaged in the practice of austerities, and as the king drew near with clasped hands, the very picture of humility and reverence, they asked him what boon he desired. The monarch explained that he wished their assistance in the performance of a sacrifice which would raise him to heaven in his bodily form. But unfortunately he not only said that he had failed to gain their father's assistance,

21

but indicated as well that in his opinion the sage had not been as cordial as he might have been. Such an observation was enough to rouse the wrath of any well-conditioned sons, and they asked the monarch in angry tones what he meant by coming to them when their father had already rejected his prayer. If their father was unequal to such a sacrifice, so were they, and Trishanku had been guilty of a great sin in coming to them. At the same time, they would like him to know that their father was competent to perform any sacrifice that had ever been offered in heaven, earth, or hell. Presumably by that observation they meant that the object on which Trishanku had set his heart was impossible of attainment, and that entrance to heaven in bodily form could not be secured by any sort of human effort. Be that as it may, Trishanku added to his folly by losing his temper also, and telling the young men that if neither they nor their father were fit for the duty he had proposed entrusting to them, he would find somebody who was. Such language was not to be endured, and before Trishanku knew what had happened to him, the ascetics cursed the king and changed him into a Chandāla. Now a Chandāla is the lowest of all outcastes. There is no human being more degraded. A Chandāla is the son of a Brāhmin woman who has had intercourse with a man of low caste. And Manu says in his *Laws* that a Chandāla must not dare even to look at a Brāhmin, and that those who have any regard for religion must shun his presence. They are not allowed to live in any village ; their only permitted wealth is dogs and donkeys ; their dress is the garments of the dead. By royal ordinance they act as public executioners, and carry to the grave the corpses of those who die without kith or kin. It was into such a fearful creature that this mighty monarch of the solar race was changed by the curse of Vasishtha's sons. In his anger he had forgotten what a terrible thing it is to

offend any member of the priestly caste. The same law-
book warns kings and princes that they must never make
a Brāhmin angry, because a Brāhmin is able by his curses
to destroy all that a king has. And it goes on to tell how
Brāhmins by their curses have destroyed the world by
fire, made the sea undrinkable, and the moon to wax and
wane. Nay, even more than that, it says that Brāhmins
should be honoured in every way, because whether they
are wise or ignorant, good or bad, every one of them is a
very great god ; indeed they are greater than the gods,
because the gods depend on the Brāhmins for their continued existence, and should the Brāhmins so resolve,
they could create new worlds and new gods. Trishanku
then should have known not to offend Vasishtha's sons,
but anger robbed him of his understanding and he found
himself changed into a base Chandāla, of horrid aspect and
clothed in rags. Round his neck there hung a garland of
human skulls ; his body was daubed with ashes gathered
at a burning ghaut. His ornaments of gold had become
iron shackles. When his ministers and attendants saw
the transformation they fled in every direction, leaving
their master entirely alone. But though his outward
appearance had been thus woefully changed, the monarch
was still master of his soul, and his resolve remained
unshaken. Not only so, but he had already decided whose
help he would invoke. He had heard of king Vishvāmitra
and the amazing austerities he was practising in Southern
India. And no doubt he had heard also of how his royal
brother had come into conflict with Vasishtha and his
hundred sons. It was Vishvāmitra's help, then, that he
was determined to obtain, and with that object in view
he set out for the south of India. In due course he reached
Vishvāmitra's hermitage, and told to willing ears the story
of his wrongs. From the way in which he spoke, Trishanku
apparently was still of the opinion that, in seeking to go

to heaven in his bodily form he was asking for no unusual boon. Indeed, he dwelt on the number of sacrifices he had already offered—no less than a hundred, and complained that despite such a great expenditure he was to get no reward. Besides that, he had never once told a lie; if Vishvāmitra doubted his word, he swore on his honour as a member of the warrior caste that he had never once told a lie. He had been a just and industrious ruler, interested in the welfare of his subjects. His character and conduct had always given satisfaction to his spiritual guides, and yet when he applied to them for assistance in attaining the object on which he had set his heart, they had spurned him from their presence and finally placed him under their curse. "In fact," said Trishanku, "I have come to the conclusion that it is no use trying to do anything. Man's toil all goes for nothing. Everything is under the control of Destiny, and Fate rules all." But despite this pessimistic observation, Trishanku's next remark showed that his purpose was still unshaken. For he appealed to Vishvāmitra to help him in the celebration of his proposed sacrifice, persuaded as he was that between them they would meet and overcome the power of Fate.

By the response which he made, Vishvāmitra showed that he was as courageous as his friend. He not only promised to assist him in the way he required, but he calmly told him not to worry. He would gather together a great company of Brāhmins, saints and ascetics from all quarters, and he would guarantee that between them they would perform such a sacrifice as would not only raise Trishanku to the skies, but raise him as he then was, with all the degrading marks of his Chandālhood still upon him.

The reader will remember that in his contest with Vasishtha, the hundred sons of Vishvāmitra had all been slain. But during his residence in Southern India his wife had borne him four other sons. These had now grown up to manhood, and in accordance with their father's instructions they went round most of the hermitages in India, inviting saints and ascetics to come and assist their father at the sacrifice which he proposed to offer on Trishanku's behalf. A very large number of Brāhmins accepted the invitation, and none of those who came appear to have objected to a member of the warrior caste assuming to himself a prerogative which belonged to the priestly caste, and to the priestly caste alone. But there was one hermitage where the messengers of Vishvāmitra received a curt refusal. And that, of course, was the hermitage of Vasishtha. In the estimation of that mighty saint, such an invitation was a double insult, and in a voice trembling with passion he asked how it was possible for any self-respecting Brāhmin to be present at a sacrifice where the presiding priest was a member of the warrior caste. No god would look with favour on the offerings of a base-born Chandāla ; and he wondered who the Brāhmins were that had consented to be present and to eat food which was the gift of an outcaste. When Vishvāmitra's sons got home and told their father what Vasishtha had said, his anger knew no bounds. With flaming eyes he cried, " What do the wicked rascals mean ? How do they dare to censure me ? I have practised the most severe austerities, and my character is without blame. But I shall be revenged. The curse that fell upon Trishanku shall fall upon Vasishtha. He, too, shall be changed into a Chandāla. And as for his hundred sons, I condemn them to an even more frightful fate. Not for one lifetime, but for seven hundred lives, I condemn them to roam the earth, friendless and forlorn, shunned and abhorred by all ; clad in dead men's clothes, feeding on dogs' flesh, ugly and misshapen in body, indulging in **every form of wicked deed.**"

Having thus relieved his feelings, Vishvāmitra addressed
the Brāhmins who came in response to his invitation. If
any of them had cherished doubts as to the propriety of
their host's intentions, they did not venture to express
them.   Indeed they told one another that if they did not
accede to his wishes, they would be cursed as heartily as
Vasishtha and his hundred sons had been.   And so the
sacrifice was begun.   What the exact nature of the
sacrifice was, we are not told.   But it is said that the sacred
texts were repeated in careful accordance with the prescribed usage, and the gods were requested to appear and
to accept their share of the offerings.   But the gods made
no response, and not one of them appeared.   When
Vishvāmitra saw that the gods were not coming and the
sacrifice had proved of no avail, he broke into another
passion of wrath.   Turning to his friend, he said that if
the sacrifice was ineffectual, they would soon be witnesses
of his ascetic power.   And indeed there was seen a sight
such as the eyes of man had never gazed upon before.
For Vishvāmitra was resolved that he would not own
defeat.   As the reader knows, the monarch had acquired
an immense stock of ascetic merit, and this he was prepared to expend in raising Trishanku to the skies.   And
so he called aloud, " Trishanku, in virtue of my ascetic
merit do thou ascend to heaven, ascend in person, as thou
art, clothed as thou art, with all the marks of degradation
upon thee."   And to the amazement of the beholders,
Trishanku was seen to rise from the ground, to rise higher
and higher, and in his bodily form, until he seemed to be
entering heaven.   But though the gods had been silent,
they were not asleep.   Indra, the king of heaven, at least
was watching all that took place.   And as Trishanku
appeared, as it were, at the very gate of heaven, the god
cried aloud, " Turn back, Trishanku, turn back.   You
cannot enter heaven.   You are not entitled to come here,

you who have been cursed by your spiritual guide." In obedience to the command of the god, Trishanku began to fall headlong, and as he did so, he cried out to Vishvā-mitra to save him. Then indeed began a contest between the might of the celestials and the might of the saint. Indra cried out, "Descend! Descend!" Vishvāmitra cried out, "Stay where you are," with the result that Trishanku hung suspended in the sky. Nor was this the end of the matter. Beside himself with anger, Vishvā-mitra created a large number of stars ; he called into being seven new *rishis* ; he even went the length of creating new gods, and swore that if Indra did not take care, he would create another Indra.

There was thus created a situation of the most serious import, which required immediate handling. The result was that not only the gods, but a large number of demons and glorified saints presented themselves before Vishvā-mitra, and in the most submissive manner begged him to reconsider his action. They respectfully observed that it was most improper to insist that Trishanku should enter heaven without first getting rid of his body, especially in view of the fact that he was labouring under the effects of a most humiliating curse. But Vishvāmitra refused to listen to any arguments. He had pledged his word to Trishanku, and his oath must be fulfilled. Trishanku must get into heaven, and the stars he had created must remain for ever in the sky, a witness to his ascetic power. He said nothing, however, about the new gods whom he called into existence, and we are left in ignorance as to their future fate. When the celestials had heard this ultimatum, they felt that there was nothing for them but to agree. And yet as we read the text it would seem as if some sort of compromise was arrived at, for this is how the answer of the celestials runs, " The stars you have created will remain shining in the firmament with Tris-

hanku in their midst " as if he had not attained heaven
itself.   In any case, Vishvāmitra expressed his satisfaction
with the answer, and when the sacrifices had been completed both gods and Brāhmins returned to their respective
abodes.   It was in this manner, then, that Trishanku's
ambition was realised.   We can still behold him shining
in the sky as glorious in his appearance as a god.

Rāmāyana, i. 57–60.
Laws of Manu, ix. 313, x. 51.

VI.

A MAN SACRIFICE.

" The slaughter of human beings as sacrifice to the gods is never seen.
Why then do you desire to sacrifice human beings to Shiva ?   You are
treating men as if they were beasts."

" By making a pilgrimage to the well, Tamraruna, you obtain the
same benefit as is got from a man sacrifice."—*Mahābhārata*, ii. 22, iii.
84.

A.

HARISCHANDRA, king of Ayodhyā, was childless, despite
the fact that he had a hundred wives. A conversation
that he had with the *rishi* Nārada only deepened his
regret that he should have no son to succeed him on the
throne. For that pious sage told him that the pleasure
which a father found in his son was greater than all other
pleasures combined. Clothes kept out cold, food nourished
the body, ornaments of gold added to one's beauty,
marriage brought with it a dowry, a wife was a friend, and
a daughter, well, she was an object of compassion, but a
son shone like a light in heaven. Indeed, a father began
to live over again in the face of his son. And a wife was
only a wife in name until she became the mother of a boy,
who achieves for his sire the gift of immortality. Even
the beasts of the field know that the creature who does
not beget offspring has no place in the world.

Happily, Nārada did not confine himself to vain words.
He advised him to go to Varuna, the god of the firmament,

and promise that if the god would grant him a son he would offer him up as a sacrifice. Without thinking of the mental agony that must subsequently ensue, the monarch addressed the god in the manner prescribed by the sage, and said that if he gave him a son he would promise to offer him up as a sacrifice. Varuna heard the monarch's prayer, and in course of time a man-child was born. He received the name of Rohita. But as soon as he was born the god appeared and called upon the king to implement his promise. Harischandra, however, replied, "Animals are not suitable for sacrifice until they are ten days old," and Varuna consented to wait for ten days. But when the ten days were over, and he came and asked that the child should be sacrificed, the king said, "No one ever thinks of sacrificing an animal until its first teeth have grown. When his teeth have grown, I shall implement my promise." The god once more accepted the excuse and waited till the teeth had grown. But, when the god came and asked that there should be no more delay, the king explained that they must wait till the first teeth had fallen. But when the first teeth had fallen and the god had come again, the king asked Varuna to wait till the second teeth appeared, and when the second teeth appeared he reminded the god that his son belonged to the warrior caste, and a man of the warrior caste was not fit to be a sacrifice until he had been endued with armour. In this way the monarch was able to evade the fulfilment of his pledge until his son reached manhood. By that time, however, he felt that he could not invent any further excuse, and he sent for his son. When Rohita heard of the awful fate that was in store for him, and that he was to be offered up as a sacrifice to the god, he seized his bow and fled to the forest.

Varuna was very angry at being thus deprived of his

victim, and in punishment for the evasion of which he
had been guilty, he afflicted the king with the disease of
dropsy. When the news of his father's affliction reached
the prince, he left the forest and entered a village. It
was apparently his intention to return home and deliver
his father from the curse that had befallen him. But
in the village he met the god Indra, in the guise of a
Brāhmin, who told him that there was no happiness for
any one who did not lead a wandering life, and that even
the best of men fell victims to the bondage of sin when
they failed to avoid human habitations. In view of the
fact that he had received this advice from a Brāhmin
whose words ought to be obeyed, Rohita resumed his
forest life. Nevertheless, he was not content, and on
several occasions he resolved to go back to his father's
house. But every time he entered a village he was met
by the disguised Indra, who gave him the same advice
as before, and sang the praises of a wandering life. This
went on for six years, and Rohita could wait no longer.

Now it so happened that just at that time Rohita
came across a *rishi* named Ajigart, with his wife and
three sons, in great distress for want of food. The youth
at once proposed to buy one of the three sons, and to give
in exchange one hundred cows. The father replied :
" I cannot consent to part with my oldest son " ; and
the mother said : " I shall not allow my youngest boy
to be sold." The result was that they agreed to give
the middle son, Shunashepha, in exchange for one hundred
cows. Taking Shunashepha with him, Rohita at once
returned to his father's house and said he had purchased
a substitute whom they would offer as a sacrifice to the
god Varuna. When the god was approached, he agreed
to the arrangement, saying that a member of the priestly
caste was of more value than a king's son.

And so everything was got ready for the sacrifice.

Vishvāmitra and Vasishtha were both present, along with others as officiating priests. A difficulty, however, at once arose. No one would consent to bind the victim to the altar. But Ajigart, the poor lad's father, appeared on the scene, and said that he would do it if he were given another hundred cows. When Shunashepha had been bound to the altar the question was asked, "Who will kill him?" And once more the unnatural father intervened and said: "Give me yet another hundred cows, and I shall slay him." This offer also was accepted, and the father began to sharpen his sacrificial knife. When Shunashepha saw that he was about to be butchered, as if he were a beast and not a man, he called upon the gods to save him. He first prayed to Brahmā, the creator, or Prajāpati, as he is called in the text. But Prajāpati told him that Agni, the god of fire, was the nearest, and that he ought to pray to him. And so he prayed to Agni. But Agni said: "Savitar (the sun) rules over all creatures; go to him." Savitar however replied: "You are being offered up to Varuna, ask him to help you." But Varuna referred him back to Agni, of whom he said that he was the most compassionate of all the gods. He added: "If you do that we shall release you." The victim therefore cried aloud to Agni, repeating, as he had done on the other occasions, appropriate verses from the Vedas. When he had thus sung the praises of Agni, the god of fire told him to ask the Vishvādevas to release him. But the Vishvādevas (all the gods) said: "Indra, the king of heaven, is the strongest and knows best what to do." In obedience to this advice Shunashepha prayed to Indra. Indra was very pleased with his adoration and gave him a golden car. But he said that if the suppliant wanted to be successful, he must gratify the Ashwins (the harbingers of dawn) before he could hope to be released. Once more, however, the youth was told that there was yet another deity whose praise must be uttered, before the gods would consent to set him free. This was Ushas, the goddess of dawn. Happily this was the final effort that Shunashepha required to make, for as he prayed to the goddess of the dawn, his fetters fell off, one after the other, and his father's sickness began to abate. By the time the last of the three verses, which he addressed to Ushas, had been uttered, all the fetters had fallen from his limbs, and Harischandra was completely healed.

Vishvāmitra, who, as we have seen, acted as one of the officiating priests, was so pleased with Shunashepha's spirit and devotion that he there and then adopted him as one of his own children. But Ajigart, the poor lad's inhuman father, refused to give his consent, and insisted that Shunashepha should return with him to the forest. The youth, however, met his father's claim with a stern refusal. "Not only did you sell me," he said, "but you bound me to the stake and would have killed me, as a butcher kills a brute beast. In your eyes three hundred cows are of more value than a son." Ajigart professed to have been very sorry for what he had done and offered to give him a third of the animals he had secured in such a base manner. But Shunashepha replied: "You say you have repented of your evil deed. What guarantee do you give that, should opportunity offer, you won't sell me again. You have done a deed that would disgrace a Shūdra, and it is not possible that you and I should be reconciled. At this point Vishvāmitra intervened with the declaration that it was indeed a horrible sight to see Ajigart standing with uplifted hand ready to slay his son.

When Ajigart had been thus dismissed, Vishvāmitra proceeded to take the step necessary to enrol Shunashepha as a member of his family. Indeed, he said he was going to give him the rank of the eldest born, thus taking precedence of his hundred sons. This was a proposal which

3

was strongly resented by the fifty oldest, but Vishvāmitra was not the kind of man to tolerate such insubordination, and he there and then disinherited them. Nor did he confine himself to that. He uttered a curse against them to the effect that they would be the fathers and ancestors of the very basest and most degraded of men. And so it came to pass. The Andhras and Pundras, as well as other races, are the descendants of these sons of Vishvāmitra, who were so foolish as to incur their father's wrath. As to the other fifty, who had happily remained silent, they accepted their father's decision and looked up to Shuna-shepha as their oldest brother. They were appropriately rewarded. Vishvāmitra gave them his blessing and said they would be enriched with cattle and children in great abundance.

Aitareya Brāhmana, vii. 3.

B.

Ambarisha, king of Ayodhyā, had made great prepara-tions for a sacrifice, but Indra came and stole away the animal that had been chosen as the victim. When he inquired from his priest what he ought to do in the circum-stances, he was told that if he could not find the animal he would require to sacrifice a man in its stead. The king accordingly did everything he could to find the beast. He travelled over many countries; he explored both cities and forests; he even offered a thousand cows as a reward to any one who would secure its recovery. But despite all his efforts, no trace of the animal was to be found. He was thus compelled to adopt the alternative which his priest had set before him, and make arrange-ments for a man sacrifice.

Now it happened when he had come to this decision, he had just arrived at the hermitage of a very eminent

ascetic whose name was Richika. The saint was the
father of three sons, and these youths, with their mother,
were present when the king came to their father's hermitage.
When he saw the young men, Ambarisha at once invited
the Brāhmin to assist him in his difficulty. He explained
how the animal he had proposed to sacrifice had been
carried off, and how the officiating priest had said that if
it could not be found a man must be sacrificed in its stead.
For these reasons the king was of the opinion that it was
the holy man's bounden duty to sell him one of his sons.
To this proposal Richika replied by saying that he would
never consent to part with his first-born, while his wife
declared that she would never allow the youngest to be
slain. Every one knew that fathers were fondest of the
oldest son in the family, but with mothers, the youngest
child was always the favourite. As the father and mother
thus discussed their preferences in the presence of their
children, Shunashepha, the second son, intervened, and,
without any pressure from his parents, volunteered to be
the victim. He somewhat cynically added that apparently the son who came between was destined to be sold.
It was a great price that the monarch had agreed to pay
for the lad—heaps of jewels, gold and silver coins by the
hundreds and thousands, in addition to many millions of
cows. But Ambarisha was only too glad to pay any price,
and placing Shunashepha in his chariot, drove off in the
direction of Ayodhyā, greatly delighted with his success.

That very day the monarch and his victim halted for
their midday rest by the shores of Pushkar, India's most
sacred lake. While the king was asleep, Shunashepha,
seeing some ascetics engaged in austerities, drew near to
watch them. To his surprise he recognised among them
his mother's brother, Vishvāmitra. In his loneliness and
sorrow the youth rushed forward and flung himself at
his uncle's feet. " Have pity upon me," he cried. " My

father and mother have forsaken me. I have no friends
left. But you are the friend of every one and the protector
of all. Save me from the extremity in which I am placed.
It is in your power to gratify the king's desire, and at the
same time deliver me from death. I, too, wish to live a
long life, and secure a place in heaven by the practice
of austerities." The heart of Vishvāmitra was deeply
touched by this pathetic appeal, and, turning to his sons,
told them that they had a splendid opportunity of doing
a heroic deed and acting as the youth's substitute. They
had devoted their lives to the practice of asceticism and
other righteous deeds. It was now open to them to crown
their achievements by gratifying the god Agni and saving
this poor child from death. Now Vishvāmitra had no
less than a hundred sons, but they one and all cried out
in protest against what they held to be a most unnatural
proposal. Indeed, they told their father that it was very
strange that he should be more interested in the offspring
of another than in his own, and his action was equivalent
to eating his own flesh and blood. Vishvāmitra's hair
stood on end as he listened to such unfilial language, and
he cursed his sons most vigorously, condemning them to
the level of the most base-born outcastes, and declaring
that they would live on dog's flesh for a thousand years.

By the time he had recovered his equanimity, Vishvāmitra had conceived a plan which he assured Shunashepha
would secure his deliverance. It was exceedingly simple.
When Shunashepha approached the stake, he was to
repeat two verses in praise of Agni, verses which he taught
him there and then, and he would be set free. Shunashepha never doubted his uncle's word. And when he
had got the two verses thoroughly by heart, he was so
impatient to be gone that he approached Ambarisha and
asked him to resume their journey without further delay.
The king was very glad to see his victim so cheerful,

and it was not long before they reached the city of Ayodhyā.

Immediately after their arrival preparations were made for the sacrifice. A garland of red flowers was placed upon the victim's brow ; his body was daubed with red sandal-wood paste ; a red garment was given him to wear ; a girdle of sacred grass was bound about his waist, and he was led forth and fastened to the stake as if he were a beast and not a man. But, as he stood there, Shunashepha repeated the verses his uncle had taught him in praise of Agni. These verses were followed by others in praise of Indra and Vishnu. The gods were exceedingly pleased with their worshipper's devotion, but it was Indra, we are told, who set him free. Not only did he set him free, but he promised that his life would be long and happy. As for king Ambarisha, he came to no harm from the failure of his sacrifice ; indeed by the kindness of the same gracious deity, he obtained more than he had ever hoped to secure by its means.

Rāmāyana, i. 62.

VII.

A HOLY MAN DRINKS UP THE OCEAN.

" Agastya said : 'It matters little whether Indra pours down rain or not. If he does not shew any regard for me, I shall change myself into Indra, and keep all creatures alive. I can even repeatedly create new worlds.' "—*Mahābhārata*, xiv. 92. 22.

IN ancient days a holy man, whose name was Agastya, built for himself a hermitage on the northern slopes of the Vindhya hills in Central India. It is said that he had two fathers, the gods Varuna and Mitra. And yet that statement can scarcely be true, because it is recorded in the very same place that Agastya once saw his dead ancestors all hanging head downwards, suspended over a pit. When the sage asked them why they were in that most uncomfortable and dangerous situation, they answered that it was because of his failure to marry and beget a son. This reply had reference to the belief that a son was necessary to secure a man's salvation.[1] Agastya was greatly shocked to learn that his neglect had occasioned so much pain and inconvenience to his ancestors, and he at once resolved to marry and beget offspring. But he could not find a woman anywhere who, in his opinion, was worthy of being the mother of his son. However, endowed as he was with a great superabundance of ascetic merit, he was able to do almost anything he liked. And

[1] The spirits of the dead require to be nourished by the funeral feasts which their sons offer. It is, of course, the Brāhmins or priests who, in the first instance at least, consume the food.

so he took the most beautiful and graceful parts of different animals, and bringing them into suitable combinations with one another, created a wife of whom he did not need to be ashamed.

But this creative act, wonderful though it was, was soon eclipsed by deeds more wonderful still, and Agastya's fame chiefly rests on his miraculous powers of digestion. In illustration of these powers, two stories are told. The first is about a wicked demon, who played a most wicked and cruel trick on certain simple-minded and pious Brāhmins. The demon was offended with the Brāhmins for not securing him a son from the god Indra, and in revenge invited them to a feast. Among other food set before the holy men was what seemed to be goat's flesh, but was really the flesh of the demon's brother, whom the fiend had killed and placed before his guests in the form of a goat. When the Brāhmins had completed their repast, the demon in a loud voice called upon his brother, " Vatāpi, Vatāpi, are you there, Vatāpi ? " Obedient to the summons, Vatāpi emerged from the stomachs of the Brāhmins, rending their bodies asunder as he came. Not long after, Agastya happened to visit this demon. He really went to ask him for assistance in securing a dowry for his bride. The demon received him graciously and brought water to wash his feet. But in his heart he had resolved to play upon Agastya the same trick as he had practised against the Brāhmins with such disastrous effects. And so he caused his brother to be slain and cooked and set before the sage. Of course the sage knew that he was not eating goat's flesh, but he went on eating it, till not a single chop or steak remained. The demon was greatly delighted, and could not conceal his joy. But his joy was soon changed into sorrow. Because when he called aloud as before, " Vatāpi, Vatāpi, are you there ? come out ! Vatāpi ! " Vatāpi never came. As for

Agastya, he laughed and said, " You are too late : I
have digested him." And all the demon ever saw or
heard of his brother was a mighty eructation which
followed this calm and crushing retort.

But Agastya's powers of digestion were put to even a
greater use on another occasion. It was during the golden
age, when the gods and demons were so often at war.
After many long and bloody fights, the demons had been
compelled to take refuge in the ocean. But from the
ocean as their hiding-place they issued forth time after
time, carrying fire and sword in all directions. Indeed,
they made the determined resolve that they would utterly
destroy all knowledge of religion and virtue from the
earth. " By destroying religion and virtue," they said,
" we shall secure also the destruction of the three worlds."
And so creeping out stealthily by night, when all were
asleep, they visited one hermitage after another and
murdered their inhabitants. They did their work so
quietly that no one knew of their coming or of their going.
But every morning fresh signs of their cruelty were to
be seen on every hand. The earth was covered with the
bones of the holy men, whose flesh had been eaten, with
broken jars and other implements of worship, while the
sacred fires and the offerings of clarified butter were
scattered and poured forth with dishonour on the ground.

Such mysterious visitations gradually filled the minds
of men with universal terror. Many hid themselves in
caves and dens of the earth ; others fled to the more
remote mountains and forests ; so great was the de-
moralisation that fear of death caused others to commit
suicide. But there were others again who knew no fear.
These banded themselves together and went out in search
of their invisible foes. Of course it was a fruitless effort.
No one could be found. The demons were hiding at the
bottom of the sea. Nor were the celestials free from

anxiety and fear. They did not realise that it was their old enemies the demons who were the cause of the mischief. But it was perfectly manifest that if the lives of the remaining Brāhmins were not saved, nothing could avert the destruction of the universe. They therefore hastened with Indra, the king of heaven, at their head, to intercede with Vishnu, the preserver-god. In approaching that mighty deity they reminded him of how on various occasions he had come to the rescue and saved a suffering world.[1] They could not explain how it happened, but night after night great multitudes of Brāhmins were being destroyed. Who their murderers were they did not know. One thing, however, was certain. If something was not done to stop it, with the destruction of the Brāhmins would go the destruction of the world. In reply Vishnu explained that he knew who the murderers were, and where they were living. They were the demons whom his brother celestials, by their prowess, had compelled to take refuge in the depths of the ocean. He would be only too happy to help them to kill the demons. But the difficulty was how to catch them. If there was no water in the sea, the whole business would be comparatively easy. They could advance over the ocean's empty bed and slay their foes. The only person, as far as Vishnu could see, who would be able to help them was the *rishi* Agastya. His powers of digestion were simply wonderful. If he could be persuaded to drink up the waters of the ocean all would be well. In obedience to this advice the gods hastened to Agastya's hermitage. Bowing humbly before the sage, they began to sing his praise. Among much else they told him that whenever they were in any difficulty, they always sought his help. And they did so with the more confidence, because he never sent any one

[1] They mentioned his incarnation as a Boar, as a Man-lion, and as a Dwarf.

away with empty hands. Agastya asked the gods to say
what boon they craved. When they had explained the
purpose of their visit in a few words, the holy man at once
agreed, knowing, as he did, that his action would confer
a great benefit on the world. Nor did he delay a single
moment. Getting up from his seat, he set out for the
shores of the ocean. He was followed by a great mixed
multitude of gods and men, all eager to witness the swallowing of the ocean. As they watched the level of the sea
getting lower and lower, the gods were filled with wonder
and praise. They told the sage that he was indeed the
creator and preserver of the world, that by his goodness
they themselves had been saved from destruction. When
the last drop had been consumed, and the bed of the ocean
exposed from shore to shore, the heavenly hosts advanced
to the conflict. It was a great fight that ensued, but the
scene they had just witnessed encouraged the gods immensely, while it had an equally depressing effect on their
opponents. The result was that nearly all the demons
were slain; only a few managed to make their escape,
disappearing, as they did, through certain clefts in the
earth, and finding a refuge in hell. When the victorious
gods returned to their benefactor, and had thanked him
anew, they not unnaturally suggested that the sage should
now disgorge the waters he had swallowed, and fill the
ocean again. But, as on the former occasion, Agastya
replied, "You are too late, I have digested the waters.
You must think of some other contrivance for filling the
ocean's empty bed." This answer filled the celestials with
mingled wonder and distress. They could not sufficiently
admire the powers and capacity of the sage. But it was
not till Brahmā had promised to bring down the Ganges
from heaven that their minds were set at rest, and the
ocean's empty bed refilled.

Mahābhārata, iii. 96.

VIII.

SAGARA'S SIXTY THOUSAND SONS.

"There is no heaven for a sonless man, and when he dies, his ancestors also perish."—*Mahābhārata*, i. 120. 15.

SAGARA, king of Ayodhyā, spent one hundred years in the practice of asceticism. His object in doing so was to persuade the gods to have mercy on him and grant him an heir to his throne. His efforts were successful. An eminent ascetic came and said that the gods had heard his prayers.[1] And in due course one of his queens gave birth to a son, while the other was delivered of a gourd. When the monarch saw the gourd, his first impulse was to throw it away. But a voice from heaven warned him not to be so foolish as to cast away his sons. In obedience to further instruction from the same heavenly source, Sagara separated the seeds within the gourd, which amounted to no less than sixty thousand in number, and placed them one by one in jars full of clarified butter. As a further precaution he placed a nurse in charge of each of the sixty thousand jars. His efforts were in the end rewarded, because from each of the jars there emerged a handsome boy. But in the long-run Sagara had no cause to congratulate himself on his numerous offspring. The son who was born at a single birth had to be driven into exile for his cruelty in casting the children of his

[1] The *Mahābhārata* says it was the god Shiva who heard his prayer.

father's subjects into a river and laughing at their dying agonies; while it is said of the sixty thousand brothers that they were fierce wild men, who were the cause of infinite trouble to both gods and men. Their strength and power were such that they were able to climb the sky and chase the celestials from their seats. Such a situation could not last for even, and Brahmā was invited by a joint deputation of gods and men to take the necessary action. Without explaining what he proposed to do, the grandsire told the deputation not to worry. They could return to their homes satisfied that, before long, Sagara's sixty thousand sons would be destroyed.

Not long after, Sagara began to prepare for a horse sacrifice. According to the usual practice, the horse chosen for the sacrifice was set free to roam over the world for the space of a year. It was watched and guarded with great care by Sagara's sons. Despite their precautions, however, when it came to the ocean's empty bed, it disappeared from view.[1] The young men at once returned to their father and reported their loss. They said they were convinced that the animal must have been stolen. And they were right in their opinion, because the god Indra came in the form of a demon and carried it off. When the monarch heard of his loss, he was both perplexed and afraid. His priests said that the animal must be recovered, and the thief punished with death. If this was not done, the ceremonies in which they were engaged would bring upon them a curse instead of a blessing. He therefore ordered his sons from his presence, and said they were not to come back unless they brought the horse with them. In obedience to their father's command, the young men searched everywhere. They traversed the whole world, they searched in every corner of its surface, but without success. When that failed they began to dig

[1] Empty, because the sage Agastya had drunk up the ocean.

deep into the earth for several hundred thousand miles, injuring or killing countless demons, serpents and other creatures in the process. They dug so deep that they went right down to hell, while the noise and clamour raised by the dying victims could be heard on every hand. Filled with dread and terror, gods and demons, sages and animals once more sought the presence of Brahmā, and asked him if he was not really going to interfere. On this occasion also, Brahmā told the appellants not to worry; but he condescended to explain what was about to take place. Before long the sons of Sagara would dig themselves into the presence of the god Vishnu. When that happened they would be utterly consumed. The gods who are spoken of as the Thirty-three, and the other members of the delegation, were greatly delighted to obtain this information, and went off to their respective abodes.

While this business was proceeding in heaven, the sons of Sagara also had ventured to approach their father and say that they had done their best and could do no more. But he drove them from his presence, and said they must not cease their search, and must not return until they had found the horse. In obedience to this fresh command they returned to their task and went on digging until they came to where the four immortal elephants uphold the world on their shoulders. These animals they greeted one after the other, but they continued their labours until, as Brahmā had said, they found themselves in the presence of Vishnu. He was standing before them in the form of the *rishi* Kapila, and grazing quietly beside him was the horse for which they had searched so long. Brandishing their spades and shovels, the sons of Sagara rushed at the *rishi*. As they did so, they called him an impious knave, and roundly accused him of stealing their property. Under the impulse of Fate they spoke as they did, and brought destruction upon themselves. The *rishi* uttered a tre-

mendous roar, his eyes blazed with anger, and in a
moment Sagara's sixty thousand sons had been reduced
to ashes.

Rāmāyana, i. 38.
Mahābhārata, iii. 106

IX.

THE GANGES DESCENDS FROM HEAVEN.

" To repeat her name brings purity, to see her secures prosperity, to bathe in or to drink her waters saves seven generations of our race, up and down. There is no place of pilgrimage like the Ganges, no god like Vishnu, and no one superior to Brāhmins."—*Mahābhārata*, iii. 85, 93, 96.

KING SAGARA waited long and anxiously for the return of his sixty thousand sons. When he could wait no longer, he called his grandson before him and told him to go and look for his uncles. The youth, following the path his relatives had ultimately travelled, came to the opening by which they had dug their way to the regions below the earth. And, like them, he saw the four immortal elephants who sustain the worlds. He spoke to each of them in turn ; and in each case his question was the same : " Do you know what has happened to my uncles, and have you seen the horse of which they are in search ? " But the elephants contented themselves with saying in reply : " You will achieve your purpose, and secure the steed which has been lost." As to his uncles and the fate which had befallen them, they were silent. Cheered by these encouraging words, the youth continued his search, and before long reached the spot where the horse was grazing. But how great was his sorrow when he saw all that was left of his sixty thousand uncles, a heap of ashes, lying on the ground. He hunted in every direction for water to enable him to make a funeral oblation, but not a drop could he find. As he stood lamenting their hard fate, deprived even of the offering without which his relatives could not hope to enter heaven, the bird Garuda, which is the vehicle of Vishnu, appeared before him and told him not to weep. His uncles would be greatly honoured at some future day, because the river Ganges would herself descend from heaven, and with her sacred waters lave the ashes of the dead, and bring them safe at last to heaven.

When the prince returned home and told his grandfather what he had seen and heard, that monarch at once proceeded to complete the sacrifice of the horse which had been so long delayed. But the one object of his life thereafter was, how the river Ganges could be persuaded to descend from heaven and emancipate the spirits of his sons. He lived for thirty thousand years after, but he died without achieving his purpose. And it is said that his grandson and great-grandson spent even greater periods in the practice of the most severe asceticism, and with the same object in view, to bring the Ganges down from heaven and rescue the souls of Sagara's sixty thousand sons.

The next in succession was more successful. In the fervour of his devotion he abandoned his kingdom and gave himself up entirely to achieving the end which for four generations had so obsessed his race. For a thousand years he stood with hands upraised. He never tasted food more that once a month all that time. He surrounded himself with the five fires, and brought his senses under control. Brahmā at last took pity on him, and, accompanied by the other gods, came and told him to ask a boon. The boon he asked for was, of course, that the Ganges would descend from heaven. But Brahmā replied that were the Ganges to fall all the distance from heaven to earth, it would be more than the latter could endure. Something must be done to break the force of the waters. There was, however, one being whose assistance might be solicited; and indeed Brahmā did not know any one else strong enough to do what he was about to suggest. It was that the god Shiva be requested to allow the Ganges to fall midway upon his head.

Having given this advice, Brahmā and the other celestials disappeared. But Bhagiratha, for such was the prince's name, at once addressed himself to Shiva. For twelve months he stood upright and motionless, bearing the weight of his body on a single toe. Throughout the year, he never ate any food and he never slept. Happily at the end of that comparatively brief period of time, Shiva came and said that he was so well pleased with his devotion that he would do what Brahmā had suggested, and allow the Ganges to fall upon his head. But the river goddess apparently had not been consulted, and she was very unwilling to leave her home in the skies. If it was not possible for her to disobey, she could cause her brother deity some inconvenience, and perhaps sweep him down to hell. And so she came, pouring her waters with furious violence on Shiva's head. That powerful deity knew what was in her thoughts, and of course was quite unmoved by her vehemence. But to punish the goddess and to tame her pride, he kept her waters wandering through his locks for years.

> " He held the river on his head,
> And kept her wandering, where,
> Dense as Himālayas woods were spread,
> The tangles of his hair.
>
> No way to earth she found, ashamed,
> Though long and sore she strove,
> Condemned until her pride were tamed,
> Amid his locks to rove." [1]

---

[1] Quoted from Griffith's translation.

When the waters were released at last, and the Ganges reached the earth, the prince mounted a swift car and drove towards the spot where the ashes of his kinsmen lay. Wherever he went, the Ganges meekly followed. The whole incident created great interest in heaven, and the gods, riding in chariots, or mounted on horses and elephants as big as towns, joined in the procession. And it was not long before heavenly nymphs, demons, giants, sages, and snakes had added themselves to the company. It was indeed too good an opportunity to lose, and as the Ganges hurried on, in the footsteps of the prince, the whole multitude of created beings bathed in her sacred waters and washed away their sins.

An unlucky incident nearly marred the success of Bhagiratha's long devotion. The Ganges happened to flow over the spot where an eminent ascetic was at that very moment offering a sacrifice, and in his anger the holy man drank the river up. It was fortunate there were so many gods and sages at hand. With one voice they began to propitiate the offended devotee. They cleverly suggested that the saint might look upon the river as his own daughter. This was an argument which seemed to make a strong impression on the holy man, because he graciously suppressed his wrath and allowed the Ganges to escape by his ears. Very soon after Bhagiratha and the goddess arrived at the dry bed of the ocean. From there they made their descent to the lower world. Bhagiratha's long penance was now approaching a successful close. Whenever the Ganges reached the spot where the ashes of the dead were lying, and had encircled them with her waters, the souls of Sagara's sons were delivered from their bondage, and mounted up to heaven. Nor was this the only benefit that was achieved. Ever since the sage Agastya had drunk up the ocean, her empty bed had never been refilled.

But now with the coming of the Ganges, that great defect in the order of nature was fully remedied and the ocean was replenished to her furthest shores.

Rāmāyana, i. 41.
Mahābhārata, iii. 107.

X.

THE FLOOD.

"The gods who spring from Manu." "Our father Manu."—*Rig-Veda*, i. 45, ii. 33.

A.

WHEN Manu, the father of mankind, was one day washing his hands, he found that a fish had got stranded on one of his palms. It was a very little fish; nevertheless it was able to address the sage, and this is what it said: "Save my life and take care of me, and in return I shall save you." "From what will you save me?" Manu asked. "I shall save you," answered the fish, "from a great flood which will sweep away and destroy all living creatures." "But tell me," said Manu, "in what way I am to take care of you." "Put me in a jar," said the fish. "As long as we are small we fish are in constant danger of our lives because we prey upon and devour one another. When I am too big for the jar, dig a tank and put me there. When the tank is too small to hold me, take me to the ocean. Once I get into the ocean, no one will be able to harm me." By the time it had grown to be a very large fish and was ready for transference to the ocean, the creature addressed Manu again. And it was to tell him that the flood would take place in a certain year, and before that time Manu must build a ship in which he was to seek refuge when the waters covered the earth. The

sage gave careful heed to the instructions of his benefactor.
He built a ship, and when the floods began, sought its
shelter. The fish appeared as it had promised, and Manu
fastened a great rope to a horn whch grew on its head.
When this had been done, the fish swam quickly toward
the north, until they reached a great mountain. " Now,"
said the fish, " I have saved your life. Fasten the ship
to a tree and get out. But take care you are not cut off
by the flood. Descend the mountain with caution, and
never go beyond the water level." In this matter also
Manu faithfully obeyed the fish's injunctions, and to this
day the path by which he travelled is known as Manu's
descent.

But the flood had wiped all living creatures off the face
of the earth, and Manu was left alone. He therefore determined that he would engage in austerities and thereby
secure offspring. And so, to that end, he cast into the
waters clarified butter, sour milk, whey and curds. These
materials hardened into a solid mass and, in the course
of a year, a woman was produced. As she rose out of the
waters she was met by the gods Mitra and Varuna. When
they asked her who she was, she said, " I am Manu's
daughter." " No! no!" said the gods, " say you are
ours." But she answered once again, " I am the daughter
of him who begat me." They would have liked to keep
her and to have a share in her. But though she both
promised and did not promise, she passed on and came to
Manu. When Manu saw her, he too put the same question
to her : " Who are you ? " and he was very much surprised
when she said : " I am your daughter." " How can that
be ? " he asked. But he understood when she told him
how she had been born from the milk and curds and whey
that he had cast into the sea. She also told him to make
use of her in the sacrifices he was continuing to offer,
adding the promise that if he did so, he would become

rich in both offspring and cattle.   And so the two continued
to live together, performing their acts of worship, engaging
in austerities and desirous of offspring.   Her name was
Idā.   It was by her that Manu became the father of the
race, and it was through her that he obtained whatever
blessings he happened to desire.

Shatapatha Brāhmana, i. 8.

B.

Manu was a very great *rishi*.   His father was the Sun
and his grandfather was Brahmā, but he excelled them both
in the length and fervour of his austerities.   He stood on
one leg for ten thousand years.   He held his arms raised
high above his head and his eyes fixed upon the ground
all that time.   One day, as he was standing in this posture
by the bank of a river, a fish spoke to him.   It was a very
little fish, it said, and its life was a burden to it because
of the dangers to which it was continually exposed.   The
big fish lived on the little fish, and it was the duty of a *rishi*,
so faithful to his vows as Manu was, to afford protection
to those who were in suffering.   Manu turned a kindly
ear to the cry of the suppliant.   He lifted the little fish
out of the water with his own hands and placed it in an
earthen vessel.   Now, small though it was, this was no
ordinary fish.   Its body was as bright as the rays of the
Moon, and in a few days it had grown so big that the
vessel in which Manu had placed it was not big enough to
hold it.   By this time Manu had become very fond of his
protégé, and cared for it as if it were a child of his own.
And so when the fish asked the sage to find a more con-
venient home for it, he put it in a large reservoir.   This
reservoir was fourteen miles long and seven miles broad,
and one might have thought that no further anxiety would
arise as to the size of its habitation.   But as the years

passed, the fish had grown so big that even there it was
scarcely able to move. It therefore made a fresh appeal
to the sage and asked him to carry it to the Ganges.
Manu did so. But in course of time the Ganges became
too small and it was manifest that the only alternative
left was the ocean. By this time the fish must have been
a very large animal indeed, but the *Mahābhārata* says that,
notwithstanding its great bulk, Manu could carry it quite
easily, and experienced great pleasure from its taste and
smell.

When the fish first appealed to Manu for protection it
told him that he would not fail to obtain a reward for his
compassion. And now, when Manu had placed it in the
ocean, the hour had come for the fish to implement its
promise. The destruction of the universe, it said, was at
hand. The three worlds would be overwhelmed in a
mighty flood, and if Manu would save his life he must build
a great and powerful boat which would be able to endure
the storm and tempest that were approaching. He was
to tell no one except the seven *rishis*. They would be
spared along with him when all other living creatures were
destroyed. In addition, he was to make a long rope and
store the ark with seeds of all kinds, kept carefully apart
from one another. The fish promised to reappear when the
ark was ready and the floods had begun. Its shape would
be considerably altered, but Manu would recognise it by
a great horn rising from its head.

In accordance with the instruction he received, Manu
built an ark, stocked it with seeds of every kind, made a
long rope, and summoned his friends, the seven *rishis*.
We are left to imagine how the flood began. The bald
statement is made that when everything was ready, Manu
set sail upon the stormy sea. And when he did so, the fish
appeared. Manu made a noose in the rope and fastened
it to the horn on the fish's head. For many years Manu

and the seven *rishis* were towed all over the raging waters
which covered not only earth but heaven. Their vessel
reeled to and fro "like a drunken harlot." But though
every living thing had been destroyed, including gods,
demons, beasts and men, the inhabitants of heaven, earth
and hell, Manu and his companions were saved from all
danger, safe within the ark, cared for by the fish. But a
day came when the waters began to assuage, and the
ark grounded on a peak of the Himālayas. And now the
fish spoke once more. Manu was bidden to fasten the vessel
to the mountain top without delay. For the fish had
something very important to say. It was to the assembled
rishis and not to Manu alone that he spoke : " I am Brahmā,
the lord of creatures, there is none greater than I. I took
the form of a fish that I might save you from destruction,
and now Manu will create gods, demons and men, that
the three worlds may be repeopled. He will create everything that has life ; movable and immovable. And
the power to do so he will acquire by the practice of
asceticism. And so it came to pass. Manu began afresh
the practice of asceticism, and by means of the power he
thus acquired he was able to begin the task of creation and
repeople the worlds.

If you listen to the story of Manu and the Fish every
day of your life, you will secure the fulfilment of all your
desires, and go to heaven when you die.

Mahābhārata, iii. 187.

XI.

THE MAN WHO WAS MADE A GOD.

" A Brāhmin is the lord of all created things. Whatever exists in the
world is his property. On account of the excellence of his origin he is
entitled to it all."—*Laws of Manu*, i. 99–100.

" It is through the Brāhmins that the spirits of the dead and the gods
become pleased."—*Mahābhārata*, xiii. 29, 10.

AMONG the many heroes who received a mortal wound in
the great battle of Kurukshetra, the greatest of all was
Bhishma. He lay for fifty-six days on the very spot
where he fell. And his body was so thickly covered with
arrows, that they formed the couch, as it were, on which he
lay all that time. Many eminent sages, and more than one
incarnation of the god Vishnu, sat round his bed. Among
the latter there was Krishna, who said that when Bhishma
died, knowledge of every kind would disappear from the
world, and the earth would look like a moonless night.
It was therefore deemed advisable to cross-examine the
dying man on a variety of subjects, so that some, at least,
of his gathered wisdom might be preserved. King
Yudhisthira was the principal interrogator, and one of his
questions was as follows : " By what means is it possible
for one of the three inferior castes to obtain the rank of a
Brāhmin ? " He had heard that the great king, Vishvāmitra, who was a member of the warrior caste, had by the
most unparalleled asceticism acquired that very great
honour. But Bhishma ignored that well-known story,

and declared that it was not possible that any one should hope for such a thing. And the reason was, that the soul had to pass through countless births before it could rise to what was the highest point of greatness open to created beings. The Brāhmin was greater even than the gods. The Brāhmin could make gods and he could unmake them. In illustration of that, he would tell the king a story about an outcaste who tried hard to be made a Brāhmin and failed, but was changed into a god instead. This person's name was Matanga, and he was supposed to be a Brāhmin. But his mother, unknown to her husband, had been guilty of criminal intercourse with a barber. One day his putative father sent Matanga to bring the sticks necessary for a sacrifice he was proposing to celebrate. Matanga travelled in a car drawn by a young ass. But on the road the animal happened to see his mother at some distance and made off in her direction, despite the protests of his owner. Matanga was very angry and struck the ass several times over the nose with his goad. When the mother saw her offspring being so grievously beaten, she sought to comfort him with the observation that one did not need to wonder at such treatment. For though the youth was supposed to be a Brāhmin, he was not really so. He was a base-born Chandāla, the son of a low-caste barber. Brāhmins were always kind and gentle to every one, and the youth by his action proved the baseness of his origin. Matanga was greatly distressed at these words of the she-ass, and getting out of his chariot asked her to say how she knew that he was a Chandāla, and not a Brāhmin. Thus appealed to, the she-ass entered into details, and proved to the youth that all she had said was true. Matanga at once went back to his father, told him what he had heard, and retired to a forest. He had already made up his mind that, however low his birth had been, he would compel the gods to confer upon him the rank of Brāhmin. It was, of course, by means of austerities that he proposed to secure the dignity. He therefore began a course of asceticism so drastic and compelling that the heaven grew hot with his devotions, and the gods began to burn. Realising what was wrong, Indra went down to earth and asked Matanga why he was robbing his youth of the pleasures to which it was entitled, and passing his days in useless grief. If he wished a boon, let him say at once what it was he wanted, and he would get it. But he must abandon a procedure that was causing so much discomfort in heaven. Matanga replied : " Make me a Brāhmin and I shall go home at once. If you grant me this favour, I shall trouble you no more." When Indra heard the amazing demand, he said that the youth was asking for the impossible, and would only bring destruction upon himself. How could a Chandāla hope to acquire a dignity and rank that gods, demons and men said was the highest in the universe.

But Matanga refused to be dissuaded from his task, and for an hundred years supported the weight of his body on one foot. This resulted in fresh remonstrance from Indra, who came a second time and advised him for his own sake to desist. On this occasion he took the trouble to explain why it was impossible. The soul passed from body to body through a chain of endless births. It began with the brute and gradually worked its way to the rank of a human being. Among human beings it began at the bottom and at the very bottom stood the Chandāla, the lowest of outcastes, the rank Matanga himself occupied. In that grade the soul spent a thousand years. At the end of that time it became a Shūdra, the lowest of the four castes, and a Shūdra it remained for 30,000 years. When the necessary number of births and years had expired, it rose to the Vaishya caste, in which it spent no less than 1,800,000 years, and then to the Kshatriya order, for 108 million years. Then and then only can the soul hope to enter the Brāhmin caste. But in this caste there are many grades, and the soul begins as a degraded Brāhmin, occupying that rank for 2160 million years. It then enters a higher order of Brāhmins, those, namely, who act as soldiers. Among these it will pass 648,000 million years. When that lengthy period of time is over, the soul becomes a Brāhmin who is able to repeat the Gāyatrī and other sacred verses, a condition which will endure for 259 millions of millions of years. When that stage is over, the Brāhmin will have become the excellent being who knows all the Vedas and other sacred books. The resources of arithmetic seem to have been exhausted, but we are told that the soul will wander in that existence for a very long period. But it is to be noted that during all that time, when the very highest pinnacle of existence has, as it were, been reached, joy and grief, desire and hatred, with other vices, will seek ceaselessly to destroy him. Should they succeed, he will fall, fall like a man who comes crashing to the ground from the top of a palmyra tree. On the other hand, he may be able to resist his foes and achieve liberation, which means that he will be born no more. No wonder then that Indra, as he concluded his long harangue, advised Matanga to abandon his efforts.

But Matanga refused to listen. Instead, he began a course of asceticism much more severe than anything he had previously attempted. He brought his mind under control, he engaged in the practice of *yoga*, and stood on one foot for a thousand years. When that interval had elapsed, Indra appeared a third time. He used the same arguments as formerly, and with the same success. But after the interview Matanga abandoned the forest and went to Gaya. There he went through the same rites as before. But the lapse of time was beginning to tell, and one day, after another hundred years had passed, he fell exhausted to the ground. By this time his veins were terribly swollen, and visible to the naked eye. He was a bundle of skin and bone. When Indra saw his fall, he rushed to the scene. Holding him fast, he addressed the stricken man in language similar to what we have already heard. Such treatment not unnaturally irritated the devotee, and he appealed to the god not to strike a man who was as good as dead. Manifestly Destiny was more powerful than human effort, when, with all his toil, he was unable to secure the rank that he desired. But he could not help wondering why it was that Brāhmins were so heedless and indifferent about the lofty status they had acquired. Why was it that they so often, by their careless-ness and sin, allowed themselves to be deprived of it. And surely it was very hard that he, through no fault of his own, but because of his mother's sin, should be born as a low Chandāla. However, he was convinced at last. It was perfectly plain that he could not hope to become a Brāhmin. He would therefore crave another boon. "Tell me what you want," said Indra. "Ask for any-thing else and it is yours."

What else could Matanga ask for than to be made a god, able to change his shape at will, to travel through the air, to have and to enjoy whatever he wanted, to receive the willing worship of Brāhmins and Kshatriyas. And so Indra made Matanga a god, and promised that he would obtain the worship of all classes of women as well, with a name that had no equal in heaven, earth and hell. But it was not possible to make him a Brāhmin. That is a dignity to which even the great god Indra himself could not hope to aspire.

No wonder the dying warrior warned his friends to see to it that they never offended a Brāhmin. No one could withstand them. Some of them were of a very gentle disposition, as soft as cotton. But others were very cunning and cruel. And, when made angry, they could by their incantations cause untold injury, could even reduce a kingdom to ashes by their frowns. The bravest of men had good cause to fear them; it was a sign of wisdom to sing their praise, because nobody who quarrelled with a Brāhmin could ever hope to end his days in peace. Yes, and in the next world our neglect would follow us, for neither the gods nor the spirits of the dead will eat the offering of the man with whom a Brāhmin is displeased.

Mahābhārata, xiii. 27–29.

XII.

THE BOY WHO WAS CHANGED INTO A STAR.

" Because they satisfied the ordinances laid down by the creator, the seven pious *rishis* shine brilliantly in the sky."—*Mahābhārata*, iii. 25. 14.

LONG, long ago, soon after the creation of the world, there was a king who had two sons by different wives. One day, when this prince was seated on his throne, fondling the son of his favourite wife, his other child, called Dhruva, approached and asked his father to take him up on his knee, beside his brother. But Dhruva's stepmother, who was standing near, intervened and rudely asked what right he had to ask for such a favour. He was only the son of an inferior wife, and must not dream of ever enjoying the privilege of sitting on a throne. Dhruva was only five years old, nevertheless he was very angry at these observations, and went off in a passion to his mother's room. When he had told his story, she urged him not to grieve. He must be reconciled to his fate. 'A kingly throne and white umbrella would never be his portion. He was not the son of the favourite wife. And she humbly acknowledged that both she and Dhruva must be suffering for sins they had committed in a former life, even as their successful rivals were being rewarded for the merit they had accumulated. At the same time, while she imparted these words of consolation, she pointed out that if he was still unable to be resigned, it was always possible to acquire

merit and make his future better than his past. She
brought her observations to an end by remarking that
prosperity was always the portion of a meek and humble
heart. To this wise counsel, however, Dhruva replied by
saying that he would so exert himself as to make his name
renowned throughout the world. He would achieve, and
by his own unaided effort, a position such as his father
had never enjoyed.

And without further delay the child set out upon his
task. Leaving his father's capital, he had not gone far
when he came to a forest, where he saw seven ascetics
seated on the ground. They proved to be *the seven rishis*.
Dhruva approached them with the greatest reverence,
and, bowing humbly at their feet, said that he was tired
of life and had come to seek their help. The *rishis* were
greatly surprised, and asked how a child not more than
four or five years old, the son of a king too, free from
disease and sorrow, whose every want was satisfied, could
be so discontented. When Dhruva had told the story of
his wrongs, the ascetics could only marvel at a child so
young cherishing such resentful feelings ; but they ascribed
it to the fact that he belonged to the passionate warrior
caste. Nevertheless, they asked him what he proposed
doing, and to say plainly how he thought they could help
him. The child replied that he wished neither wealth nor
royal dignity. But he was resolved to reach such a station
as no one before him had ever acquired. The seven *rishis*
each severally replied to this appeal. And their answers
were all to the same effect. The person who propitiated
Vishnu could get anything he desired. " You have told
me," said Dhruva, " the god I ought to worship ; recite
to me the prayer that will please him best." When they
had first of all explained to the child that he must concentrate his mind steadily and keep it under control,
emptying it of all " external impressions," they repeated

these words: "OM, glory to Vishnu, whose essence is divine wisdom, whose form is inscrutable, who is manifest as Brahmā, Vishnu and Shiva." He must recite it constantly, in a voice which would be inaudible to others.

When he had received these instructions, Dhruva took a respectful farewell of the *rishis* and went off to a place called the grove of Madhu, situated on the banks of the river Jumna. At this sacred spot, where Vishnu himself dwells, and which cleanses the worshipper of all sins, the child began the practice of penance, and engaged in the contemplation of the deity in accordance with the forms prescribed by the sages. And as a result, Vishnu so filled his heart that the earth could not bear the weight of the god-possessed devotee. When he stood on his right foot, one half of the world sank down; when he stood on his left foot, the other hemisphere bent beneath the burden. Again, when he stood on his toes, the whole world, with its mountains, rivers and seas, shook and was troubled. The celestials were equally distressed, and in consultation with Indra, took steps to interfere with and destroy the powerful penances of Dhruva. One of them assumed the guise of his mother, and begged him to desist, as he was injuring his health. Childhood was intended to be spent in play. When he grew old, he could pray as much as he liked. Besides, he was leaving her all alone, unprotected and helpless. But Dhruva was so engrossed in his meditations that he never even saw the false disguise which would have lured him from his prayers. Nor did he see, or if he saw he did not heed, the horrid evil spirits, the goblins and jackals, calling out to one another, " Kill him, tear him in pieces, eat him up! " All these illusions, vomiting fire, brandishing swords, and uttering awe-inspiring cries, made no impression whatever on his mind, and the gods had to confess themselves entirely baffled. They accordingly resolved to go and see Vishnu, in the

hope that he would help them. When they had praised
that deity in the usual manner, they explained how much
they were distressed by the austerities of Dhruva. They
could not tell what he was aspiring to. It might be that
he sought to overthrow Indra or the Sun. Perhaps he
would be satisfied with the lordship of the ocean, or the
wealth of the god of riches. Vishnu, however, soon set
the minds of the celestials at rest. He said they need
not be afraid. Dhruva was plotting against none of the
deities they had mentioned. Neither Indra nor the
Ocean, neither the Sun nor the god of riches, had any
cause for anxiety. The child had other ambitions, which
he proposed to satisfy, and their gratification would bring
his penances to a close. The deities were greatly delighted
to receive this information, and after making appropriate
farewell salutations, went off, headed by Indra, to their
respective heavens.

When the gods had departed, Vishnu addressed his
worshipper, and bade him ask a boon. When he heard
the voice, Dhruva opened his eyes and was filled with
awe and rapture on realising that he was privileged to see
the four-armed god. His one thought was, " How can I
praise him as I ought " ; and he answered, " Give me
power to do this and I am content, because my heart is
overflowing with devotion to thee." In reply, Vishnu
gently touched Dhruva with the shell he always carries
about with him, and the child at once began to sing a
hymn of praise. In this hymn Vishnu's forms were said
to be like the five grosser elements (earth, air, fire, water
and ether), mind, intellect, consciousness, nature and
spirit. He was also said to be Brahm, devoid of qualities,[1]
and the primeval male with a thousand feet, a thousand

---

[1] Brahm, " devoid of qualities," is the supreme soul of the universe.
He must be carefully distinguished from Brahmā (final a is long), the
creator god.

eyes and heads. The three Vedas, sacrifice, oblations,
curds, clarified butter, horses, cows, sheep, goats and
deer were all born from him, while the four castes sprang
from his head, arms, thighs and feet. The sun came from
his eyes, the wind from his ears, fire from his mouth,
heaven from his head, the sky from his navel and the
earth from his feet. In fact, the whole world had its
origin in him, even as the seed of the fig-tree contained
the fig-tree itself in germ. When he had brought his
hymn to a close, Dhruva protested that in obtaining a
vision of the god he had obtained all he wanted. But
Vishnu graciously observed that while that no doubt was
true, he wished him to say what boon he yet desired.
Thus encouraged, Dhruva told the story of his wrongs at
the hands of his stepmother, and said he was resolved to
achieve a position higher than that held by all others,
and one, too, that would last for ever. The god replied
that his prayer was granted. Some of the celestials only
lived through the four ages, some for many millions of
years. But Dhruva's life would continue for the whole
duration of a universe. Those who worshipped Vishnu
obtained emancipation, and one so devout, so absorbed
in devotion as Dhruva was, did not look on heaven as a
reward of any real value. He therefore proposed to raise
him to a *station* [1] which was higher than heaven, higher
than the three worlds; higher than the Sun, moon and
stars, higher even than the dwelling-place of the *seven
rishis*. His mother, too, would be changed into a star,
and for a period of time equal to his own, would dwell
beside him in the skies, while those who sang his praise,
both morning and evening, would acquire great religious
merit. The *Purāna* tells us nothing more about Dhruva's

---

[1] This *station*, so mysteriously referred to in the text, is the *Pole star*,
still spoken of in India as Dhruv-tārā. The *seven rishis* are said to inhabit
the seven stars of the *Great Bear* or *Plough* constellation.

encounter with the god. It says, however, that, in virtue of this boon, Dhruva still occupies his lofty position in the skies, and that those who repeat the story of his translation to these upper worlds, will, in this life, be blessed with every kind of happiness, and after death, purged of all their sins, obtain a place in Indra's heaven.

Vishnu Purāna, i. 11–12.

XIII.

THE KING WHO BECAME A LIZARD.

" No man is the dispenser of his own destiny. The actions done in a
former life are seen to produce fruits in this. The soul is born again with
its accumulated load of *Karma*. By performing only virtuous actions it
attains to the state of the celestials. By a combination of good and
bad actions, it acquires the state of human beings. By indulgence in
sensuality and similar vices, it is born among the lower animals."—
Mahābhārata, iii. 208. 22, 30.

A.

WHEN Rāma, in obedience to the clamour of the citizens,
repudiated his wife a second time and sent her as an
exile into the forest, he was so overpowered by grief that
for the space of four days he was unable to attend to his
kingly duties. But the recollection of an ancient story,
and of what·happened to a king who failed to fulfil his
royal tasks, recalled him to a proper sense of his duty.
This at least is the tale which he told to his brother,
Lakshmana. There was once a very pious king whose
name was Nriga. On one occasion, when on a pilgrimage
to Pushkar, he distributed ten million cows among members
of the Brāhmin caste. Each cow was attended by her
calf; both calves and cows wore ornaments of gold.
Now it so happened that a cow, the private property of a
poor Brāhmin, got mixed up with the cows which the
king had given away in alms. Her owner spent a long
time searching for her, and at last found the animal he
had lost, standing in the cattle shed of a caste fellow.
When he called the cow by name, she at once recognised

her owner's voice, came out of the cattle shed and followed
him along the road. But the Brāhmin, in whose shed
she had been standing, was not prepared so easily to lose
what he believed to be his property, and went off in pursuit,
shouting out, "That cow is mine. I got it from the king."
A very heated altercation ensued, with the result that
they both found themselves at length outside the gate of
the king's palace, resolved to appeal to him in person.
Unfortunately, they were kept waiting a very long time,
and when they were finally admitted to his presence they
were so angry that instead of stating the cause of their
complaint, they cursed the king. What they said was,
"Because you have kept us waiting so long and failed
to listen to our complaint, we curse you to be changed
into a lizard, and to remain in that condition for many
thousands of years. You will only obtain deliverance at
the hands of the god Vishnu, when he will appear on earth
in the form of Krishna ; and that will not happen till the
approach of the fourth age." When they had given this
violent expression to their feelings, the two Brāhmins left
the palace. As the cow was an old and feeble creature,
they decided to settle their dispute by giving her as a
present to another Brāhmin. The king's ministers were
very much distressed when they heard of what had
happened to their master, and they were not slow in
giving expression to their grief. But Nriga himself was
perfectly calm. He told them there were two things he
wished them to do at once. The first was, to instruct
the royal architect to build for him three houses, in which
he would live according to the season of the year ; one
for the hot weather, one for the rains, and the third for
winter. Fruit trees and flowering shrubs were also to be
planted for several miles on every side of these habitations.
By making such arrangements the monarch hoped to
soften the hardships of his condition. His second wish

was to have his son's coronation arranged for without delay. When the three houses had been erected and his son placed upon the throne, Nriga gave his successor some very good advice as to how he should rule his kingdom and observe the laws prescribed for his caste. In particular, he called his attention to the very grievous punishment that had befallen him for what he considered a very slight offence. "Nevertheless," he said, "don't weep for me. We are all in the hands of Time, which dispenses happiness and sorrow. We cannot evade our destiny. We must accept what fate has assigned to us. And don't forget that it is our acts in a previous life which are responsible for what happens to us in this." With these parting counsels the monarch bade farewell to his son and ministers of state, and retired to the houses which the architect had erected for him. When he had told this awful tale, Rāma said once more to his brother, "Just think of it. King Nriga is still suffering from that curse. Go at once and see if there are any suppliants waiting at the palace gate. Kings who do not attend every day to the affairs of their kingdom fall into that fearful hell where no wind ever blows."

Rāmāyana, vii. 63.

B.

Nriga, king of Ayodhyā, was very devoted to Brāhmins, and gave cows without number to these holy men. If it is possible to count the sands of the seashore, the stars in the firmament, or the drops of rain, you may be able to tell the number of cows which that pious monarch gave to Brāhmins. And yet this very religious and generous king was changed into a lizard, and condemned to lie at the bottom of a dry well for thousands and thousands of years, and all because of a very venial sin. Nor was he freed from his sufferings till Krishna, the

incarnation of Vishnu, delivered him at the beginning of
the fourth age.[1] This is how it happened. One day
Nriga resolved to present a thousand cows to Brāhmins.
They were of many colours—white, black, brown, grey
and yellow, with silver hoofs and golden horns. Each of
them was covered with a garment of silk, and with each
of them there went a gift of food and money. Unfortunately, as the recipients were taking away the cows to
their own homes, one of the animals strayed and could
not be found. But unknown to the king and his servants,
she made her way back to her old quarters. On the
following day the monarch had resolved to give away
another thousand cows, and among them was the cow
which had been gifted the previous day. Her owner was
still searching everywhere for his lost gift, and happened
to meet the second day's drove as it was leaving the
palace. Examining them carefully one by one, he discovered the animal he had lost, and at once laid claim to
it. " This cow is mine," he cried. " I got her yesterday
from the king." But her new owner with equal truth
was able to reply, " This cow is mine, I got her from the
king to-day, and I won't let you have her." Such being
the situation, they very soon became enraged at one
another, and with mutual shouts of recrimination and
abuse they both sought the king's presence and laid the
facts as they each knew them before the king. Nriga
was very much distressed. Bowing before them with
the utmost reverence, he ventured to suggest a way out
of the difficulty. It was that they should come to an
amicable settlement, while he himself would undertake to

[1] From the time of Nriga to the beginning of the fourth age, when he
obtained deliverance, a period of close on one million years must have
elapsed. The four ages, according to Hindu chronology, amounted to
over four million years. A fairly serious punishment for keeping two
Brāhmins waiting and giving away the same cow twice.

give one hundred thousand rupees to the Brāhmin who
would agree to surrender his rights over the animal. But
both Brāhmins loudly proclaimed that they would never
agree to such an unworthy proposal. Gifts were not to
be so lightly contemned. Gifts were sacred things. The
king had solemnly presented them with a gift and they
had received it as solemnly, and in return they had
solemnly blessed his majesty. The cow obtained under
such pious conditions could not be surrendered for money.
And they would very much prefer to leave the animal
with the king.

When the Brāhmins went off in this manner, leaving
the cow behind them, Nriga was very much depressed to
think that he had been guilty of so grievous an offence.
What he had done, he had done unwittingly. Nevertheless he felt that he must do something to wipe out his
sin, with the result that he became even more pious and
more generous than he had been before. But, alas! as we
shall see, his efforts were of no avail. Because when he
died and went into the presence of the lord of Death, he
discovered that his sin had not been removed. Death
treated him with great courtesy. He got up from his
chair to receive the new arrival and very politely asked
him to sit down. Indeed he treated him in a most loving
manner, and said that he had acquired a very great deal
of merit, while his sins were very few. And so he said
to him, " In recognition of that fact, I propose to give
you the option of saying which you will have first; the
reward of your virtues, or the punishment of your sins."
To this offer the king answered that he would take his
punishment first, and enjoy himself afterwards. " If
that is your decision," said the lord of Death, " hear what
I have to say. Once upon a time, though quite unwittingly, you twice gave away the same cow in alms to
Brāhmins. For this sin you will be changed into a lizard

and will live in a dry well in a forest near the banks of
the Gumti river. At the end of the third age, when
Krishna, the incarnation of Vishnu, descends to the earth,
he will deliver you from your afflictions." As soon as the
lord of Death pronounced this sentence, he who had been
the mighty monarch of Ayodhyā was transformed into a
lizard and found himself lying at the bottom of a dry well,
where he kept himself alive by feeding on the small
creatures that he found there.

After the lapse of several ages, Vishnu was born in the
form of Krishna. One day when he was hunting with his
sons and grandsons near the Gumti river, the young folk
got very thirsty and went ranging through the forest in
search of water. At last one of them found a well, but
when he looked over the side he saw to his disappoint-
ment that it was empty. His curiosity, however, was
excited by seeing a great lizard lying at the bottom.
"Come, brothers," he shouted, "come and look; here
is a great big lizard at the bottom of a dry well. Let us
tie our turbans together and let one of us go down and
get the lizard up." The proposal was eagerly accepted.
The young men tied their turbans together, and one of
them descended the well. But they discovered that the
lizard was much too heavy for them to raise it in such a
fashion. They were resolved, however, not to own defeat.
As one of them said, "We won't go away till we have got
this creature out." They therefore procured ropes from
a neighbouring village and fastened them round the lizard's
body. But though they pulled their hardest, the lizard
would not budge. In the meantime their grandfather
appeared on the scene, and when he heard the story from
his grandsons, Krishna got down into the well. The
young men no doubt thought that their grandfather
was going to help them. But as soon as Krishna placed
his foot on the lizard's body a wonderful transformation

took place. The lizard was changed into a very handsome man. Kneeling before Krishna's feet with joined hands, the transformed lizard gave thanks to his deliverer in words of adoration. He knew who Krishna was. He called him the Ocean of compassion, because he had remembered him in his low estate. But he was interrupted by the grandsons calling out, " What has happened ? what has happened ? What offence did this man commit for which he was changed into a lizard ? " And so Krishna, turning to the king, said, " Tell my grandsons why you have suffered from this calamity. Who are you ? Where do you come from ? And what sin did you commit ? " " You ask me these questions," said the king—" you ask me these questions, you who know all. Nevertheless, in obedience to your command, I obey." And so he repeated for the benefit of the young men the story which is recorded above, and he added the observation that during the intervening ages he had done nothing else save meditate on Krishna's lotus feet. On the conclusion of the story, king Nriga got into a celestial car which was already waiting for him, and went off to heaven. But Krishna did not fail to emphasise the moral of this tale. Never injure a Brāhmin; never take any of his property. Be patient with his faults; pay him every attention; always show him reverence. Remember, if you ever take back anything you have once given to a Brāhmin, you will suffer as great a punishment as befell this pious king; and don't forget that there is no difference between a Brāhmin and me. If you reverence a Brāhmin you reverence me, and when you die you will go to the highest heaven.

Bhāgavata Purāna (*Prem Sāgar*, 65).

XIV.

THE MARRIAGE OF EARTH AND HEAVEN.

" The man, who eats only twice a day, never taking any food or drink
in the interval, and does this for six years, abstaining all the while from
injuring any creature, and regularly pouring libations on the sacred fire,
will dwell for a million years in Brahmā's heaven, and enjoy the society
of the celestial nymphs."—*Mahābhārata*, xiii. 107. 7.

Pururavas, a prince of the lunar race, was held in high
esteem for his liberality, piety and truthfulness. But he
was even more renowned for his personal beauty. It was
his beauty which led him to form a connection with
Urvasi, one of the nymphs of heaven. Urvasi, in consequence of a curse uttered against her by the gods Mitra
and Varuna, had been compelled to come and live in the
world of mortals. When she reached the earth and saw
Pururavas, she was so smitten by his beauty that she lost
all desire to return to heaven. Pururavas was equally
charmed with Urvasi, and when he proposed that they
should live together, the nymph at once consented, but
with certain reservations. They were three in number.
She had two rams to which she was greatly attached.
These must always be kept beside her bed, and on no
consideration taken away. She must be supplied with
clarified butter as her only food. And thirdly, she must
never see him naked. Pururavas accepted the three
conditions, and the happy pair lived together for sixty-
one thousand years. If that were possible, their love

76

for one another increased day by day. But though Urvasi had forgotten her friends in heaven, they had not forgotten her. The Gandharvas, who sing the praises of the gods, and the Siddhas, or glorified saints, as well as her sister nymphs, felt lonely without her and they resolved to get her back. As they knew the terms of the contract which Urvasi had made with the king, they decided that the best plan would be to secure a violation of it and, to begin with, to carry off the rams. One of the Gandharvas therefore went down to the earth, and, under cover of darkness, approached the bed where the nymph and the king were sleeping. Seizing one of the rams, the Gandharva carried it off. But the animal made such a noise that Urvasi awoke, and discovered that she had been robbed, to use her own phrase, of one of her children. The king, of course, heard the cries of the lady, but he remembered also that he was naked, and dare not get out of bed. But when the Gandharva came and stole the second ram, Urvasi's anger knew no bounds. She said she was manifestly living with one who was both a coward and a knave. If she had had a real husband, it would have been otherwise. He would surely have protected her and her children. These taunts overcame the caution of Pururavas, and, hoping that in the darkness Urvasi would not be able to see him, he got up out of bed, resolved to pursue the thief and recover the animals. The prince had not reckoned on the cunning of the denizens of heaven. At the critical moment they filled the room with a great flash of lightning. Urvasi saw the prince naked ; the conditions of their contract were cancelled, and the nymph disappeared. When they saw that their object had been achieved, the Gandharvas released the rams in which they had no further interest, and went off to heaven. Pururavas at once secured the animals, and returned to the house greatly pleased at achieving his purpose, as

he thought, with so much success. But to his horror
he found that the nymph had disappeared, and no trace
of her was to be found. Crazed with sorrow, and naked as
he was, he searched for her everywhere, in every corner
of the world. At long last he found her at Kurukshetra.
She was in the company of several other nymphs to whom
she remarked, as her late paramour drew near, that she
had spent many happy years in his society. The nymphs
said they were not at all surprised, as he was a very handsome man indeed, and they would be very glad to have the
opportunity of following her example. When Pururavas,
however, appealed to Urvasi to come back and live with
him, she said it could not be. As it happened, she was
already pregnant at the time. But if he came back at
the end of a year she would present him with a son, and
consent to spend a night with him. Pururavas was
compelled to accept this very limited offer. And as time
passed he was allowed to spend one night every year for
six years with Urvasi. In this way he became the father
of six sons. When the sixth son was born, Urvasi told
the king to ask a boon. To this the lover replied that
there was one thing only lacking in his life. He had
overcome his foes. He was possessed of wealth and power.
He was strong in mind and body. He had troops of
friends and a great army. But he would never be happy
unless she consented to live with him for evermore. It
was the Gandharvas who had authorised Urvasi to offer
the king a boon. They now came forward and presented
him with a vessel full of fire. As they did so, they told
him to divide it into three, to fix his mind on the idea of
living with Urvasi, and to offer oblations, adding that if
he did so he would get what he desired. At first Pururavas
was quite satisfied with this assurance and set off for home.
But as he journeyed through a forest he began to think
that he had been a fool. It was Urvasi he had asked for,

and in place of her, he had got nothing but a vessel full
of fire. So he put the vessel on the ground and went off
empty-handed to his dwelling. But at midnight, when
he awoke, he began to think that he had made a blunder,
and getting up out of bed, set out then and there for the
forest. But he found that the vessel had disappeared.
In its place, however, two young trees had sprung up,
the one growing out of the other. These he took to his
palace, resolved that by rubbing them together he would
produce fire and worship it. As he rubbed the pieces
together he recited the *Gāyatri* verse. His efforts were
entirely successful. He elicited fire, divided it into three,
offered oblations with it, and secured a place among the
Gandharvas, never more to be separated from his love.

Vishnu Purāna, iv. 6.

XV.

THE MEETING OF THE AGES.

" In the fourth age, outcaste kings will reign over the earth. Men
will be small in body, shortlived and weak. Girls of seven and eight
years will give birth to children, and boys of ten or twelve beget offspring.
Virtue will lose her strength, and sinful men will prosper exceedingly."
—*Mahābhārata*, iii. 188.

THERE was once a king in Western India who had a very
lovely daughter. She was so beautiful indeed that he could
find no prince who, in his opinion, was worthy of being
her husband. He therefore resolved to go to heaven and
get the advice of Brahmā. When the monarch, who took
his daughter with him, arrived in heaven, he found that the
celestial choirs were singing the praises of the god. He
therefore quietly waited till the singing ceased before he
ventured into the immediate presence of the creator.
Brahmā received him very graciously, and asked him
what he wanted. The king explained that he had so far
been unable to find a suitable husband for his daughter,
and had come for advice. He mentioned several names,
however, of princes who he thought would not be altogether unworthy. But when he mentioned the names,
Brahmā smiled and said : " How long do you think you
have been waiting for the choristers to cease. The princes
you speak of are dead millions and millions of years ago.
Your wife and kinsmen, your friends and ministers and
subjects, have all been devoured by Time." " What

am I to do ? " said the king. " How am I to find a husband for my daughter ? It seemed to me as if I had not
been waiting for more than half an hour." Happily
Brahmā was able to make a thoroughly satisfactory proposal. " It is true," he said, " that your ancient capital
has been wiped out of existence, and all the people of your
age and race. But there is upon the earth another race of
men now living, and on the site of your old capital another
city stands. And its king is not only a great and powerful
prince, but a portion of the god Vishnu. His name is
Balarāma. Go to him, and ask him to marry your
daughter, I am sure they will be worthy of one another."

Brahmā thereupon began to sing the praises of Vishnu.
He identified him with the supreme, eternal Spirit, by
whose favour Brahmā acted as creator, while Vishnu
himself was the preserver, and Shiva the destroyer of the
world. He also identified him with Time, with the great
serpent on whom the universe rests, with fire which bestows
growth and warmth, with air which yields activity, with
water which satisfies our needs, with ether which gives
space for things to move, and with the earth which gives
nourishment to all. Indeed Vishnu was the world, and
the world was in him. He was the man primeval, without
beginning and without end.[1]

In obedience to the god's instructions, the king and his
daughter returned to earth. But when they reached
their native country they were very much surprised to
find that the race had degenerated greatly in the interval.
They were small in stature, and weak in both mind and
body. With such a bridegroom in prospect, however,

[1] Brahmā, Vishnu and Shiva constitute the Hindu triad. It is elsewhere said that Balarāma was the incarnation of a white hair, and
Krishna, his brother, the incarnation of a black hair of Vishnu. It is on
Krishna, and not on Balarāma, that the worshippers of Vishnu usually
lay most emphasis.

neither father nor daughter was prepared to be too critical, and the marriage was immediately arranged and carried through. But the husband did not care to have a wife so very much bigger than himself. He therefore took his ploughshare and cut a piece off both ends of his bride. When he had seen his daughter thus happily married, the father retired to the Himālaya mountains, where he spent the rest of his days in the practice of asceticism.

Vishnu Purāna, iv. 1.

XVI.

THE GREAT GOD SHIVA.

"A serpent for his Brāhminical cord, his throat black with poison, a wreath of dead men's skulls about his breast, in such ghostly attire was arrayed the great god Shiva. . . . He who loves not Shiva's lotus feet, can never dream of pleasing Rāma (Vishnu)."—*Rāmāyan of Tulsidās,* i. 64.

WHEN the god Shiva and his wife Umā were sitting one day on the top of a mountain, the lady happened to notice that the other celestials and their wives were setting off in a body on some expedition. She asked her husband if he knew where they were going and for what purpose. "Yes," he said, "they are going to attend a horse sacrifice that is being celebrated by Daksha, one of the Prajāpatis. "But if the gods are to be there, why are you not going ? " she said. "You are the greatest of all the celestials ; have you not been invited ? " "Ah," said Shiva, "you are reviving a very old story. The celestials long, long ago made an agreement among themselves that I was to get no share in any of the sacrifices." This answer made Umā very angry, and she said it was a very queer arrangement, which sought to exclude the most powerful of all the gods. Indeed she was so overwhelmed with anger and grief that she said she would not speak to her husband again if he did not take steps to rectify such an unjust arrangement. This attitude on his wife's part made Shiva realise that he must do something. He therefore got up

and, summoning all his *yoga* powers, hastened to the place
where Daksha was sacrificing. He was attended by many
of his goblin followers, and, on his behalf, they extinguished
the fires with blood, threw down the sacrificial stakes, ate
up those who were celebrating the sacrifice, and, seizing
the celestial ladies, pushed them discourteously about.
A great number of bottles were broken, with the result
that rivers of milk and treacle began to flow. Mountains
of meat and dishes, containing food of every kind, were
scattered far and wide. The sacrifice itself, in the form
of a deer, took refuge in flight. Shiva was very angry
when he saw the sacrifice running away, and he set off in
swift pursuit. As he ran, a drop of perspiration formed
on his brow. And where it fell to the ground, a great
fire blazed forth. From the fire a terrible-looking creature
emerged, small in stature, with blood-red eyes and a green
beard. This creature took up the pursuit of the sacrifice
and consumed it utterly. When he had consumed the
sacrifice, he turned upon the gods and *rishis*, who fled in
all directions, seeking safety wherever they could. At
this point Brahmā intervened, and begged Shiva to recall
the mighty creature that his wrath had produced, promising
if he did so that the gods would, from that day forward,
give him a share in every sacrifice. The problem, however,
was what should be done with the creature that had been
born from Shiva's anger. If he remained as he was, he
was strong enough to destroy the whole creation. Brahmā
therefore proposed to divide him into a large number of
parts, and thereby minimise his strength. To this proposal
Shiva graciously gave his consent. The product of the
god's anger was divided into many parts, and under the
name of Fever they continue to live among beasts and
men. But Fever is found showing itself in different aspects
and working in different ways. For instance, it enters
into all creatures at birth and death. But the liver disease

in sheep, the hiccup from which parrots suffer, the soreness
that appears on the hoofs of bulls, with many other afflictions and ailments, are all due to Fever. And Fever was
originally the anger which was produced by Shiva at the
sacrifice of Daksha.

There are two versions of this story given in succeeding
chapters of the *Mahābhārata*. The first indicates that
neither gods nor *rishis* had any thought of inviting Shiva
to the sacrifice, but the second version says that a *rishi*,
called Dadhīcha, asked why Shiva had not been invited.
In fact, he said that the sacrifice was not worth celebrating
if Shiva (Rudra) was not present. Daksha replied that
there were eleven Rudras in all, and he knew every one of
them, but he did not know who this great god was whom
Dadhīcha was talking about. He was offering a sacrifice
to Vishnu, the master and lord of all the gods, the god
without a peer. Apparently Dadhīcha was in a minority
of one, and he departed from the company, saying he was
certain that some great calamity would befall them if they
worshipped one who ought not to be worshipped, and
refused to worship him who ought to be adored.[1] When
Shiva appeared on the scene very soon after and destroyed
the sacrifice, Daksha's memory underwent a rapid improve-
ment. He humbly besought forgiveness, and asked the
god to confer upon him a boon. He also proceeded to
repeat the 1008 names of Shiva. The god was greatly
pleased with this act of adoration, and said it would confer
as much benefit on his worshipper as if he had performed
a thousand horse sacrifices. Best of all, he imparted to
his worshipper a new religion which the gods and demons,
he said, had elaborated from the Vedas and the philosophies of Sānkhya and Yoga. These supernatural creatures had long used it in the practice of their austerities.

---

[1] The reader will observe that Dadhīcha and Daksha respectively deny
divinity to Vishnu and Shiva.

It was full of mystery, and, for that reason, stupid people criticised it. He admitted that it was a creed opposed to the duties laid down for the four castes and the four modes of life with which it had very little in common. But it was the true means of liberation for all that. Unfortunately there is no indication that Shiva expounded this new religion, for the text says that immediately thereafter the god disappeared from view. But there is this advantage : if you read this story and recite the names of Shiva you will never be troubled by fever, and more than that, you will never experience the slightest evil all through life. You will be healed of your diseases and pains ; no ghost or demon will disturb your dwelling ; you will obtain the fulfilment of all your desires ; and when you die you will go to heaven, and never be born again in the form of either beast or bird.

Mahābhārata, xii. 283, 285.

XVII.

THE GOD INDRA KILLS A BRĀHMIN.

"No greater crime is known on earth than killing a Brāhmin."—*Laws of Manu*, viii. 381.

"The horse sacrifice, which is the king of sacrifices, removes all sin."—*Laws of Manu*, xi. 261.

THERE was once a Brāhmin of the name of Twashtri. He was not an ordinary Brāhmin by any means, and the references to him are highly mysterious, because it is said he was the lord of all beings and the chief among the gods. Be that as it may, he entertained so great a hatred for Indra that he created for himself a son who, he hoped, would be able to rob Indra of his throne. This son had three heads, and each was devoted to one particular task. With one he read the Vedas, with the second he drank liquor, and with the third he gazed so earnestly that it seemed as if he would swallow all the points of the compass. His character and disposition were as remarkable as his appearance. He surpassed all others in the fervour of his asceticism, as well as in the meekness and piety of his soul. Not unnaturally Indra grew very anxious as he watched this astonishing youth daily adding to his strength, a strength that was calculated to absorb the whole universe. It was manifest that if the god did not do something, and do it very quickly, his own power and dignity would be lost for ever. And it seemed to him that the only way in which he could destroy his rival was by the allurements of the flesh. He therefore summoned to his presence the most beautiful nymphs that were to be found in heaven, and bade them go and tempt the sage. They went as they were directed, but they came back with the humiliating confession that they had done their best and failed. The youth was absolutely impervious. Passion had no power whatever over one whose senses were so completely under control. When Indra received this information, he came to the conclusion that murder was the only alterr ‘ive, and professing that the sacred books gave him authority for such an act, he threw his thunderbolt at his rival and slew him. But even in death the body of the young Brāhmin shed over the world such a glorious light that Indra continued to be afraid. It seemed as if the youth were still alive and endued with miraculous power.

Now it so happened, as Indra stood gazing at the body of his victim, a woodcutter passed that way, carrying an axe on his shoulder. Addressing the traveller, Indra ordered him to cut off the dead man's heads. But the woodcutter refused. " Why should you ask me," he said, "to do such a dishonourable deed ? Besides, I must ask you who you are, and why you have slain this man. Are you not aware that it is a very great sin to kill a Brāhmin ? I wonder that you are not afraid." " In answer to your question," said the god, " I beg to let you know that I am Indra, king of heaven. This man was my enemy. Do as I tell you. I shall not feel either comfortable or safe till I see these heads severed from the body. As for the sin of killing a Brāhmin, I shall see to that also, and wipe away the stain by the performance of some rigid penance." Having received this explanation, the woodcutter, in obedience to the god's command, cut off the three heads, and, wonderful to relate, a great number of birds, pigeons, sparrows and parrots flew out of the different mouths and necks of the dead man.

Greatly relieved and comforted to think that his enemy was now dead without hope of revival, Indra went off to heaven. But his troubles were not by any means over. The young man's father had yet to be reckoned with, and he was determined to have revenge. Twashtri accordingly called into being a powerful demon to whom he gave the name of Vritra, and who, he thought, would be able to destroy the murderer of his son. The demon was of immense stature. His head touched the sky. As soon as he was created the demon went and challenged Indra to immediate combat. A terrible battle ensued, and in the end the demon was victorious. Indeed he seized the king of the celestials, threw him into his mouth, and swallowed him. When the gods saw their leader disappear down the throat of the demon, they were filled with terror, and did not know what to do. At last they fell on a brilliant expedient. They created a *yawn*, the first yawn that ever was, and the yawn had its first effect upon the demon. He couldn't help himself, and as he opened his mouth to yawn, Indra quickly contracted his body to a very small size and jumped out of the demon's gaping jaws. With Indra once more in the open, the battle was renewed. But his valour was of no avail, and realising that there was no hope of victory, Indra took refuge in flight. Greatly disconcerted by this second defeat, the gods took council with the *rishis*, when they unanimously decided that the wisest thing to do would be to place the whole situation before Vishnu, the god who can never be destroyed. In accordance with this decision, they set off in a body, both gods and *rishis*, to the top of Mount Mandara where Vishnu was sitting at that time. As they approached his presence, they began a hymn of praise in which they dwelt upon the mighty deeds Vishnu had already accomplished at the churning of the ocean, and elsewhere. They said, too, that he was supreme over all

the gods and lord of all the worlds. When they had told
their story and expressed their conviction that Vishnu
alone could save them, that deity replied that they must
have recourse to a policy of conciliation. The demon
had apparently, by the power of Twashtri, so pervaded
the universe, that it would not be easy to destroy him.
He therefore proposed that the *rishis* and the celestial
minstrels should go to the demon and make offers of peace.
What these particular proposals were to be, Vishnu did not
say, but he mysteriously remarked that he himself would
enter the weapon by which Vritra eventually would be
slain.

In obedience to these instructions, the *rishis* and
heavenly minstrels went to interview Vritra. They
pointed out that he and Indra had been fighting for a
very long time, and with—so they said—very uncertain
results. They were convinced that the demon could never
subdue the god. Would it not be very much better for
them both, and for everybody else, if they could agree to
terms of perpetual peace. Both heaven and earth had
been put to a great deal of trouble by this constant
fighting. When Vritra angrily intervened and said that
he would never consent to be Indra's friend, the *rishis*
expressed their surprise at such an observation. " Why
not ? " they said. " It is a most attractive sight to see
virtuous persons dwelling together in love and friendship."
It was an opportunity no wise man would ever surrender.
There was no wealth which one should seek more earnestly,
and everybody knew what a fine character Indra was ;
eminently virtuous, truthful, high-minded and blameless ;
of excellent judgment, and a lover of all that was good.
They therefore hoped that the demon would entertain
no doubt as to Indra's good intentions and consent to a
lasting peace.

" Well then," said the demon, " I agree to make peace

but only on the terms that I now specify. Give me a
solemn undertaking that Indra will not attack me with
any weapon made of either wood, stone or iron; with
any weapon made for hand-to-hand fighting or fighting
at a distance, nor with anything that is wet nor with
anything that is dry. And this also he must promise,
that I shall never be attacked either by night or by day.
If you promise this, then I shall agree to make peace."
When the *rishis* had given their promise, the demon said
he was very glad that there was to be no more fighting.
Indra expressed himself in similar terms; but such were
not his real feelings, and he gave himself continually to
the devising of some loophole by which he could at once
evade the terms of peace and slay his foe. As he was
pondering over this difficult problem, it so happened that
Indra found himself, one evening, standing on the sea-
shore, and not far off he saw the demon whose life he
sought. All at once the thought came to him : "The
sun is sinking in the west, darkness has begun to fall, but
one cannot say that the night has come or that it is any
longer day. If I could only slay the demon now, between
the darkness and the light, I should not have broken my
pledge." And so he continued to ponder and pray to
Vishnu for guidance. Suddenly a great mass of foam
rose out of the sea ; rose to a great height as high as a
mountain. And as Indra looked at it he realised that
this mass of foam was neither wet nor dry, just as it was
not a weapon made of either stone, iron or wood. If
Vishnu would only enter the foam, and if he launched
the foam at Vritra, then he would be able to slay him
with a weapon different from any that had been forbidden
by the terms of peace. Vishnu had promised to help
him, and said that he would enter into the weapon that
Indra wielded. This foam then must be the weapon
that the mighty god had planned. In any case, he would

try, and try he did; for he laid hold of the foam and hurled it at the demon, and because Vishnu was in the foam, it possessed a strength and power which no one could resist, and Vritra fell lifeless to the ground. When the gods saw that their enemy was dead, they crowded round the victor with their congratulations and praise. Nature also showed her satisfaction. The sky was filled with light, a pleasant breeze began to blow, and even the beasts of the field rejoiced. But Indra did not fail to say to whom the credit belonged. It was Vishnu, the greatest of all the gods, who had given them the victory.

Nevertheless, despite his gladness, the heart of Indra was ill at ease. He could not forget that his soul was burdened with a great sin. He had killed a Brāhmin, and he did not know how he was to be delivered from the consequences of that awful crime. As the days passed he became more and more depressed, and eventually he disappeared. Nobody knew where he had gone. Search was made for him in every direction, and no trace of his whereabouts could be found.

Mahābhārata, v. 9, 10.

XVIII.

PRIDE GOES BEFORE A FALL.

"The man for whom the gods are preparing defeat is deprived by them of understanding, and evil appears as good to the mind which is polluted by sin."—*Mahābhārata*, ii. 81. 8.

THE disappearance of Indra filled the universe with consternation. Prosperity and happiness are impossible without a king. Anarchy is sure to prevail. The inhabitants of the earth suffered very grievously without Indra's guiding hand; rain ceased to fall, the world was changed into a desert, and even the trees of the forest perished for lack of moisture. But heaven also shared in the distress; both gods and sages being overwhelmed by gloomy anticipations of the inevitable end. Naturally an attempt was made to persuade one of their number to assume the sceptre which Indra had so ingloriously abandoned, but not one of them was prepared to accept the vacant post. At last it was decided to offer the sovereignty of heaven to Nahusha, a monarch of the lunar race. Nahusha had acquired a great reputation for his many virtues and the capacities he had shown as a ruler of men. But he professed great reluctance when the subject was raised, observing, not unreasonably, that such a thing had never happened before, and that no mortal was equal to the task. However, the celestials assured him that, once he was crowned and anointed, he would feel very different. The superhuman qualities and

powers, with which both gods and demons were endowed,
would be transferred to him. With such assurances,
Nahusha consented to the coronation and, sure enough,
he soon discovered that every day added to his powers.
But, alas! he began to put these powers to a bad use.
Instead of attending to his lofty duties as monarch of the
worlds, he spent his days in sloth and sensual enjoyments,
wandering about the garden of heaven with a miscellaneous
crowd of nymphs and minstrels, or sitting listening to
their songs and old-world tales of gods and heroes. Things
had been bad before, they were now much worse; and
to crown his wickedness, Nahusha cast sinful eyes on
Indra's queen. This lady, whose name was Sachi, bore
an honoured name. The breath of slander had never
touched her reputation, and she fled from the presence of
the voluptuary. In her distress she sought counsel with
Brihaspati, the priest of the gods, who promised that he
would not see her wronged. But Nahusha was determined not to be baulked of his desire. He therefore
ordered the gods to his presence and told them to see to
it that the lady came and did as she was bidden. The
celestials tried to plead her cause. It was most improper,
they said, for any man to wrong another's wife, and they
hoped that his majesty would not set such a bad example
to his subjects. Unfortunately Nahusha was able to give
an only too complete rejoinder. He reminded them of
the sins of which his predecessor had been guilty, and
asked what they had done to check him in his frequent
amours. And so he said, "Bring the woman at once, or
I shall make you suffer for it." Unable to help themselves,
the gods went to the house of Brihaspati and told Sachi
that she must obey the command of the king of heaven.
But Brihaspati refused to let her go. "This queen," he
said, "has come to me as a suppliant, and I never refuse
to hear a suppliant's cry. And you celestials know what

Brahmā has declared, that no one can ever prosper
who ignores the prayer of those who are in distress."
At the same time, however, the priest of the gods suggested that something might be achieved by a temporising
policy. One never knew what a day would bring forth,
and he proposed that Sachi should go and tell Nahusha
that she must get time to think about his offer. In
accordance with this plan, Sachi approached the monarch
and spoke as she had been advised. She added that
among her other difficulties she would like to find out
what had happened to her husband, and where he had
gone. But she promised that if her inquiries proved
unsuccessful she would submit herself to his will and
become his wife. Nahusha was so pleased to see her, as
he thought, in a yielding mood, that he granted her
request, and he did so the more readily because he was
confident that Indra would never be found.

But Sachi was resolved that Indra should be found,
and with that end in view she addressed her prayers to
the goddess of Night, and by the kindness of that gracious
being she was guided to the hiding-place of Indra. It
was a long journey over mountains and rivers, to the
shores of the farthest sea, and beyond that to an island
in the midst of the sea ; and in the midst of the island to
a lake, and in the midst of the lake to a great mass of
lotuses, thousands and thousands of them, all in bloom ;
and in the midst of the lotuses there was one particular
lotus in whose stem the great god Indra lay concealed.
Of course he had contracted himself tremendously, and
Sachi had to do the same before she could secure an
entrance and cast herself at her husband's feet. She lay
prostrate before him and never said a word. At last
the silence was broken by Indra saying, " Why have you
come, and how did you find me ? " When Sachi had
told her dreadful tale, and besought her lord to hide

himself no longer, but come out and slay the man who
would do him wrong, Indra replied that it was impossible
for him to do anything in the meantime but stay where
he was. The reason he gave was that Nahusha by this
time was much stronger than he. The offerings that had
been made to him and the superhuman qualities and
powers with which gods and demons had endowed him,
had caused Nahusha to acquire wonderful strength. But
he had a plan in his mind which, he was confident, would
rob the monarch of all that he had acquired. If it could
be brought to a successful issue he was confident that
Nahusha would be eventually cast out of heaven. Indra
did not venture to reveal how he thought it would work
out ; he merely contented himself with saying, " Go back
to Nahusha and say, ' Come to me in a palanquin such
as was never seen before, and I shall do what you desire.
My former husband drove in a chariot that was drawn
by horses and elephants, but you are much greater than
he. Command the seven *rishis* to carry your palanquin,
and then you will have something that we can boast of ;
something that is absolutely unique.' " In obedience to
Indra's instructions, Sachi returned to heaven, and, as we
shall see, approached Nahusha and spoke as her husband
desired.

While she was absent in her search, the gods also had
been busy. They had come to the conclusion that they
must secure the help of Vishnu. ' Somehow or other,
Indra must be purged of the sin he had incurred by killing
a Brāhmin. If that was once wiped away they felt that
his courage would be restored, and he would be able to
resume his place in heaven. As usual the celestials found
that Vishnu was both willing and able to help them. He
at once declared that what Indra needed to do was to
offer a horse sacrifice. By doing that, his sin would be
removed and all their wishes realised. The gods were so

delighted to hear of the expedient that they began the sacrifice on their own account, and so great was its efficacy that Indra, in his distant hiding-place, felt its beneficent effects, and knew that a burden had been lifted off his soul. But having achieved so much they were determined not to rest content till they saw Indra face to face. They therefore, through the agency of their own special priest, Brihaspati, proceeded to perform another sacrifice which called Agni, the god of fire, to their aid. Agni searched everywhere, but had to confess defeat. A second effort, however, was more successful, and the god of fire returned to his colleagues with the joyful tidings that Indra was hiding in the lotus beds. The celestials hastened to the place without delay, and began to sing the praises of their king. Every hymn they uttered added to Indra's strength, and yet when he cross-examined them as to what had happened in his absence, they had sorrowfully to admit that Nahusha had become very powerful indeed. He seemed to have absorbed every energy and attribute that the god had ever possessed ; not only so, but they had to make the lamentable confession that he had put them into such a state of terror that they went in fear of their lives and were wandering about in disguise. However, four of the most powerful gods gave an undertaking that they would enter into a copartnery arrangement and, joining force with Indra, do their best to slay Nahusha.

But just as they had decided to take this action, one of the seven *rishis* came hot foot into their presence. It was the mighty saint, Agastya, who once drank up the ocean, and he had a wonderful story to tell. Nahusha had done as Sachi had asked him to do. He had summoned the seven *rishis* to his palace and told them to carry his palanquin. It had all happened that very day. The *rishis*, knowing what would be the ultimate result, had obeyed the commandment of the king, and bore his

7

majesty through the streets of heaven. As they moved
along, however, they asked him a question. It was about
certain hymns in the Vedas. Did Nahusha think they
were genuine ? and the infatuated fool, out of sheer per-
versity, said that they were not. This wicked answer
roused the anger of the holy men, and they did not fail
to reprove him for his sin. But rebuke, even from one
of the seven sages, Nahusha was not prepared to tolerate,
and to show his contempt for them he stretched out his
foot and touched one of them on the head. It was Agastya
himself who was subjected to the gross insult, and, as
Agastya said, that insult to a *rishi* was more than enough
to rob the monarch of all the strength and power he had
acquired. What was still better, it was now possible to
curse him, and without losing a moment that is just what
Agastya did. " You have done three things which you
ought not to have done," said the sage. " You have said
that the Vedas are not genuine, you have touched me with
your foot, and you have made the seven *rishis*, each of
them the equal of Brahmā, carry your palanquin. I
therefore curse you to fall down from heaven to earth,
where you must dwell for ten thousand years in the form
of a serpent. When that period has elapsed, you will be
allowed to come back to heaven."

It is needless to narrate how delighted the gods were
to receive this information. They at once set off for the
upper world, with Indra at their head, glad to be relieved
of all further responsibility for the government of the
skies.

                                    Mahābhārata, v. 9, 10.

XIX.

VISHNU'S INCARNATION AS THE MAN-LION.

" The man who has read all the Vedas and knows all the philosophies,
is but the worst of fools, if he is not devoted to Vishnu.   He who has faith
in him, and is devoted to his service, has practised all the pieties, even
though he has never studied the Vedas or performed a religious sacrifice."
—*Garuda Purāna*, 236.

HIRANYAKASHIPU, king of the demons, had secured a boon
from Brahmā, the creator god.   The boon was to the effect
that he should never be conquered or slain by either god
or demon, animal or man.   Trusting to this promise, he
began to wage war with the celestials, and he was at length
so successful that he became the lord of heaven, earth
and hell.   He dispossessed Indra of his throne, and assumed
to himself the functions of the sun and moon.   He acted,
too, as the god of riches, and the ruler of the lower world.
The deities were so hard pressed that they were compelled
to take refuge on the earth, where they wandered in fear
of their lives, and in mortal guise.   In his pride of heart,
the demon king made proclamation that no one was to
worship any god or being except himself, and that all
offerings and sacrifices were to be made to him.   Siddhas,
Gandharvas and snake deities acted as his attendants,
while the nymphs of heaven danced before him as he sat
eating and drinking in his crystal palace.   But there was
one person in his realm who failed to give the demon king
the honour and dignity he claimed, and that was his own

son Prahlāda. This boy had been committed to the care
of a Brāhmin teacher and dwelt in his house. But one
day Prahlāda came to visit his father and was told to
give a brief account of all that he had learned. Prahlāda
at once replied that the substance of all he had learned was
to adore Vishnu. The demon's eyes flashed with anger
as he listened to these words, and he charged the Brāhmin
with the guilt of teaching his son to praise his father's
greatest foe. But the man assured the king that he was
in no way responsible, and Prahlāda himself boldly claimed
that his teacher was no other than Vishnu himself, "the
instructor of the whole world," the supreme spirit, "the
creator and protector, not of me alone, but of all human
beings and even, father, of you." When the demon asked
his son what evil spirit had taken possession of him and
caused him to blaspheme, the boy replied that it was
Vishnu who had entered his heart, "pervaded all the
regions of the universe, and by his omnipresence, influenced
the conduct of all beings," including both his father and
himself.

One might have expected that the demon would have
issued orders for his son's punishment. But he merely
told his servants to take him away to the house of his
preceptor. But after some time had passed, Prahlāda
was sent for again and bidden to recite some poetry. The
boy responded by reciting a hymn in praise of Vishnu.
When he had finished, his father ordered his attendants
to seize him and put him to death. It is said that thousands
of demons, brandishing huge swords, rushed at the apparently helpless boy. But though they struck him again
and again, they caused him not the slightest injury or pain.
And he addressed them very calmly, saying that Vishnu
was in their weapons and in his body, and that the
one could not do the other any harm. When he saw
what had happened, Hiraṇyakashipu tried to persuade

Prahlāda to abandon the worship of Vishnu, and said, if he gave him a promise to that effect, he would do him no further injury. But the boy asked what harm could happen to him, when he had a friend and helper who was able to save him in every circumstance. The result was that the king called in other methods of punishment. Great snakes were told to bite him, and they bit him accordingly in every part of his body. But again he felt no pain. Indeed, as the snakes themselves confessed, his skin was not even scratched, while their fangs and jewelled crests were either broken or destroyed. The demon next summoned to his aid the elephants of the skies, each of them as big as a mountain, and ordered them to attack his son with their united tusks. But though these mighty creatures bore him to the ground and trod him underfoot, they too failed to injure him in the slightest degree. Indeed, Prahlāda called his father's attention to the fact that the tusks had been blunted in the attempt to pierce his flesh, a wonderful fact due to no strength of his, but because he had called upon Vishnu in the hour of his affliction. The king, though foiled once more, was convinced that his son would be unable to resist the burning fire, and he caused great piles of brushwood to be built round the prince, and ignited. But here also, though the wind god blew his hardest at the request of the demon, Prahlāda once more declared that he felt no pain, and that the air was as cool and fragrant as if it had been blowing over lotus fields.

At this stage the Brāhmins intervened, and asked the king to restrain his wrath, pointing out that those who came under its influence could not obtain a place in heaven. At the same time, they undertook, if the king would set his offspring free, to devote themselves to his instruction, and make him realise the impropriety of worshipping his father's greatest foe. He should remember that, after all,

Prahlāda was only a child. Youth was prone to many
errors, and people of experience should be tolerant towards
its faults. They added, however, that if he still refused
to abandon the worship of Vishnu, they would take the
necessary steps to bring about his death. In response to
this appeal, the demon king gave orders for his son being
set free, and conducted to the house of his preceptor.
When he reached his teacher's dwelling, however, Prahlāda
at once began a series of discourses, on what he called the
supreme truth, which were addressed to an audience of
young persons, who, like himself, were members of the
demon race. In these addresses he dwelt on the fact that
birth and death were the portion of all living things,
passing, as they did, from infancy and youth to gradual
but inevitable decay. But while that was manifest to all,
there was something equally clear to every student of
scripture, and that was that the dead were born again.
And this brought him to the truth that " pain was in-
separable from every period of existence." Men in their
foolishness spoke of the pleasure they obtained in quench-
ing their hunger and thirst. But they did not understand.
Fire was agreeable when we were cold, no doubt, and
water was pleasant when we were thirsty, and food was
grateful when we were hungry. But we would like the
opposite equally well if our circumstances were changed.
And we can see that those " whose vision is darkened by
delusion " find delight in suffering, while the man who is
paralysed and cannot walk would be only too glad to
experience fatigue. In the same way, he who cherished
affection for any one was opening the door of his heart to
many miseries ; planting a thorn that would expose him
to many pricks. It was the same with the man who
possessed wealth. He was harassed by the constant
thought that it might be lost or stolen or destroyed. As
he had said already, birth itself was a great misfortune,

while the dying man had to look forward, not only to the judgment-seat of Yama, but to the pains of another birth. Indeed this world was a very sea of sorrow, in which Vishnu was our "only hope." Perhaps his hearers might reply that they were too young to understand such high matters. It was true that their bodies were young, but their spirits were eternal. And in any case he who addressed them was also a child, and he had resolved that he would not put off to old age the discussion and understanding of what was so important. When old age came, he would not have strength of body or mind sufficient to deal with them. But that was always the way with men. They put off from day to day. They were always finding some excuse. Childhood and youth were absorbed in play and pleasure. And they arrived at old age, to find themselves ignorant and powerless. In the end they would die, with their thirst unquenched. Why then should his young friends not follow his example, and begin to meditate upon Vishnu right away? He was proposing nothing distasteful; Vishnu was the giver of happiness and of prosperity. He removed the sins of those who thought upon him night and day. If they fixed their hearts on him, they would be able to "laugh at every care." Prahlāda also dwelt upon the duty of hating nobody. All living things were "objects of compassion." If any one happened to be more fortunate than ourselves, we ought not to envy him his happiness, rather we should be pleased to see him so well off, and soon we should discover that the "suppression of malignant feelings is itself a reward." Even if we believed that the deity is distinct from his creatures as some do, our enemy was an object of pity and not of hate. But the conclusion of the whole matter was that Vishnu did not differ from us, but was the same as ourselves. "He is identical with all things," and the whole world is his manifestation. This was Prahlāda's concluding appeal.

He begged his hearers to lay aside the angry passions of
their race, and try hard to obtain the perfect, pure and
eternal happiness which neither god nor devil, neither man
nor beast, neither fever nor ophthalmia, neither dysentery
nor spleen, neither hatred nor malice nor desire, would be
able to destroy. If they fixed their hearts on Vishnu,
they would achieve a " perfect calm." Wealth, pleasure,
virtue were things of little moment. But the fruit they
would gather from the tree of wisdom was beyond price.

When the demon king heard of these efforts on the part
of his son to corrupt the minds of the rising generation,
he ordered his cooks to mix deadly poison in Prahlāda's
food. But the poison did not cause him the slightest inconvenience. Hiranyakashipu therefore called upon the
Brāhmins to implement their promise, and destroy his
recalcitrant offspring by the employment of those incantations which, they said, could not possibly fail. But
though they approached him, chanting verses from the
Sāma-Veda, and called into existence a terrifying female
form who smote him on the breast with a fiery trident,
they were as unsuccessful as the cooks had been. Indeed,
even more so, for the trident broke into a hundred
pieces, and the magic that the priests had employed
turned against themselves and consumed them. Prahlāda
was greatly distressed at seeing the destruction of the
priests. As he said himself, he cherished enmity against
no one, and he had nothing but the kindest feelings for
the fire that had sought to burn, the elephants that had
tried to crush, and the cooks who had failed to poison him.
He therefore addressed a prayer to Vishnu, asking him to
restore his persecutors to life. Vishnu heard his prayer,
and the Brāhmins at once rose to their feet, very grateful
to Prahlāda for his generous treatment. When they had
bowed before him and called down all sorts of blessings,
they hastened to the king and told him what had happened.

Hiranykashipu now sent for his son once more, and told him to explain how he had become possessed of such wonderful power. Was it the result of magic, or had he been endowed with it from birth? This naturally led to a fresh discourse from Prahlāda on the greatness of Vishnu, who had taken possession of his heart. But he emphasised, more than he had done on previous occasions, the fact that he cherished no feelings of hatred towards any of those who had sought to injure him. Indeed, he wished harm to no one, knowing as he did that those who caused harm to others, in thought, word or deed, were sowing the seeds of a future birth, whose harvest would be reaped in pain. No suffering that any one might inflict would be able to disturb him. The priests had told him that he did not need to worship the gods, or to depend on the eternal, when his father was lord of the three worlds. But it was only by glorifying Vishnu that one could obtain anything, be it wealth or offspring, virtue or emancipation. When Prahlāda had finished this further discourse, his father caused him to be thrown from the battlements of the palace. Now the walls of the palace were many miles in height, and one would have thought that his body would have been dashed to pieces when it fell on the rocks below. But the Earth, the nurse of all creatures, received him gently on her lap, and he rose up quite unharmed. A great enchanter was next invited to try what he could do. This person tried his best. He employed an infinite variety of enchantments, some of which must have been very powerful, as Vishnu found it necessary to send his famous discus to protect the boy; but every one of them, including a terrible cold wind, failed of its purpose, and the magician had to own defeat.

After these fruitless efforts there was a lull in the persecution, and Prahlāda was once more permitted to return to his teacher's house, where he received daily instruction

in the science of government. When Hiranyakashipu
was informed that his son had acquired a thorough knowledge of the science, he sent for him and addressed to him
a series of questions dealing with such matters as the treatment of friends and foes ; the attitude a ruler should adopt
towards his subjects, his counsellors, and the other officials
and employèes of the state ; as well as the methods to be
adopted in waging war, in the building of forts, and the
reduction of aboriginal tribes. To these questions, which
seem to have been addressed to him all at once, Prahlāda
replied that though he had been fully instructed in all
these matters, he was unable to approve of the views which
his teacher held concerning them. That honoured person,
for instance, had said that conciliation, gifts, punishment
and the sowing of dissension were the four contrivances
by which a man achieved his purposes. But he hoped his
father would not be angry when he said that he knew
"neither friends nor foes." Vishnu was everywhere,
and in every one, and it was therefore impossible to speak
of any one as being distinct or separate from oneself. And
it was accordingly waste of time to study such unprofitable
subjects as his teacher had prescribed. Such knowledge
was ignorance. The only knowledge worth acquiring
was that which led to emancipation. He had no desire
for either wealth or dominion, though he was convinced
that those who cared for neither of these things would
obtain both in a " life to come." All around him he
could see men toiling to be great. But it was destiny,
not human effort, that was the cause of greatness, and
there were kings, both cowardly and ignorant, ruling
over kingdoms to whom the science of government was
unknown.

Hiranyakashipu, who had listened in silence to this
long speech, could contain himself no longer. He rose
from his throne and kicked his son upon the breast. Boiling

with anger, he called for several of his most distinguished
followers to bind his son and cast him into the sea. This
they did, and in addition piled great rocks on the top of
Prahlāda, as he lay, chanting the praises of Vishnu, at the
bottom of the ocean. If it is impossible to kill him, cried
the angry father, we shall see to it that he shall lie there
for thousands of years, imprisoned beneath a mass of
mountains. For a time it seemed as if the earth would be
submerged beneath the waves. The sea was so distressed
that it rose to an alarming extent. But apparently that
peril was obviated, and Prahlāda spent the days of his
long imprisonment dwelling unceasingly on the greatness
of the god he adored. In this fresh hymn he said, in
addition to much else, very similar to what has been
recorded already, that Vishnu was both knowledge and
ignorance, truth and falsehood, action and non-action,
and he ended by declaring that he was so identified with
Vishnu that he was Vishnu himself. " Glory to him," he
said, " who I, also, am ! "   " I am all things ; all things
are in me."   " Brahm is my name." [1]

The next chapter proceeds to tell us that as a result of
recognising Vishnu " as identical with his own spirit,"
Prahlāda forgot his own individuality. The consequence
was that the bonds with which he was bound could hold
him no longer. They were snapped asunder, and despite
the rocks and mountains which had been piled on top of
him, Prahlāda rose to the surface of the sea. As he did
so, the ocean was violently agitated, its inhabitants were
filled with fear and the earth trembled. And, finally,
when the youth had uttered another hymn, Vishnu
appeared before him " clad in yellow robes," and told
him to ask a boon. The only boon that Prahlāda thought

[1] The reader will note that it is Brahma (Brahm), the supreme soul of
the universe, with whom Prahlāda identifies all things, including both
Vishnu and himself. Brahmā (final a long) is the creator god.

worth asking, was that in a thousand births his faith in
the god might remain unshaken by any earthly passion
or desire. When that prayer had been granted and he
was told to ask a second boon, he begged that his father
might be forgiven for the way in which he had tried to
drive him from his devotion. Prahlāda enumerated the
various persecutions to which he had been exposed, but
thanks to the divine favour none of them had done him
any harm. This boon Vishnu also granted, and told his
worshipper that he would grant him yet another boon.
But Prahlāda said he wanted nothing more, knowing, as
he did, that his faith in Vishnu had already secured for
him the one thing he desired, and that was "*freedom from
existence.*"

When the god had departed, Prahlāda directed his steps
to his father's presence. Hiranyakashipu was apparently
delighted to see his son, and said that he repented of his
former cruelty. But in course of time the controversy
broke out afresh. Prahlāda refused to abandon the worship
of Vishnu, and the demon once more declared that his
son must die. But it was the demon who died. No doubt
he was trusting to Brahmā's promise that neither god nor
demon, neither beast nor man, would ever be able to destroy
him. He had not, however, realised the infinite wisdom
and resources of the mighty god he held in scorn. And
so it proved at last. One day as the demon was arguing
with his son, as he had done so often before, as to the
universality of Vishnu's presence, he rose from his throne
and smote a pillar in his royal hall. "Vishnu is everywhere, you say," he cried mockingly. "If he is everywhere, why is he not in this pillar, and why don't I see him
if he is?" As he uttered these blasphemous words, his
question was answered in a way he did not expect. Vishnu
himself appeared from the midst of the column, but clothed
in a marvellous form. In one part of his body he had

the shape of a man, and in another the shape of a lion. He had a thick and shaggy mane, eyes as red as fire, a mouth as huge and deep as a cavern, a tongue as sharp as a two-edged sword, and nostrils that rose and fell with every breath. He champed his jaws, too, and contracted his eyebrows in a way that was awful. His head touched the sky, his body was covered with yellow hair, he had a hundred arms, each a host in itself, while his finger-nails were powerful weapons of offence. The demons who stood around took refuge in flight. Their master alone showed no sign of fear. He realised, of course, that he was in the presence of Vishnu. But he merely said : " Is this the great magician who thinks he will be able to slay me ? His efforts will be all in vain." As he uttered this taunt, he rushed upon the Man-lion. He looked like an insect falling into a fire ; the fiend was absorbed in the glory of the god. And yet when Vishnu seized him and raised him in his arms, such was his agility that he slipped through the fingers of the god like a snake that escapes from the talons of a vulture. The celestials, who had crept out of their hiding-places to witness the combat, became alarmed. But there was no cause to fear. It is true that the demon thought he had achieved something, and grasping his mace rushed at Vishnu once more. He made his attack with amazing vigour. But the Man-lion seized him as a reptile seizes a rat, and holding him in a close embrace, carried him to the gate of the palace. And there, when he had played with him for a little, he tore his body to pieces with his claws. As he did so, the mighty god rolled his eyes in fury, and licked his lips with his tongue. His mane was covered with the demon's blood. He looked like a lion that has killed an elephant. To complete the picture, we are told that he made for himself a garland of the demon's entrails, and hung it round his neck.

It doesn't matter what sins a man may have committed,

if he listens to or reads this story of Prahlāda—and once is enough—he is cleansed from all his sins. But it is specially efficacious when the moon is new or at the full. If you read it then, you will acquire as much merit as if you had given a cow to a priest.

Vishnu Purāna, i. 16–20.
Bhāgavata Purāna, vii. 8. 12–30.

XX.

VISHNU'S INCARNATION AS RĀMA.

"Rāma is one-half of Vishnu."—Rāmāyana, i. 18.

THE gods and demons were constantly at war, but never were the celestials put to greater trouble than at the hands of Rāvana, an exceedingly handsome and powerful demon with ten heads. This Rāvana and two of his brothers, like others of their kind, were remarkably devout, and surpassed both gods and men in the number of their sacrifices and the fervour of their austerities. The youngest of the three stood on one leg for five thousand years, and for another five thousand years worshipped the sun. The second brother spent the same period of time seated between the five fires in summer, and standing in water during the rainy season and winter. But Rāvana excelled them both. He never tasted food for ten thousand years, and at the end of every thousand years cast one of his ten heads into a sacrificial fire. When he was about to cast his tenth head into the fire, Brahmā, the creator, who was his great-grandfather, appeared and told him to ask a boon. The demon at once asked for immortality, but Brahmā said that such a boon was more than he could grant. He obtained, however, his second wish, which was that he should never be overcome in battle by either god or demon. In his pride he never dreamed of asking for immunity against beasts and men. In addition to granting his prayer, **Brahmā** gave him back the nine heads which he had cast into the fire so many thousands of years before.

Rāvana had now obtained his heart's desire, and yet when his friends wanted him to attack his stepbrother, the god of riches, he professed certain qualms of conscience. But he was reminded of the fact that the gods and a certain class of demons, who had fought with the gods for ages, were as closely related to one another as he was to the god of riches, being the children of the same father though of different mothers.[1] Be that as it may, Rāvana cast aside all his scruples, drove his brother out of Ceylon, where he had his capital, and took possession of his wonderful aeroplane. From Ceylon as his citadel, the demon next began a long series of campaigns against demons, gods and men. In these battles so many millions were slain, that their spirits jostled one another on their way to heaven. Many more or less divine beings were among the slaughtered, but apparently he was never able to slay any of the gods.

On the other hand, Brahmā intervened on several occasions and prevented his fellow deities from destroying Rāvana. For instance, he invaded the lower world, determined to fight with and slay the god of death. In that land of gloom he saw the dead undergoing a great variety of torture, and crying aloud in their agony. Some were swimming about in seas of blood, others were compelled to traverse deserts of burning sand, others were preyed on by dogs and worms, others were afflicted by hunger and thrist. But there were some who reaped the reward of their good deeds, enjoying the society of beautiful women, living in ease and luxury, eating

[1] These demons were the elder brothers of the gods, who robbed them of their sovereignty in the world which had once been theirs   See Legend I.

and drinking, singing and dancing the whole day long. Rāvana's battle with the god lasted for seven days and seven nights, and he would most assuredly have been slain had Brahmā not interfered. The creator insisted that the pledge he had given to the demon must be observed. The moral order of the universe could not be overturned. It would be too bad an example to set to the world. In obedience to Brahmā's command, the lord of death stopped fighting. Indeed he did more than that ; he ran away. He did not see what else he could do. But his action had the unfortunate result that Rāvana ever after asserted that he had put Death to flight. He made the same claim with regard to Vishnu, and on two separate occasions that mighty god and Rāvana met face to face, and Vishnu, mindful of Brahmā's boon, simply made himself invisible. But when they met a third time, Vishnu smote him to the ground and sternly told him that the boon he had received alone stood between him and destruction. Rāvana was so overawed that he got up and went away without a word. But before he left, he saw the three worlds, with gods and saints, demons and men, all gathered together within the stomach of the god.

Indra, the king of heaven, had a less fortunate experience when Rāvana invaded the upper world, attended by a mighty host. Indra appealed to his brother deities for help. Vishnu said that as far as he was concerned, he could not render any assistance. The time was coming when he would do so, and with complete successs. But he encouraged his colleagues to take the field and to do their best. A very long battle ensued, in which Indra was captured by Rāvana's eldest son and carried off to Ceylon. Once more Brahmā had to appear on the scene. He said the young man had shown wonderful prowess, and ever after would be known as the conqueror of Indra. But some respect must be shown to the king of heaven, and

8

the prisoner set free. By way of compensation, however, Rāvana's son got a chariot and horses, with the promise that so long as he remained in the chariot he would never die. It is satisfactory to note that when Indra was released, Brahmā told him that his captivity at the hands of a demon was by way of punishment for the immoral life he had lived.

The one god with whom Rāvana did not attempt to fight, was Shiva. At an earlier period in his career, that god made such a remarkable manifestation of his glory that Rāvana was compelled to sing his glory for a thousand years ; while a later passage tells us that he made a golden phallus, which is the emblem of Shiva, worshipped it with flowers, and danced before it with uplifted hands. Shiva was so pleased with such devotion that he gave his worshipper a celestial weapon, a gift which made him more presumptuous than he was before.

Such a state of matters, however, could not last. It was perfectly manifest that something had to be done, and once more it was Vishnu who came to the rescue. At a conference which was held in heaven, Brahmā was very frankly told that it was the promise which he had made to Rāvana which was the cause of all their trouble. They could have killed him easily if it had not been for that. As it was, the whole universe was in a state of terror. The sun did not dare to shine or the wind to blow because of him, while fear kept the waves of the ocean still. They therefore hoped that their grandfather would devise some plan by which Rāvana could be outwitted and slain. Brahmā replied that so far as he could see, they must secure the services of some mortal sufficiently strong and powerful to contend with Rāvana. There was no other way out of it. Rāvana had secured immunity from gods and demons, but there was nothing to prevent him from being killed by a man. Just as

Brahmā made this observation, Vishnu, the preserver
god, appeared on the scene. He was riding on the great
bird Garuda. Whenever they saw him the whole gathering began to sing his praise, and as he took his seat alongside of Brahmā they declared that he, who was the hope
and refuge of the world, must go down to earth and,
assuming the form of a man, slay the wicked demon who
had harassed them so long. Without a moment's hesitation—no doubt he had clearly resolved on what he was
about to do—Vishnu declared that he would do as they
requested, go down to earth and live among men for
eleven thousand years. And long before that time was
over, he would root out and destroy, not only Rāvana,
but all his sons and grandsons, his ministers and friends.

Now it so happened that there was a king in northern
India whose name was Dasharatha. He had so far been
childless, but at that very moment he was celebrating
the horse sacrifice in the hope that by so doing he would
secure at least one heir to his throne. The gods had heard
about the sacrifice, and they suggested to Vishnu that
he should divide his divine essence into four, and be born
as the offspring of Dasharatha's queens. In accordance
with this advice, Vishnu at once went down to the earth
and appeared before Dasharatha. It is said that he rose
out of the sacrificial fire, a mighty and awe-inspiring
creature, as big as a mountain, clothed in crimson garments,
with a great head of hair, a long beard, and a red face.
He carried in one of his hands a large cup filled with a
mixture of rice, milk and sugar. Addressing the king,
he said : " I have come to you from Brahmā ; he has
heard your prayer. Divide the contents of this vessel
among your three queens. By drinking it they will
become pregnant and give birth to sons." When he had
communicated this message, Vishnu disappeared. Greatly
delighted with his success, the monarch hastened to his

palace. To his senior queen he gave half the contents of
the cup, and in course of time she gave birth to Rāma,
who, because his mother secured the larger portion of
the sacred mixture, was called *one-half of Vishnu*. The
two other queens received the rest. One of them gave
birth to twins, and they were therefore supposed, each of
them, to represent one-eighth of Vishnu, while the remaining brother possessed one-fourth of the divine
energy.[1]

But Brahmā was determined that Vishnu should not
go alone. The celestials also must play their part. He
therefore proposed that they should cohabit with female
bears and monkeys as well as with the nymphs of heaven,
and produce thereby armies that would assist Vishnu in
his human form to fight with Rāvana and his hosts.
Brahmā added that he himself already had a son who
was the king of the bears, and had come out of his mouth
one day when he was yawning. In obedience to these
proposals not only the gods, but great multitudes of
glorified spirits, celestial minstrels and bards, did as they
were required, with the result that many millions of
bears and monkeys were born, and in virtue of their
divine fatherhood they were, of course, not ordinary bears
and monkeys. Some of them were the size of mountains,
and able to cover hundreds of miles at a single bound.
They were able also to assume any shape they chose, able to
travel round the world, to lift up in their hands the largest
hills, and to swim the broadest seas.

How they fought and prevailed, is told in the *Rāmāyana
of Vālmīki*. But the central figure of the poem is Rāma.
The fact that his brothers shared in the divine essence is
almost entirely forgotten, and it is he, and not his brothers,
whom later ages have adored.

Rāmāyana, vii. 9–46, i. 15–18.

[1] Their names were Rāma, Lakshmana, Bharata and Shatrughna.

XXI.

RĀMA'S LOYALTY TO TRUTH.

"Truth is the root of all religion."—*Rāmāyana*, ii. 18.
"If Truth and a hundred horse sacrifices were weighed together, Truth would weigh the heavier. There is no virtue equal to truth, and no sin greater than falsehood."—*Mahābhārata*, i. 74, 102.

WHEN Rāma and his three brothers were born, their father had reached the advanced age of nine thousand years. It was therefore not unnatural that as soon as his sons were grown up, he should wish to be relieved of the burden of sovereignty. Rāma was the oldest and the best loved of the four, and the proposal that he should be installed as his father's colleague and successor afforded great delight to all classes of the people. The streets of Ayodhyā were thronged with happy multitudes who dwelt on the blessedness that would be theirs when Rāma sat beneath the white umbrella. But while preparations for the coronation were in progress, the mother of Bharata, Rāma's stepbrother, appeared before the king and craved the fulfilment of a boon which he had granted her many years before. In one of the many battles between the demons and the gods, the king, who had gone to the help of the celestials, was grievously wounded and would probably have died, had Bharata's mother not carried him off the field. Though told on that occasion to ask a boon, she had never done so. Her opportunity, however,

had come at last, and when she sought the fulfilment of
this ancient promise, her husband replied that he was as
ready to grant it as he had ever been. Unfortunately it
was not the practice to ask what the boon was to be, and
in his infatuation the aged king allowed himself to be
bound by the strongest oaths that he would do whatever
she asked, however hard or difficult it might prove. And
so he swore by the sun, moon and stars, by earth and sky,
by day and night, by saints and devils, by the spirits of
the dead, by the household deities and the Thirty-three
gods, and by everything that had life, however small,
that he would grant her prayer. When the queen had
bound the king by oaths which she knew he dare not
break, she put forward her demand. It was that the
coronation rites begun for Rāma should be completed on
behalf of her own son Bharata, while Rāma should, before
the close of another day, be sent into exile and ordered
to live in the forest as a hermit, for the space of fourteen
years.

As the monarch listened to these awful demands he was
overwhelmed with grief. He raged and stormed at the
queen. He called her a poisonous snake in human form.
He threw himself at her feet and begged for mercy. He
swore that he would not grant so wicked and so cruel a
boon. In reply, the queen told him that he could not
break his plighted word. In particular, she dwelt on the
greatness of truth. All justice, human and divine, was
founded on truth. A life based on truth was the only
life that achieved abiding happiness. But despite her
exhortation, the evil-minded queen was very much afraid
that her husband would never implement his promise.
She therefore caused a messenger to be sent for Rāma.
She was confident that he would insist on carrying out
his father's pledge. And when Rāma came, and was
told what had happened, her highest hopes were

realised. The noble-hearted prince showed not the least
resentment. He said that he would gladly surrender
everything he possessed to a brother so well beloved as
Bharata. And he would do so all the more willingly
when it was in obedience to his father's will. And so
before another sun had set, Rāma, accompanied by his
wife, Sītā, and his brother, Lakshmana, had started for
the forest.

It so happened that when these events took place,
Bharata, for whose advancement his mother had planned,
was absent from the capital. When he got home a few
days later in obedience to an urgent summons, he found
that his father had died of grief, and that he was expected
to assume the reins of government. This, however, he
indignantly refused to do, and with the least possible delay
followed his brother to the forest. He was accompanied
by his father's queens, the ministers of state and many
thousands of his father's subjects. His one desire was to
make it plain that he was in no way responsible for his
mother's crime, and that he would never be satisfied till
Rāma returned home.

The story is very beautifully told of how Bharata pleaded
with his brother to return. He had never heard of a
more sinful act performed at the behest of an evil-minded
and crafty woman. Now that the sin had been committed,
it was their duty as loyal sons to conceal it to the best of
their ability. On the other hand, if they acted in obedience to their father's foolish and unjust decree, harm could
only result. Rāma alone was qualified to govern the
kingdom. The citizens were determined that he alone
should reign. It was the invariable rule that the oldest
son should succeed his father on the throne. In response
to these appeals, which were warmly supported by the
late king's ministers, Rāma remained unmoved. He said
it could not be. They spoke as if he were greater than

Destiny. He was a man and nothing more. How could he fight against the decrees of Fate, decrees which had destined his brother to the throne and himself to the forest. There was one thing, and one thing only, which men could do and should do ; and that was to devote themselves to the cause of righteousness. Their father's command must be obeyed ; their father's promise to Bharata's mother must in no way be evaded. He therefore insisted that Bharata should return to Ayodhyā and perform those rites and ceremonies which it was a son's sacred duty to see were duly celebrated, and by which their father would be delivered from the pains of hell. It was a fair division of labour. Bharata would sit beneath the shade of the white umbrella dispensing justice to the citizens of Ayodhyā, while Sītā, Lakshmana and himself would be equally happy, living the hermit life.

At this stage one of the ministers intervened. He was a Brāhmin and a philosopher. Indeed he is spoken of as the chief of the twice-born sages. This distinguished personage expressed his surprise that Rāma should cherish such weak and foolish ideas. Why should he be swayed by the opinions that prevailed among the vulgar ? Why did he talk of the duties men owed to their kith and kin ? Why did any one pay reverence to his father and mother ? Man was born alone and died alone. Life was very brief. We were like travellers, staying for a night in one place and then moving on to another. At the best, the link which bound us to parents, wealth and other possessions was of the most slender kind, and the wise man made little of it. It was therefore very foolish to choose hard-ship and difficulty in obedience to what he called the demand of duty, when he had royalty, with all its luxury and happiness, within his grasp. His father was dead, and the dead had no claim on the living. His father was one and he was another, and if he gave up Ayodhyā

for the sake of his father, he would get nothing in its
place. There had been many tears shed. For his
part, he wept when he thought of those who, in
foolish adherence to what they called their duty,
involved themselves in present suffering to obtain, not
heavenly rewards as they supposed, but annihilation
at the hour of death. Rāma had spoken of the rites
for the dead. What purpose did they serve ? Funeral
oblations made day after day with so much earnest
solemnity, were just a waste of good food. Dead men
did not eat. And there was no hereafter. The whole
business was the invention of clever rascals who played
upon people's feelings to secure their own enrichment.
And so they talked about the need of worshipping the gods,
about the power of gifts and austerities, about the observ-
ance of rites and ceremonies and denying the flesh. Seeing
there was no future life, he advised the prince to listen to
his counsel. Forget all about another world, enjoy the
passing hour and what it brings. Pay heed to the things
you can see and handle, to what is perceptible by the
senses alone.

To these ignoble appeals Rāma replied that the philosopher was seeking to obliterate all distinctions between
good and evil, and at the same time pretending that there
was justification for so doing. Was it the same thing
to be pure and impure, good and bad, high-minded and
base ? And how could he ever hope to get to heaven if he
broke the promise he had so solemnly made. It was the
duty of kings, more than of any other class of men, to cling
to deeds of righteousness. Subjects followed and imitated
the action of their rulers. It was truth that sustained
the order of the world ; it was by the power of truth that
princes ruled. Truth was the foundation on which the
temple of justice was reared ; nay, it was the source of all
goodness. Without truth, the making of gifts and sacri-

fice, vows and austerities, yea, even the holy books of
revelation, all and each were every one of them vain.
It was truth that made our homes and our land secure.
It was falsehood that plunged them into distress.   And
therefore he refused to listen to appeals based on covetous-
ness, ignorance and foolishness.   Truth was the inspirer
of the soul, and both the gods and the spirits of the dead
refused to accept the offerings made by men who were un-
faithful to their plighted word.   There were three stages
in the progress of every sin.   Born in the heart, it was
achieved by the hand and found its support in the tongue
that spoke falsely.   The philospher had spoken with great
cunning, but his proposals were dishonourable and base.
However, he would not listen to them for a moment.   He
was well content to live in the forest, enjoying the society
of the gods and the spirits of his ancestors.   He would
achieve his object by obeying his father's command, remembering it was by the multitude of sacrifices that Indra
obtained the first place among the gods, and by their
hard asceticism that the great saints of old secured the
happiness of heaven.   Justice, constancy, sympathy,
truth, reverence for the gods and Brāhmins, and the
exercise of hospitality, these were the virtues that crowned
a man's life with true success.   He was sorry that his
father had ever given the speaker rank and honour in his
palace.   He looked upon a Buddhist as no better than a
thief.   The whole pack of them were haters of righteousness and truth.   It was most unwise of kings to allow such
wicked unbelievers an entrance into their presence.   In
the good old days, twice-born men had acquired fame by
other methods than those now proposed, and as a result
their names were known and honoured still.   He would
walk in their path and follow their example.

When Rāma had thus spoken the philosopher declared
that he renounced his atheistic beliefs ; indeed, he said,

that he had only assumed them for the purpose of trying to dissuade him from his purpose ; because in his heart of hearts he scorned and hated atheists as much as any one could do.

Rāmāyana, iii.

XXII.

RĀMA AND SĪTĀ.

"Sitā is Lakshmi, and thou art Krishna and Vishnu, the preserver of the people."—*Rāmāyana*, vi. 119.

WHEN Sītā heard of the fate that was in store for Rāma, she announced her intention of accompanying him to the forest. He did all he could to prevent her, pointing out the hardships and dangers she would have to endure. But the loyal-hearted wife asked what she had done to earn her husband's scorn. She was not ignorant of the duties that devolved upon a wife. No woman should ever think of forsaking her husband. There was no refuge or safety for her apart from him. She was going with him ; nay, she would go before him in the pathless woods, treading down the grass and thorns that would impede his progress. Her parents had taught her well, and she knew where a wife's place was. In his society the forest was better than a palace ; better than heaven itself without him. They would be very happy there, bathing in the cool springs of water, feeding on fruit and honey, gazing their fill at mountain, stream and sea. Was it only fourteen years of exile ? A thousand years would pass like a single day. He need not worry so far as she was concerned. Her one desire in life was to be with him, and if he did not let her share his exile she would die. Rāma did all he could to shake Sītā's resolve. He once more

enlarged on the dangers of the forest life. He knew
nothing of the joys that she was describing. Sleep was
almost impossible, because of the multitudes of creeping
things. There were flies, scorpions and snakes without
number. Beds of leaves afforded little comfort. And
they would often be in great straits for food. As for fruit,
they would have to be content with what the wind shook
from the trees ; while the gathering of flowers as an offering to the gods, as well as the unremitting attention they
must give not only to religious rites, fasting and prayer,
but to hermits and guests, would prove a grievous burden.
To these arguments Sītā turned a deaf ear. She told him
he had said enough, and that he need say no more. She
was afraid of nothing but separation from his love. When
he was with her she was in heaven. When he was absent
she was in hell.

To such an appeal, Rāma could offer no more objections.
He said that till that moment he had never realised how
much she loved him, while it was his own love for her that
had made him eager to save her from the dangers to which
she would be exposed. But now that he had consented to
her going, they must delay no longer. He had been told
to leave the capital before sunset. And so when they had
said farewell to the aged king and to Rāma's mother, the
three exiles, clad in forest garb, set forth upon their
journey. By this time the whole city had become aware
of the approaching calamity. The streets, the roofs and
windows of the houses were thronged with weeping multitudes. In particular, they bewailed the fact that Sītā,
whose face had been so carefully veiled that even the spirits
of the air had never seen it, was walking through the public
streets and seen by all. Indeed the populace became so
excited that they resolved to accompany the exiles and
to share their banishment, and it was with the greatest
difficulty that Rāma persuaded them to stay at home.

When the exiles arrived at the hermitage where they had resolved for a time at least to settle, they received a cordial welcome from the ascetics in the neighbourhood. One ancient lady received Sītā with special cordiality, and expressed her great. pleasure at meeting a woman so devoted to her lord. And yet she felt it necessary to enlarge on the fact that a woman must always look upon her husband as a god, and pay him every token of respect, quite regardless of what his character or conduct might be. In this lady's opinion nothing was more disgraceful than for a wife to seek to rule the home, and yet she had heard of such women, dead to all sense of decency, lording it over their husbands and making those who should command, obey. No woman who acted in that fashion could ever hope of going to heaven. We hear very little of how the princes and Sītā passed their years of exile. They wandered from place to place, spending sometimes a year, sometimes a few months, sometimes only a few days, in one particular spot. And though certain passages tell of how Rāma slew a large number of demons who had been persecuting the hermits and disturbing their religious rites, it would appear that their forest life was comparatively peaceful and free from danger or strife. In the thirteenth year, however, the situation began to change. By this time they had arrived in Central India and had chosen a very beautiful and peaceful spot where they resolved to spend the remaining months of their banishment. But, alas! only a few days after their settlement there, a great ugly, female fiend saw Rāma and fell violently in love. She pressed her claims with such vehemence and was so rude to Sītā, that Rāma, who could not kill a woman, resolved to punish her by cutting off her ears and nose. Wounded and bleeding profusely, the fiend fled to the place where her brother and many thousand of demons were encamped, and told the story of her wrongs. In obedience to her appeals, the demons attacked Rāma, but they were all destroyed. Unfortunately those demons were the servants of Rāvana, the ten-headed monarch of Ceylon, for whose destruction Vishnu had been born into the world. And when Rāvana heard of the destruction of his followers he made preparations for war. But his ministers told him that it was folly for him to think that he could ever conquer Rāma in battle. Rāvana was very angry at such a statement. He had already met and overcome the greatest of the gods, and he wanted to know who this Rāma was, against whom he could not hope to be victorious. Nevertheless, he yielded to persuasion and agreed to do as his ministers proposed, and that was, to carry off Sītā as a prisoner to Ceylon. She was the loveliest of womankind. There was not a goddess in heaven to compare with her. Once robbed of Sītā, Rāma would die of grief.

In accordance with this suggestion, Rāvana mounted his aeroplane, and was soon in the neighbourhood of the hermitage. By means of a series of stratagems which were carried through by some of the demon's followers, first Rāma and then his brother were tempted to penetrate deeper and deeper into the forest. Sītā, when thus left alone, was committed to the care of a vulture with which they had formed a very close friendship. But the vulture was sixty thousand years old, and fell asleep at his post. The result was that Rāvana had seized Sītā and placed her in his aeroplane before the vulture was wakened by her cries for help. The aged bird, however, put up a brave fight and was successful in breaking the car to pieces and slaying Rāvana's attendants, before he fell, mortally wounded, to the ground. And so it happened that it was in his arms and not in his aeroplane that Rāvana carried the princess to Ceylon.

When Rāma returned and found the cottage empty of

his love, he was beside himself with grief. Fitting an arrow to his bow, he swore that he would destroy the three worlds if the gods did not reveal to him the hiding-place of Sītā. Sun, moon and stars, mountains, rivers and trees, every kind of spirit, good and bad, gods, demons and men, he would destroy them all, if they did not give him back his wife. In past days he had been of a gentle, benevolent disposition, and he supposed that was why the gods had held him in contempt. He had observed that people paid no attention to the Creator just because he was compassionate and kind. But as far as he was concerned, he would in future act on a different plan. He would be absolutely without pity, and have one object in life only, the obtaining of vengeance for the loss of his blameless spouse. He knew that the world was destined to perish some day in the great dissolution of all things, but he would anticipate that awful day, and if the gods did not restore Sītā before another sun had set, the three worlds, with all they contained, would be swept out of existence.

Lakshmana appealed to his brother to be calm and not talk so foolishly. Where was the justice of punishing the three worlds because some person unknown had carried off Sītā. It was the special duty of kings to see to it that the innocent did not suffer for the guilty, and he was confident that neither gods nor demons, neither mountains nor rivers, had been responsible for the wrong to which they had been exposed. To these exhortations Laksh-mana added others equally wise. His brother must not forget that suffering was the appointed lot of every man who came into the world. If Rāma could not endure the sorrow which had befallen him, how were ordinary mortals to withstand the assaults of grief. And looking higher, let him think of the gods themselves. These mighty beings, also, were subject to the control of Fate, and of them also, no one could say that unmixed happiness had been their lot. He therefore appealed to him to refrain from useless grief and do what was the task of the moment, assist him to make a thorough search. In obedience to his brother's counsel the broken-hearted husband had not travelled far when he found the vulture bleeding profusely and at the point of death. By great good fortune the bird was still able to speak and make the prince acquainted with the fact that Sītā had been carried off by the demon monarch of Ceylon. Anxiety to recover his wife, however, did not prevent the princes from performing the funeral rites of their deceased friend with scrupulous care. They gathered fuel, they built a funeral pyre, and with their own hands set fire to the wood, as if the vulture had been a member of their own caste. They also repeated the sacred texts appropriate to the occasion, and when the body was consumed, made offerings to the spirits of the dead. For this purpose they hunted and slew several deer, whose flesh they spread out on sacred grass with the prayer that the departed might obtain an entrance into heaven. The ceremony was brought to a close by the performance of the water oblation. When all was over, the heroes bathed in the river Godāvari, which flowed past their hermitage.

Having performed these pious tasks, the princes set out in the direction Rāvana had been seen to travel. They passed through a number of impenetrable forests where fresh adventures awaited them, and at last emerged on the shores of a lovely lake whose beauties recalled to Rāma's heart the joys he had had with Sītā. And had it not been for his brother's earnest appeals, Rāma would have lost all hope of recovering his wife. Eventually they met the king of the monkeys and his distinguished lieutenant, Hanumān, both of them the offspring of the gods. When they had heard Rāma's story they undertook

9

to befriend him and to place at his disposal the whole of
the monkey race. It will be remembered that when
Vishnu promised to appear on earth as Rāma, he did so
on the understanding that the gods and other celestials
would cohabit with bears and monkeys and produce
thereby an army which would assist him in his contest
with Rāvana. And so it came to pass. The many millions
of bears and monkeys, for the former are also included,
which flocked to Rāma's standard, were all of divine origin.
It took some months, however, to gather them together,
and Rāma had well-nigh fretted his heart out with impatience before he saw them standing on the shores of
Southern India and looked across the intervening sea
that lay between them and Ceylon. Having arrived there,
the problem was, how to cross the straits, a distance of
seven hundred miles. Not more than two or three of the
monkeys were able to jump so far. But a bridge was soon
constructed. Indeed the whole work, including an excellent roadway, was completed in five days. It was an
embankment rather than a bridge, being composed of
mountains and trees which the monkeys and bears uprooted
and cast into the sea. As Rāma and his hosts marched
across the bridge, the gods appeared in person. Each of
them sprinkled the hero with holy water and expressed
the hope that he would be victorious in his fight with
Rāvana. No purpose would be served by recounting the
many battles that took place. It is enough to say that
Rāvana, and practically the whole of his followers to the
number of many millions, were defeated and slain. So
fierce was the contest that Rāma and his brother did not
escape without sustaining many grievous wounds. On
one occasion indeed, it was thought that they were dead.
But Hanumān went off to a certain mountain in the
Himālayas in search of a very powerful medicinal plant
which was known to grow there. Unfortunately the herb

knew that Hanumān was coming and made itself invisible.
But Hanumān uprooted the mountain on which the plant
was growing, and carried it off with trees and elephants
still on it, just as they were. When he got back to Ceylon
he held the mountain to the nostrils of Rāma and his
brother, who sat up at once, healed of all their wounds.
The mountain was then applied in the same way to the
noses of the bears and monkeys who had been killed in
the battle, and with equally miraculous results.

Now that Rāvana was dead, one would have supposed
that Rāma would have hastened to Sītā's prison-house.
But we find instead, that Rāma's mood had changed. He
gave the cold command that Sītā was to be brought into
his presence. And when she did appear, he spoke no
word of love. He told her merely that he had removed
the insult from his name and killed the cause of his disgrace
as his duty demanded. But he could have nothing more
to do with her, and she could go where she liked. No
man with any self-respect could take back a wife who had
lived so long in another's house. Rāvana had held her in
his arms and looked at her with lustful eyes. As she
listened to this cruel speech, Sītā wept many bitter tears.
But she had the courage and wisdom to defend herself
vigorously. If she had known that her husband had ceased
to love her, she would have committed suicide. It would
have saved everybody a great deal of trouble and fewer
lives would have been lost. It was a poor requital for all
the love and devotion she had shown him. Her heart
had always been his and his only. He professed to be a
judge of character ; he was ignorant of hers. He had seen
other women and distrusted them. Was that any reason
why he should distrust the whole sex ?

When she had uttered this brave defence, Sītā turned
to her brother-in-law and asked him to erect a funeral
pyre. There was, she said, no other alternative. She

had no wish to live longer now that her husband had cast such undeserved insults on her fame. Lakshmana looked anxiously at Rāma in the hope that he would interfere, but his only movement was a gesture to show that Sītā's request should be obeyed. The bears and monkeys could not control their grief and wept aloud, and it was manifest that Rāma also was deeply moved. His eyes were full of tears and he never spoke a word. When the fire had been got ready, Sītā entered the flames with the touching appeal, " As my heart has never gone away from Rāma, do thou protect me, oh fire, the witness of the people." But Sītā did not perish. Supernatural aid was close at hand. Brahmā, the creator god, accompanied by Indra, Shiva and a great multitude of the celestials, appeared on the scene, riding in their cars. Raising their hands in wonder, they asked the prince why he, who was the protector of the worlds and so endowed with wisdom, treated his wife in such an amazing fashion, and allowed her to enter the fire. Did he not know that he was the first of all the gods and the creator of the three worlds. To these questions Rāma replied, " I know myself to be a man, Rāma, the son of Dasharatha. Let Brahmā tell me who I am, and whence I have come." In response to this request the creator once more told Rāma who he was, the great god Vishnu, who is manifest in all creatures, in cows and Brāhmins, and possessed of a thousand legs, a thousand heads and a thousand eyes ; the sacred letters OM, the foremost of the Vedas. He had already appeared on earth in various incarnations, and now he had achieved yet another blessing to the world by the destruction of Rāvana. As for Sītā, she was the goddess Lakshmī, his heavenly spouse. When Brahmā had finished his address, the god of fire rose out of the flames with Sītā in his arms and addressed the prince. His words were to the effect that Sītā was absolutely free

from stain. It was true that she had lived in Rávana's
palace for many months, but she had always been true
to her husband in thought, word and deed. Ráma was
greatly delighted to receive this comforting assurance.
But in justice to himself, he said it was necessary that
Sítá should undergo some purification. If this had not
been done, people would have cast aspersions on her name
and say that he had been indifferent to the claims of
morality. Sítá was as dear to him as his own life, and in
his heart he knew, and had always known, that no evil had
ever come near her. She was his, he knew it, even as the
sun's rays belonged to the sun. When husband and wife
had been thus happily reconciled, Shiva and Indra added
their congratulations. By the special favour of the gods,
Ráma's father was allowed to have a brief interview with
his sons and daughter-in-law. He told the latter not to
be angry with her husband. He had acted in a very
strict way, but it would have a wholesome effect on other
women, and help them to remember that a husband was
a god.

When the gods had gone back to heaven, Ráma resolved
to return to India at once. The fourteen years of exile
had by this time expired, and there was no reason why
they should not return to Ayodhyá. It was a long and
difficult journey. But it will be remembered that Rávana
had a wonderful aeroplane which he had stolen from his
stepbrother, the god of riches. The aeroplane was of a
very great size, and contained a large number of spacious
and splendid rooms, beautifully furnished with seats and
cushions. It was as big as a mountain, and in view of its
size, Ráma was able to invite the bears and monkeys to
go with him as fellow-passengers. As they journeyed
through the air, Ráma pointed out to Sítá the bridge
that had been built across the straits, and both together
gazed down upon the places where they had spent their

years of exile. When the car passed over the capital of
the monkey king, Sītā begged her husband to descend and
invite the monkeys' wives to go with them to Ayodhyā.
This was done, and with these friends added to their
company, the brothers and Sītā came at last within sight
of their father's capital, the citadel of the solar race.
Words cannot describe the joy with which the people
welcomed Rāma. They raised a shout that could be heard
in heaven. The houses and streets were decked with
flags and flowers, while every man and woman that was
able to travel went forth to meet and welcome their
king. And nobody was more delighted than Bharata,
Rāma's noble-hearted and unselfish brother, who, during
the intervening years had governed in his name. It was
Bharata also who insisted that Rāma's coronation should
take place without delay.

When the coronation was over and the bears and
monkeys had returned to their proper haunts, Rāma
assumed the task of sovereignty. He lived happily with
his brothers, and in his hours of leisure wandered in the
gardens of his palace with Sītā by his side. As the months
passed, Rāma noticed a change in his wife's condition,
and one happy evening she told him that she was with
child. Greatly delighted to receive this news, the king
asked his wife if there was any desire of her heart that he
could gratify. And she said nothing would give her more
satisfaction than to pay a visit to the hermits in the forest.
Even one night spent in their society, on the bank of the
Ganges, would afford her great delight. Rāma was only
too pleased to gratify her wish, and promised to make
the arrangements for her going the very next day. Having
made this promise, Rāma passed to the outer courts of
the palace where he spent the night listening to the
conversation of his ministers and friends. That evening
Rāma observed that kings were often criticised and blamed

by their subjects. He wondered if anybody had ever blamed him. And so, turning to one of the company, he said, " Has anybody ever blamed me ? " In answer to such a direct question, it was difficult to avoid making a reply, and the person addressed said, " Yes, you also are blamed. The people blame you for taking back Sītā. They say that she was a prisoner in Rāvana's capital, that the demon held her in his arms, and that you don't seem to care. You are quite happy and free from all sign of jealousy. They can't understand your conduct, and think that your action will have a bad effect on their own wives." Rāma was deeply distressed to hear these observations, and when he had asked the rest of the company if it was really true that the people made such criticism, he dismissed the gathering and retired to his own apartments.

But he had already resolved what he was to do. Sending for his brothers, he told them what he had heard. He did not for a moment question Sītā's virtue, and he knew that after Rāvana's death they had received conclusive proof that her character was without a stain. The gods themselves had appeared in person and given ample assurance of her chastity. But in view of what the people were saying, he had decided that he must repudiate Sītā, and therefore he requested Lakshmana to take her away to some remote place and leave her there on the following day. By great good fortune it had been already arranged that she should visit one of the hermitages for a single night. Under the impression that she was setting forth upon this brief and pleasant outing, Lakshmana was to escort her to the hermitage of Vālmīkī. Once she reached that place, it would be his duty to tell her that she was not to return. In conclusion, Rāma told his brothers that they must not in any way attempt to interfere with or to alter his decision. If they tried to do so, he would never speak to them again. As he uttered this last in-

junction, the heartbroken king rose and left the room.
He sighed like an elephant, and his eyes were full of tears.

All unconscious of the fate that was in store for her,
Sītā was ready at dawn to set out upon her journey to
the forest. Lakshmana was waiting to escort her. No
mention is made of Rāma being present to bid her farewell,
or of any desire on Sītā's part to see her husband and
say good-bye. They had not gone far before Sītā's right
eye began to throb, a bad omen which caused her much
distress. But Lakshmana laughed away her fears, and
said she had no cause to be alarmed. On the second day
they reached the bank of the Ganges, that sacred stream
whose waters remove all sin. And now it was Lakshmana
who required comfort, for we are told that he began to
weep, and it was Sītā who acted as his comforter. She
knew it was because they were separated from Rāma. And
she felt the separation as much as he did. But he must
not be too cast down. They would spend one night only
at the hermitage, and then return home. By this time a
boat had been got ready to ferry them across the river.
When they reached the farther shore, and Sītā was proceeding in the direction of Vālmīki's hermitage, Lakshmana
stopped her and said that he had a very melancholy
duty to perform. He wished her to understand that he
was a very unwilling agent in the matter, but Rāma's
commands must be obeyed. When he had gone so far,
the prince broke down completely and could not say
another word. But at last he was able in broken accents
to explain that Rāma had resolved to disown her once
more. Though he was absolutely convinced that she
was entirely innocent, her husband had decided that she
was to be left in charge of Vālmīki in obedience to the
wishes of the citizens of Ayodhyā. Sītā was overwhelmed
with grief and fell senseless to the ground. When she
recovered consciousness she spoke very touchingly of her

past experience of forest life, happy in the love and tenderness of her lord. But now she was to live alone. She could not bear the thought. Her natural desire was to cast herself into the Ganges and be at rest. But that could not be, as she bore beneath her breast that which would prevent the termination of her husband's race. A woman's husband was her god. It was her duty therefore to work for his welfare, even if it involved the loss of her own life. Râma knew that she was innocent. He had renounced her for the sake of his good name. She would support him therefore in his efforts to preserve it from all stain. She was sorry, however, that the people of Ayodhyā had been so uncharitable and unjust. Realising that it was best for both that they should separate at once, Lakshmana re-entered the boat, and when he reached the other shore, mounted his chariot and drove off as quickly as he could. But whenever he looked back he saw the helpless queen rushing wildly along the river bank, casting herself in a paroxysm of grief upon the ground. Her cries soon attracted the attention of Vālmīki's disciples, who hurried to their master with the information that they had seen a lady, as beautiful as a goddess, abandoned and alone, the very image of sorrow. Now Vālmīki was a great ascetic, and by virtue of the merit he had acquired, knew all that was happening in heaven, earth and hell. He was already acquainted with the calamity that had befallen Sîtā, and was aware that she was coming to his hermitage. He therefore approached the queen with words of kindness, and told her not to grieve. She was to look upon that place as her home. Everybody who lived there would treat her as if she were their own daughter. As he said this, Vālmīki escorted the queen to where the wives of his fellow ascetics were gathered, and committed her to the care of these ancient dames. In course of time Sîtā gave birth to two boys, and gave to them the names

of Kusha and Lava.[1] But Rāma was not informed that
sons had been born to him, nor did he ever inquire as to
his wife's progress and happiness. If, however, you ask
why Rāma should have been guilty of such cruelty, listen
to this explanation, an explanation which afforded great
satisfaction and comfort to Lakshmana's tender heart.
The wife of an eminent sage once gave shelter to certain
demons who had fled before the wrath of the gods. In
punishment for her crime, Vishnu cut off the lady's head.
When the sage saw his wife's lifeless body he uttered a
curse against Vishnu. It was to this effect. "Because
you have killed my wife, I condemn you to be born among
mortals. And because you have robbed me of her society,
so too will you be robbed of the society of your wife for a
long period of time."

When Sītā's two sons were twelve years old, news came
to the hermitage that Rāma was about to celebrate the
horse sacrifice. During the intervening years, Vālmīki
had been busy composing his great poem, the *Rāmāyana*,
the epic which sets forth in inspired verse the story of
Rāma's glorious career, and he had taught it so carefully
to the two boys that they were able to recite it from
beginning to end. The kind-hearted sage knew that his
opportunity had come at last. He would take the boys
with him to Ayodhyā. It would be easy to get an opportunity for them to recite the poem. And he told them
that when they stood in Rāma's presence, and he asked
them who they were, they were to reply, "We are the
disciples of Vālmīki," and nothing more. Everything
came to pass as their foster-father had planned. The two
lads were summoned to Rāma's presence and told to recite
the poem. Their wonderful likeness to Rāma was apparent
to every person in the audience, and it was the unanimous

---

[1] The Maharajas of Udaipur and Jaipur in Rajputana claim descent
respectively from Lava and Kusha.

opinion that nobody could perceive the least difference
in either face or form. Their father, however, made no
comment. But when the recitation, which occupied
quite a number of nights, was complete,[1] Rāma sent for
Vālmīki and said, "If Sītā is innocent and has led a pure
life in the forest, let her come to Ayodhyā and offer proof
to that effect." Vālmīki's reply was that Sītā would
certainly obey her husband's behest, for she knew and
believed that a woman's husband was her greatest god.
This conduct on Rāma's part is spoken of as wonderful,
and his ministers told him that nobody else would act
in such a noble and generous way.

The trial was fixed for the following morning. Great
crowds gathered to witness such an unusual event. Every
one was deeply moved and stood absolutely motionless as
Sītā appeared on the sacrificial ground, accompanied by
Vālmīki. She advanced with downcast head, her hands
folded together, and her eyes full of tears, "meditating
upon Rāma." Suddenly the silence gave place to a great
shout of admiration and pity. Some praised Rāma, some
praised Sītā, others praised both. Vālmīki was the first
to speak, and he testified not only to Sītā's purity, but to
the fact that Kusha and Lava were Rāma's own sons.
He swore that he was speaking the truth. He had never
sinned once in all his life, either in thought, word or deed.
But if he was telling a lie, then he prayed that he might
lose all the merit he had acquired through many thousand
years of stern asceticism. To this statement Rāma
answered that he was quite sure that Vālmīki was telling
the truth, nevertheless he felt it necessary that Sītā should
produce proofs as to her chastity. Before they left
Ceylon, the gods had intervened and given the most satisfactory assurances. But the people had slandered her

[1] The poem consists of about four thousand pages in the English translation.

since, and in consequence he had been forced to send her
away. He knew that the boys were his. But it would be
better for everybody concerned if Sītā gave her personal
testimony in the presence of that assembly. By this
time the gods had heard of what was going on, and they
appeared in large numbers with Brahmā at their head.
With the coming of the gods a most remarkable change
in the atmosphere was felt. A delightfully cool breeze
sprang up; people said they had never experienced anything like it. It was the kind of wind that blew in the
age of gold.

Sītā made a very brief reply. "I have never even
thought of any one but Rāma, and by the strength of this
virtue I ask the earth goddess to give me room. I have
always in thought, word and deed worked for Rāma's
welfare. And in proof that this is so, I ask the earth
goddess to receive me." She obtained an immediate
response. The earth at once opened before her, and serpent
deities, bearing on their heads a beautiful throne, appeared.
The earth goddess came with them. Taking the poor
princess in her arms, she placed her on the throne, which
sank into the earth and disappeared from view. The
gods, by their words of praise, showed that they approved
of what Sītā had done. As for Rāma himself, he was
plunged in grief. But his grief soon gave place to wrath,
and he swore that if the earth did not restore Sītā to his
arms, he would submerge her with all her mountains and
forests beneath the waves. He had brought her back
from Rāvana's prison-house. He was resolved that he
would bring her back from hell. As he went on talking
in this fashion, Brahmā asked him to control himself. He
should remember that he was the god Vishnu. Sītā
had gone to the land of the snake deities, and he would
meet her again in heaven. With these words of consolation, Brahmā and his brother deities departed, while

Rāma, taking his two sons with him, retired to his palace where he spent the night mourning the loss of his much loved queen. Though he lived for many thousands of years he never married another wife, and in the performance of his religious ceremonies always kept a golden image of Sītā by his side.

Rāmāyana.

XXIII.

RĀMA'S ASCENT TO HEAVEN.

" For a thousand years Rāma celebrated many horse sacrifices . . . numberless cow sacrifices and various other sacrifices."—*Rāmāyana*, vii. 112.

RĀMA's reign on earth lasted for eleven thousand years. It is said that these were years of great happiness. Whatever his feelings may have been after the loss of Sītā, there is no doubt as to the satisfaction and prosperity of his subjects. They never experienced any sort of trouble or distress. Parents never had to perform funeral rites for their children, because every one lived for a thousand years, surrounded by hundreds of their sons and grandsons. Nature joined in the universal joy. Trees were covered with fruits and flowers the whole year round ; pleasant winds blew, and rain fell whenever it was required. And yet, strange to say, there emerge at least two incidents which seem to question the accuracy of our picture. We read of a hungry Brāhmin trudging from door to door, seeking charity and finding none. And what is equally wonderful, another member of the same caste rails against the prince because of his son's death, a boy of fourteen years. In no other kingdom save Rāma's, he says, are such untimely deaths ever heard of. But apart from these two incidents, it would appear that sorrow and disease did not exist. Indeed the story of this long and prosperous reign is confined to a few pages, and Rāma's most serious

tasks were the slaying of a Shūdra who had been so presumptuous as to practise asceticism, and the settling of a
dispute between an owl and a vulture as to the ownership
of a nest.[1]

As for Rāma's brothers, they each in course of time
carved out for themselves kingdoms in different parts of
India. Bharata's conquest was the most impressive.
The territory he acquired was in the north-west of India.
In a battle which lasted for seven days, thirty millions
were slain. The gods said they had never seen anything
like it. Bharata divided the country he conquered between
his two sons, and erected for each of them a capital city
which continued in after days to give honour to their
names.[2] But neither Bharata nor the other brothers
were happy away from Rāma, and when their sons grew
to manhood they spent most of their time in Ayodhyā.
In their joy at being in his society, they felt no regret at
separation from their sons. In this manner the eleven
thousand years gradually passed away. Rāma performed
many sacrifices, and especially remarkable is the statement
that the sacrifice of the cow was offered times without
number.

But the longest reign must end at last. And one day
Time came to Ayodhyā in the guise of an ascetic. He told
Lakshmana, who was standing at the palace gates, that he
wished to see his brother. When he was escorted to the
royal presence, the king presented the usual offerings and

[1] The owl said she had owned it since the creation of the world; the
vulture, since the birth of the first man.

[2] They were called Takshashilā and Puskalāvatī. They both appear
in the pages of authentic history. The king of the former (Taxila) made
submission to Alexander the Great when he invaded India. It was
afterwards in the possession of the Bactrian Greeks, descendants of the
Greek colonists whom Alexander left behind him. Taxila was long
famous as the site of a university of ancient learning. The recent
excavations at Taxila, 20 miles N.W. of Rāwalpindi, are well known.

caused his guest to sit on a throne of gold. But when the king asked him to state the object of his visit, the ascetic replied that the welfare of the gods demanded that their interview should be in private. The strictest secrecy was necessary, and should any one venture to invade their privacy Rāma must promise to put that person to death. In obedience to this request Lakshmana undertook to act as doorkeeper, and see to it that no one attempted to enter the room where the interview was being held. When these precautions had been taken, the ascetic, who so far had concealed his name, announced that he was really Time, Rāma's own son, born to him from the womb of Māyā or *illusion*, when as the god Vishnu he reigned in heaven. He was there that day as the ambassador of Brahmā to remind him of the fact that the years of his appointed sojourn on earth had reached a close, and that his brother deities were anxiously awaiting his return to heaven. If he wished to remain longer among men, he was to say so; but Brahmā had thought it his duty to send him word. In reply, Rāma, addressing the messenger as his son, said he was very pleased to see him. As to the question of his return, he had already been revolving that matter in his mind when Time arrived, and he was quite prepared to resume his proper tasks, as soon as may be, in the upper world.

While this conversation was proceeding within the palace, another ascetic appeared at the outer gate. The new arrival was Durvāsa, a very eminent but very bad-tempered saint. When he announced his desire to speak with Rāma, Lakshmana ventured to remark that his brother was engaged in private conversation with another ascetic, and could not be disturbed. But the sage, true to his character, said that if Lakshmana did not go at once and arrange for an immediate interview, he would blast with his curse, not only Rāma and all his house, but the whole

city and inhabitants of Ayodhyā as well. When he heard
this terrible threat, Lakshmana, though he knew that
death would be his portion, resolved that it was much
better that he should perish rather than that his family
and race should be destroyed. He therefore went and
told the king that Durvāsa wished to see him and would
not be denied. Rāma accordingly said farewell to Time,
and hastened to receive his second but very impatient
visitor. Bowing before him with folded hands, he meekly
asked him to say what he wanted. "I am very hungry,"
said Durvāsa. "I have just completed a thousand years'
asceticism, and throughout that long period I have never
broken my fast. Bring me food, a large quantity of food,
that I may appease my hunger." The monarch at once
gave orders for the very best food to be prepared, and
when the ascetic had eaten his fill, he thanked Rāma for
his hospitality and retired to his hermitage.

But with the departure of the saint, Rāma remembered
on what terms he had granted an interview to the first
ascetic. Lakshmana had interrupted their conversation,
and therefore Lakshmana must die. Afraid that Rāma,
out of love for him, would refuse to implement the agreement, Lakshmana told his brother not to be distressed.
They must fulfil the promise they had made. They were
in the hands of Destiny, and men's actions were controlled
by what they had done in a former birth. Fortunately
Rāma remembered that he did not need to slay his brother.
Wise men had said that to renounce a person was equivalent
to killing him. And so he uttered the words, "I renounce
thee." Being thus abandoned by his brother, Lakshmana
at once left the palace and proceeded to the banks of the
river Sarju, where he stood for a short time in the attitude
of devotion. He next closed his mouth and nostrils, as
well as the other apertures of his body, in such a way that
it was impossible for him to breathe. The gods by this

time had appeared on the scene and, in a way that is not explained, conveyed Lakshmana to heaven. But it is said that the celestials were very glad to see him, remembering, as they did, that he was a fourth part of Vishnu.

Rāma was very sad at the loss of his brother, and he told Bharata, who was in Ayodhyā at the time, that he had no desire to live longer on the earth. He was resolved to go that very day to be a dweller in the forest. It was his intention to make Bharata his heir to the throne. But Bharata absolutely refused. "There are your two sons. Divide your kingdom between them and build cities for them to dwell in. As for me, I am going with you. Even heaven would cease to be heaven for me if you were not there. Not only so, but you must send word to Shatrughna, our remaining brother, for I am certain that he, too, will wish to go with us." And so it was arranged. Messengers were sent to Muttra to summon Shatrughna, and before he was able to join them, seven days had passed. But by that time Rāma's sons had been installed in their respective kingdoms, and cities had been built for them to dwell in. But new aspirants for the privilege of accompanying Rāma had now put in a claim. When the citizens of Ayodhyā heard that Rāma was going to leave them, they refused to be left behind. And not only they, but the bears and monkeys, who had assisted Rāma in his fight with Rāvana thousands of years before, also appeared and said, "We, too, are going with you. We cannot allow you to forsake us." The poem now makes it manifest that Rāma was going a longer journey than to the forest. He was going to heaven, and this the citizens and the bears and monkeys also realised. It was thus a very great company indeed that followed Rāma. Ayodhyā was left entirely empty. The citizens, with their wives and children, the ministers of state, the eunuchs and women of the zenana, the

bears and monkeys, even the beasts of the field and the
birds of the air, joined in the procession. The pilgrims
sought the banks of the river Sarju. Rāma walked in
front. Lakshmi, the goddess of prosperity, his heavenly
spouse, was on his right hand, the earth goddess was on
his left. He was attended by the four Vedas, the Gāyatri
verse, and the sacred letters OM, with sages and demons
bringing up the rear, all of them wonderfully happy at
the thought that they were journeying with Rāma to
the very gates of heaven. When they stepped into the
water, Brahmā, the creator god, appeared. He was
attended by his brother deities, and a variety of semi-
divine beings riding in celestial cars to the number of
many millions. Brahmā addressed Rāma by the name
of Vishnu, and said that they had come to welcome him
back to heaven. They recognised that he was the refuge
of all creatures, beyond the reach of thought and knowledge, the immortal and imperishable lord. When
Brahmā had thus spoken, the other celestials, with Indra
and the god of fire at their head, bowed down in worship.
They said that by his coming they were freed from sin,
and the desire of their hearts had been fulfilled. It was
thus that Rāma and his brothers entered heaven. But
as they passed within the skies they did not forget their
humbler friends. Rāma, or as he is now called, Vishnu,
asked the creator to allot to each of them a suitable place
in the upper world. In response to this request, Brahmā
replied that the citizens of Ayodhyā, their wives and
children would go to a particular region which was next
his own; a blessed spot, which even the most degraded
were privileged to enter if they saw all things as Vishnu.
As for the bears and monkeys, he remembered that they
were the offspring of the gods, born to help Rāma in his
fight with Rāvana, and he therefore proposed that they
should be reunited with their celestial sires. And so

indeed it came to pass. Not even the beasts and birds
which had followed their owners from Ayodhyā were
forgotten. Men and women, old and young, sages and
demons, monkeys and bears, with beasts and birds of
every kind, as they plunged into the waters of the river
Sarju, were divested of their bodies, and went to dwell in
heaven with the gods.

The childless man who reads even a single verse of this
poem will secure a son, while those who read a verse of it
every day will be freed from all their sins.

Rāmāyana, vii. 114–124.

XXIV.

VISHNU'S INCARNATION AS KRISHNA.

" Revere the actions of Hari (Krishna), but do not give your mind to
the doing of them."—*Prem Sāgar*, c. 34.

" If he held up Gobardhan, which was a mere ant-hill, for seven
days, I do not regard that as anything remarkable."—*Mahābhārata*, ii.
41. 9.

AT an assembly of the gods held on the top of Mount
Meru, the Earth appeared as a suppliant. She was
grievously burdened, she said, by great numbers of demons.
The demons had left their proper haunts and begun to
dwell among mortals and to plague mankind. Some of
them wore the guise of celestials, but others had taken
birth as human beings and been born as sons of kings.
She gave the names of quite a number of them ; but
mentioned, in particular, an individual called Kansa. In
a previous birth this powerful demon had been slain by
Vishnu, and now he was king of Muttra, having deposed
his father and assumed the crown. The father was a
worshipper of Rāma, while the son was a devotee of
Shiva. It was because his father refused to abandon his
creator and the remover of his grief, and become a follower
of Shiva that Kansa deposed him, and issued a proclamation that no one should ever make mention of Rāma's
name, or pay to him any sort of worship. Since that
announcement had been made, things had grown much
worse ; cows and Brāhmins were in a state of distress ;

indeed the Earth declared that if the gods did not come
to her help, she would sink down to the lower regions.
In concluding her appeal, the goddess reminded her hearers
that not only they, but demons and serpents, indeed every
living thing, were merely portions of Vishnu.

Recognising the seriousness of the situation, Brahmā
proposed that they should go in a body and tell Vishnu
what the Earth had said. He was confident that that
mighty deity would do what he had often done before,
go down to earth in a small portion of his essence and
remove the evils of which they had heard so pathetic an
account. In accordance with this decision, the gods went
off to the Sea of Milk, which was Vishnu's favourite abode.
When they arrived, the god was asleep, but the celestials
gathered round his couch and began to sing his praise.
In their hymn of adoration, they said that he was Brahm,
the Eternal Spirit, that he was the four Vedas, that he
was the smallest of the small and the largest of the large,
that he could not be seen, could not be described, could
not be conceived, that he was all that had been, and all
that would be ; the protector and the saviour of the world.
Before they were finished, the god had wakened from his
slumbers and addressing the creator, told him to say what
they wanted. He was not to be afraid to speak. His
prayer would surely be heard. As he said this, Vishnu
revealed his eternal form, a sight which brought Brahmā
to his knees and evoked another outburst of devotion.
When he was at last able to speak, Brahmā told his story,
ending with the cry, " Show thy favour to us ; deliver the
Earth from her oppressors. Tell us your counsels and we
shall humbly obey." Vishnu made an immediate response.
He plucked out two hairs—it is not recorded from what
part of his body—and said, " These two hairs, one white
and the other black, will go down to the earth and deliver
her from her oppressors. The white hair will be born as

the seventh son, and the black hair as the eighth son of Devaki, the wife of Vasudeva, and the cousin of Kansa. It will be my black hair that will slay the demons. When he had made this announcement Vishnu disappeared from view, while the gods, bowing before his invisible presence, returned to Mount Meru.

The scene now changes to earth, and to the town of Muttra, where Kansa soon got information of his impending doom. According to one narrative, the very eminent sage, Nārada, who earned the title of the mischief-maker because of his gossiping ways, and who was constantly travelling between earth and heaven, went and told Kansa that Vishnu had announced his intention of being born as the eighth son of his cousin Devaki. But another account is that Kansa one evening took his cousin and her husband for a drive, when a voice from heaven cried aloud and said, "What a fool you are, Kansa. Do you not know that the eighth child to which this woman will give birth will cause your death ? " The king at once drew his sword and was about to kill his cousin right away. But her husband intervened and said, "Do not kill her. I promise that I shall hand over every one of her children immediately after their birth to be dealt with in whatever way you please." Confident that Vasudeva would keep his promise, the king had mercy on his cousin and spared her life. But not unnaturally he placed her under close supervision. As far as the first six children were concerned, Vasudeva faithfully adhered to the agreement. He delivered them to Kansa, who caused them to be put to death.[1] As the reader will remember, the seventh child was to be the personation of the white hair of Vishnu ; and when he was about to be born, the god sent the goddess of sleep to transfer the embryo to the womb of another of Vasudeva's

---

[1] The text says that these infants were really demons transferred to the womb of Devaki by the command of Vishnu.

wives. He added, that a rumour would spread to the
effect that Devaki had miscarried; and apparently Kansa
accepted this rumour as founded on fact. With reference
to the eighth child, however, it was necessary to take
greater precautions, because it was the eighth child whom
Kansa had special cause to dread. But here again the
great and mighty god had all his plans prepared when the
critical moment arrived. He instructed the goddess of
sleep what she was to do. The father was to take the
newly-born child, carry him without the city walls to a
place on the farther shore of the river Jumna, where a
cowherd's wife had just given birth to a daughter, exchange
the infants and hurry back to his own house. Such a
scheme was attended by many difficulties. Kansa had surrounded the house with guards, and guards were stationed
at each of the city gates. But the goddess caused them
all to fall into a deep sleep, and Vasudeva both came and
went without experiencing the least inconvenience.[1] Of
course the goddess was his companion from beginning to
end of the undertaking, while the great serpent, Shesha,
who upholds the world, followed in the rear, extending his
mighty hood over the little company and shielding them
from the torrential rain that was falling at the time.

When Vasudeva got back and placed the female infant
in his wife's arms, it cried aloud. The cry awoke the
guards, and one of them ran to Kansa's palace, with the
news that a child had been born to Devaki. Kansa at
once appeared on the scene, seized the infant and dashed
its head against a stone. But it rose high in the air, a
great and mighty form, crying out, "Your efforts have
been all in vain. He who will slay you has been born.
Take heed what you do. You have to fight, not with

---

[1] Whenever he was born, the infant told his parents who he was.
Prior to the birth the gods also appeared in person and sang his mother's
praises, declaring that she was equal to the celestials.

men and demons, but with the greatest of the gods."
When he saw that he had been deceived, the king gave
orders to his followers to make a thorough search in every
corner of the world, and wherever they found an unusually
healthy and vigorous boy, to see to it that he was put to
death. As for his cousin and her husband, he set them
free, with the observation that no purpose would be served
by keeping them prisoners any longer. Eight children
had been born and he had killed them all, with the exception of the one he was most anxious to destroy.

As soon as he obtained his freedom, Vasudeva hurried
to the encampment of the cowherd, where he found both
the man and his wife rejoicing over the fact that a son had
been born. His purpose was to persuade the cowherd
and his companions to return to their pastures without
delay. This was not a difficult task, as they had already
fulfilled the object of their visit to the capital, the payment
of their annual tribute to the king. Before the cowherd
left, Vasudeva asked him to take care of his seventh
child also, and rear him as his own son. In this way the
two brothers were brought into companionship; and they
grew up to manhood together, dwelling in the forest pastures
and caring for the cattle of their foster-father. The elder
child was called Balarāma, while the younger, that is, the
eighth child, was called Krishna, a word that means
black, and black was the colour of the hair from which
he sprang.

Many were the pranks which Krishna played during
his childhood and youth. For instance, when he was still
an infant, a female demon came in the middle of the
night, picked him up from the place where he lay asleep,
and gave him her breast to suck. She had caused the
deaths of many infants by the same evil conduct, but
she met her match in Krishna. The infant seized her
breast with both hands and went on sucking till he had

sucked her life away. Her shrieks of pain and terror
roused the whole encampment, but Krishna would not let
go till he saw her dead at his feet. And yet both his
father and mother were greatly alarmed, and they did not
put him back in his bed beneath the waggon till they had
sprinkled cow dung on his head, and fastened an amulet
round his wrist, with appropriate prayers to Vishnu in
his various forms. Not long after, his mother happened
to offend him. Awaking out of his sleep and feeling
hungry, he called aloud for nourishment. But such was
his impatience that he began to kick his feet about in all
directions, with the result that the waggon was overturned and the waterpots broken. Such a fresh exhibition
of strength filled the encampment with amazement. But
it was not long before another adventure of the infant
eclipsed all that had gone before. This incident we are
about to relate happened some months after, when he
was learning to crawl. His mother was never able to
keep him out of mischief. If he was not covering himself
with ashes and dung, he was in among the feet of the
cattle and pulling their tails. At last, when he and his
brother paid no attention to their mother's injunctions
and threats of punishment, she tied a rope round Krishna's
middle, fastening the other end to a large wooden mortar.
Thinking that such a contrivance would hold him fast,
she went off to attend to her household affairs. But
Krishna was not to be so detained. Left to himself, he
went on crawling and dragging the heavy mortar after
him. At last he passed between two trees which grew
close together. The mortar stuck between them. Krishna
went on pulling, and the mortar held its place. The
result was that the two great trees were uprooted and
came crashing to the ground. When the cowherds rushed
to the spot, they found the child unharmed, and laughing
aloud, as he thought of what he had done. But the head

men of the tribe were very much disturbed. They said it was an exceedingly bad omen, and it was not the first. There was the death of the female fiend, the overturning of the waggon, and now two trees had fallen, when there was no wind to blow them down. They therefore resolved to break up their encampment and seek some place where no such omens would disturb them.

The district which they chose for their new settlement was called Vrindhāvan, and there Krishna and Balarāma had even more wonderful adventures than any they had formerly experienced. One of them was an encounter which Krishna had with a great water-snake whose home was in a deep pool of the river Jumna. His parents and the cowherds were sure the child would perish. And indeed it seemed as if Krishna himself was anxious as to the result. But his brother Balarāma called upon him to remember who he was, the eternal God, the very centre of creation. When Krishna, thus exhorted, put forth his divine strength and crushed the snake, the creature in its agony cried aloud for mercy. In doing so, it declared that Krishna was the god of gods, the Supreme Spirit, in whom all the celestials dwell and of whom the universe was only a very small part. By way of excuse for its evil ways, the snake said that when it showed itself cruel and remorseless, it was merely fulfilling the law of its being, and no sin attached to it when it conformed to the nature with which it had been endowed ; indeed, if it were to do otherwise, it would be guilty of punishment. In response to such a weighty appeal, which was earnestly supported by the serpent's wives, Krishna spared its life on condition that it went to the ocean and lived there in the future. On another occasion, when Balarāma fell into the hands of a powerful demon and was seized with a momentary fear that the fiend was going to carry him away, Krishna had to remind him that he too was the

cause of all that existed, and that in their dual forms
they were the soul of the universe and would continue to
exist when that universe was destroyed. Having been
thus exhorted to lay aside all thoughts of his mortality
and remember who he was, Balarāma destroyed his
adversary.

Krishna's most remarkable feat, however, was a trick
which he played on the god Indra. It was in the days
that followed the rainy season, when the cowherds had
gathered in large numbers to offer a sacrifice to that deity.
Krishna, out of a desire to make Indra angry, asked the
cowherds what was the object of such a sacrifice. They
replied that Indra was the god of the clouds and of the
waters, and they wished to show their gratitude and
secure his future favours. " That may be quite a wise
proceeding for farmers and traders, whose livelihood
depends upon the soil. But our source of livelihood,"
said Krishna, " is in our cattle, and we wander freely
among the forests and among the hills. It is the spirits
of the woods and mountains whom we should worship.
If we do not propitiate them, they will become angry
with us, and coming in the forms of tigers and other wild
animals, destroy both us and our cattle. What have we
to do with Indra ? Leave him to the farmers and others
of that kind. But let us worship our cattle and the hills
on which we roam." And so pointing to a mountain
called Gobardhan, which raised its great height in front
of them, he said, " Let that mountain be the object of
our devotion. Let us offer to it an animal sacrifice,
and feed it with flesh and milk." The cowherds were
delighted with the proposal. They abandoned their
worship of Indra. They made a great feast to which they
summoned many thousands of Brāhmins, and when they
had worshipped the mountain, they adorned their cows
with garlands and solemnly walked round them. In the

performance of these religious rites, Krishna played a double part. Because he went and sat on the top of the mountain where he received the worship of his fellow cowherds, calling himself the mountain and consuming a great deal of the food that was offered, but while doing so he also climbed the mountain with his companions and worshipped his other self.

As Krishna both hoped and expected, the god Indra was very angry when he saw himself flouted and deprived of his rightful due. And he resolved that he would have revenge. He therefore summoned the clouds to his presence, and though the rainy season was over, commanded them to pour forth their waters on the impious and ungrateful cowherds. In obedience to their lord's behest, the clouds discharged great volumes of rain, which fell without ceasing for seven days and seven nights. So great was the deluge that the whole earth was under water. But whatever may have happened to others, Krishna and his friends experienced no trouble of any kind. For here is what he did. He lifted up the mountain and, holding it aloft on the little finger of his left hand, told the herdsmen to drive their cattle and waggons under it and take refuge from the storm. This they did, and as long as the tempest lasted they, with their wives and children and cattle, dwelt secure. It was certainly a most amazing spectacle; and accustomed as they were to Krishna's miraculous deeds, this, the greatest of them all, filled them with wonder and praise. They told him that he really could not be a man of mortal birth. He must be either a god or a demon, or one of the heavenly minstrels at least. To this assertion, Krishna at first made no answer, but after a little he said : " I am sorry you should be ashamed of your relation to me. I am not a god, nor a demon, nor a heavenly minstrel. I was born one of yourselves, and you must be content to know that

I am your kinsman." When he saw how he had been outwitted, Indra thought it would be advisable to go down
to the world and come to terms with his supplanter. By
the time he reached the earth the rain had ceased, the sun
was shining, and Krishna had put the mountain back in its
place. Indeed, when Indra arrived at Vrindhāvan, he
found Krishna herding cattle in the jungle, surrounded
by his rustic companions. But though the supporter
of the world appeared in the guise of a cowherd, Indra's
more spiritual eyes were able to distinguish Garuda the
vehicle of Vishnu, spreading out his wings above the head
of the incarnate god. Whatever his feelings may have
originally been, Indra had no thought of quarrel. Indeed,
the first thing he did was to confess that he had done
wrong in deluging the earth with rain. He then went
on to say that he was very glad indeed that Krishna had
saved the lives of so many cows, and on behalf of these
sacred animals announced that Krishna would thereafter
be known as *Indra of the cows.* In confirmation of this
statement the king of heaven took a pitcher and sprinkled
Krishna with holy water, while the cows, which by this
time had gathered in large numbers, poured forth such
quantities of milk, that it flowed like a river all round the
world. Having thus accomplished so successfully the
object of his journey, Indra, after a parting embrace,
mounted his elephant and went back to heaven.

Krishna and his brother, like the other boys in their
encampment, followed the cattle to their pastures, and
there they spent many happy days, making garlands of
forest flowers and binding peacocks' feathers in their
hair ; playing at games, leaping and jumping, laughing and
shouting as other boys are wont to do. And when the day
was over and they had driven the cattle home, they joined
in the amusements by which the cowherds wiled away
the evening hours. But as the years passed, new desires

began to surge in Krishna's breast. He was approaching
adolescence, and sought the presence of the other sex.
This was first manifested in his treatment of a number of
young women, the wives and daughters of the cowherds,
when they were bathing in the river Jumna. They had
gone to a sequestered spot, leaving their garments on the
shore. Krishna happened to be in the neighbourhood,
and hearing the noise of their laughter, he crept forward
to watch and listen. As he gazed at them from behind a
thicket, Krishna formed the strange resolve that he would
steal their clothes. This he at once did, and making
them into a bundle, took up his position in a tree. When
the women emerged from the water and found that their
garments had disappeared, they were very much alarmed.
And their alarm was increased when they saw that Krishna
was watching them. Hurrying back into the water and
concealing their nakedness as well as they could, they
begged him to have mercy on them and give them back
their clothes. But though they pleaded long, and said
they would report his evil conduct to their fathers and
husbands, Krishna replied that they would get their
clothes back on one condition only, and that was that
they came out of the water one by one, and with hands
upraised. This incident is but the introduction to other
similar deeds ; for we are told that the wives and daughters
of the cowherds cast aside all modesty and restraint,
abandoning their household tasks and following Krishna
to the forest whenever they heard the sound of his flute.
And this they did even when their husbands interfered and
told them not to go. For they would escape under cover
of darkness, and did not return to their homes till the
approach of dawn warned them of their danger. At
times Krishna would rebuke them for their incontinence,
and tell them to go back to their husbands, because they
knew that a wife should not desert her lord and master,

however ugly or stupid he happened to be. But such
reproof only deepened their longing, and they said they
were prepared to abandon everything and everybody,
rather than be absent from his side. Nor did they fail
to get their reward. By such devotion they not only
obtained the salvation of their souls, which they were not
in search of, but they secured what they were anxious
to obtain—the satisfaction of their desire. On other
occasions Krishna would tell them to come and dance.
And it was no ordinary dance. The place they chose was
a level spot on the banks of the Jumna, and it did not
matter how many women were present, there was a
Krishna for each of them, round whose neck they cast
their arms, and when they kissed, each woman was confident that she had her lover all to herself.[1]

About this time the *rishi* Nārada went to Kansa once
more and told him what had happened to the seventh and
eighth sons of Devaki, and how they were living as cowherds in Vrindhāvan. Kansa was very angry, and bitterly
reproached Vasudeva for the deceit of which he had been
guilty. But he did not give up hope. For, as he said,
they are not yet full grown, and perhaps some of my famous
boxers will be able to slay them. And that no time might
be lost, he sent one of his nobles to the cowherds' encampment to summon the two young men to Muttra. This
nobleman was very unlike his master. He congratulated
himself on the fact that he would soon be standing in the
presence of a portion of the deity, and that he would
be permitted to touch him who is the soul of all. In any
case, when he arrived and told his message, Krishna and
Balarāma at once accepted the challenge, and set out for
the capital. By the way, when they were bathing in a

[1] Mention is made of a cowherdess to whom Krishna was specially
devoted. Her name was Rādhā, and to the present day she shares with
Krishna the devotion of their worshippers.

river, the two brothers revealed their divine forms.
Balarāma was specially wonderful, for he appeared in
his real and original character as the chief of serpents with
a thousand heads, and attended by others of his race.
His mighty form, with its multitudinous coils, acted as a
couch on which Krishna reclined. Krishna himself did
not appear as wonderful as his brother. But the nobleman observed that he had four arms, wore yellow garments,
and that his breast and arms were adorned with the
proper crests and ornaments of Vishnu.

When they approached the wall of Muttra, Krishna
and Balarāma got out of the chariot in which they had
made the journey, and entered the town on foot. At the
gateway, they met Kansa's washerman carrying his master's
garments home from the wash. Krishna at once laid hold
of the bundle, and when the washerman offered resistance
and began to give abuse, he struck him dead. As a number
of the cowherds had by this time arrived and joined themselves to his company, Krishna divided the garments
among them, after having selected a portion for his brother
and himself. Nor was this their only adventure before
they reached the palace, because Kansa sent against them
a wild elephant, whose driver was ordered to tread the
brothers under foot. But Krishna caught the brute by
the tail and Balarāma by the trunk, and when they had
played with it as they used to do with calves in their childhood, Krishna swung it round his head at least a hundred
times and then dashed out its brains. These and other
incidents, equally remarkable, naturally caused a great deal
of excitement in the city, and it seemed as if the whole of
the inhabitants had gathered round the arena where the
brothers were to accept the challenge of Kansa's famous
wrestlers. Some of the populace, when they saw the lads,
spoke with anxiety as to the result, and said it was
cruel to expect that two young striplings should contend

II

against such experienced foes. But others evidently knew
that Krishna and Balarāma were not ordinary persons,
and reminded their neighbours of what they had accomplished when they were scarcely out of the cradle. Their
mother, Devaki, was among the spectators, and the same
conflicting thoughts seem to have perplexed her mind, for
we read that she looked longingly and anxiously in their
direction, and again comforted herself by remembering
that her sons were portions of Vishnu. And now the
stage is set, and the wrestling match begins. Nor was
it long before Kansa realised what would be the issue, for
he ordered the musicians to cease their play. But the
gods, who were watching from the sky, at once ordered
the minstrels of heaven to strike up, and themselves called
out words of encouragement to the brothers. And the
spectators had not long to wait. As they had treated
the elephant, so did the youthful cowherds treat their
opponents. They seized them by the waist, swung them
round their heads and dashed them to the ground. When
he saw that his first two champions were dead, Kansa
ordered others forward, but they also were slain, and
before he had time to flee, the demon king found himself
in Krishna's grasp. Rushing at him, where he was seated
on his throne, Krishna seized him by the hair of his head,
knocked off his tiara, threw him to the earth and got on
top of him. The weight of him who is the upholder of
the universe was too much for Kansa, and he was dead
in a moment. Krishna, still holding him by the locks,
dragged the dead body into the middle of the arena. The
spectators were greatly shocked to see their king treated
in such an ignominious fashion, but the few who ventured
to interfere shared their dead master's fate, and no further
attempt was made to resist the conquerors. Very soon,
Kansa's father, who had been so unjustly deposed by his
unfilial son, was restored to his kingdom, and Krishna was

receiving the congratulations and worship of his parents, who said : "Thou art no son of ours. The whole universe from Brahmā to a tree is contained in thee."

Though the inhabitants of Muttra, as a body, seem to have welcomed Krishna's intervention, there were others who were resolved that such an act must not go unpunished. And Kansa's father-in-law, on no less than eighteen separate occasions, brought an army against Muttra and besieged it. He was driven off each time with great slaughter. But the defence had weakened the inhabitants so greatly, that when they heard that the Greeks were coming to attack them, the citizens decided, on the advice of Krishna, to abandon their state and capital, and set up a new settlement on the western shores of India. The place they chose was Dwāraka, where they built for themselves a city on land which Krishna received from the ocean. This city was so powerfully placed and defended, that they were secure from all their foes. From this new centre, Krishna and his brother continued to distinguish themselves by their many miraculous deeds. For instance, Balarāma, when in a state of intoxication, ordered the river Jumna to come to him so that he might bathe in her waters. The river refused to obey, but Balarāma not only laid hold of her with his ploughshare and dragged her into his presence, but compelled her to follow him wherever he went. As for Krishna, mention must be made of a brief excursion to heaven which involved the celestials in a very serious defeat. When he went to the upper world, Krishna travelled on the great bird Garuda. He was accompanied by one of his wives. Unfortunately the lady when in the garden of Indra saw a beautiful tree, which she greatly coveted. It was one of the products secured at the churning of the ocean. To please his wife, Krishna uprooted the tree and placed it on Garuda's back, intending to take it back to Dwāraka. But Indra's wife protested violently, and the monarch of the skies, accompanied by his brother deities armed with clubs and swords, maces and darts, made a powerful attack on Krishna. He cut all their weapons to pieces, however, with his discus, and put the deities to flight. Garuda, the vehicle of Vishnu, was of great assistance to his master, using his beak, his wings and claws in a very drastic manner. Though Indra's wife was very angry at her husband's cowardice in running away, the gods recognised that it was no disgrace to be defeated by the creator, preserver and destroyer of the world, and they begged Krishna to do them the favour of taking the tree back with him to his earthly home. So far as one can learn he never revisited his friends, the milkmaids, but he formed other alliances of the same kind. Because we are told that he carried off, by strength of hand, the affianced bride of one of his enemies, just before the marriage was about to take place ; and he married sixteen thousand princesses who had been taken captive by another. Though he had so many wives, not one of them had ever any cause to complain of neglect. For one so powerful and wonderful was able to multiply himself to any extent he chose, with the result that each of the many thousands thought that she was wedded to him alone. And so indeed it was, for he visited them all at the same time in the apartments which he had allotted to each. He was blessed with a numerous progeny, being the father of no less than one hundred and eighty thousand sons, while his grandchildren were so numerous, that thirty-eight million schools had to be erected for their instruction.

Vishnu Purāna, v.
Bhāgavata Purāna (*Prem Sāgar*).

XXV.

KRISHNA ON THE BATTLEFIELD.

"Honest men carry on war without crookedness or cunning."—
Mahābhārata, ii. 59. 11.

"As to those acts of the gods and the ascetics, a pious man should
never imitate them, or, when he hears of them, should never censure
them."—*Mahābhārata,* xii. 292. 18.

THE central theme of the *Mahābhārata* is the great battle
that took place between the five brothers of the house
of Pāndu, and their hundred cousins knows as the Kurus,
for the sovereignty of Northern India. In this contest
many millions of men were engaged, and kings and princes
from all parts of India took part. The cousins competed
eagerly for the assistance of their common relative,
Krishna, and from a desire to be as far as possible impartial,
Krishna said that to one side he would offer an army of
a hundred million soldiers, and to the other he would offer
himself, not as a combatant, but as friend and adviser.
He gave the first choice to Arjuna, the messenger of the
Pāndus, who, without a moment's hesitation, chose
Krishna. The ambassador of the Kurus thought this a
very foolish choice, and went off greatly delighted with
the army Krishna had given him. Krishna acted as
Arjuna's charioteer right through the battle, which lasted
for eighteen days. But when, from time to time, he saw
the battle going against his friends, he found it very
difficult to refrain from breaking the pledge he had given,

not to fight. Indeed, on one occasion he left the chariot
which he was driving, and was advancing against the
foremost of the Kuru warriors [1] when Arjuna had to
bring him back by main force, pointing out that all men
would call him a liar if he broke his plighted word.
Krishna was very angry at his actions being thus interfered with, but he could not deny the justice of the argument. On the other hand, his presence was a great source
of encouragement to the Pāndus. More than once it
required all his efforts to persuade the Pāndus to go on
fighting. Arjuna, for example, bewailed the folly of such
useless slaughter. Why should they kill their friends and
kinsmen ? He would not, if he could help it, take the
life of one of them, were it to gain the sovereignty of the
three worlds. In despair he cast aside his bow and
arrows, and, sitting down in the chariot, he declared that
he would fight no longer. Krishna, however, begged him
to remember that he belonged to the warrior caste. He
would never be allowed to enter heaven if he displayed
such cowardice. Wise men did not grieve for either the
living or the dead. As for people killing and being killed,
nobody was ever killed. The soul lived for ever. And
none of those he saw before him or around him, had ever
ceased to exist, or would cease to exist hereafter. These
observations led to a series of questions which Arjuna
addressed to Krishna, and with the answers which the
god made, are said to compose the philosophic poem
known as the *Bhagavadgītā*. This episode seems to
have taken place in an interlude of the battle. In any

[1] This warrior, as Krishna advanced, joined his hands in worship and
praised the day that should see him so highly honoured as to be slain by
him who was the god of gods. On another occasion when the Kurus
tried to capture Krishna, he suddenly manifested his divine form.
Thousands of gods issued from his body, each of them the size of a thumb.
From his eyes, mouth and nose Rudra (Shiva) emerged, while Brahmā
sat upon his brow.

case, Krishna's answers were sufficient to dispel the doubts of Arjuna, for he once more took up his bow and arrows, and addressed himself to the fight.

Though Krishna had promised not to take an active part in the battle, he had distinctly stated that he would act as an adviser to the Pāndus. The advice which he gave was specially noticeable in connection with their unavailing efforts to kill a person of the name of Drona. Now, Drona was a Brāhmin by caste, and his skill and prowess were so great that Krishna declared he must be slain if victory was to be secured. But the difficulty was how to kill him. With his single arm he had killed millions of men, and hundreds of millions of horses. Finally Krishna said, "You must take refuge in deceit." And so he proposed that one of the Pāndus should go and tell him that his son was dead. Such a piece of news would absolutely unnerve him, and it would be quite easy to take his life. Arjuna, for whom Krishna was acting as charioteer, said that he would never consent to such a dastardly deed. And Yudhisthira, the oldest of the brothers, was equally reluctant. He only consented with the greatest unwillingness when Krishna said, "If you don't do something of the kind, you will be most certainly overthrown." Eventually, to meet the moral difficulty which the princes felt to be very serious, another of the brothers, named Bhīma, killed an elephant which had the same name as Drona's son, namely, Ashwatthāman. He then approached the father and in an awkward manner said, "Ashwatthāman is dead." In speaking as he did, Bhīma was guilty of deceit. Knowing what was true, he yet uttered what was false; but his deception had the desired effect. The old man, when he was told that his son was dead, was smitten to the heart and his limbs dissolved like sand in water. After a little, however, he began to wonder if it could possibly be true. His son

was so brave and powerful he could not believe it possible
that any one could slay him, and he resumed the battle
with all his old vigour. But the statement he had heard
rankled in his mind, and he advanced to speak to Yudhisthira, the eldest of the Pāndus. In former days Yudhisthira had been a pupil of Drona's, and Drona had formed
the highest opinion of his loyalty to truth. He was certain
that he would not tell a lie, even to secure thereby the
sovereignty of the three worlds. And so he approached
Yudhisthira, persuaded that he at least would tell the
truth. Krishna, however, was on the watch. When he
saw Drona approaching, and conscious of the purpose
that brought him, the god warned the prince that if he
did not tell a lie on this one occasion, his followers and
allies would all be slain and his empire brought to ruin.
He strengthened his appeal by saying that it was not a
sin to tell a lie in connection with a marriage, or to save
the life of a cow or a Brāhmin. And so, anxious to win,
yet afraid to lie, Yudhisthira replied to Drona's question,
" Yes, Ashwatthāman is dead," but he added under his
breath the word " elephant." Such equivocation served
its purpose. Drona put his trust in Yudhisthira's reputation for truthfulness, and believing that his son was really
dead, he fainted away. Though he ultimately recovered
consciousness and killed another twenty thousand men,
he was slain that same afternoon.

This sinful deed, however, did not take effect without
a manifest token that the moral order of the universe
had been outraged. Up to that day the chariot of
Yudhisthira had always travelled two inches above the
surface of the ground. But when he uttered this falsehood, his steeds touched the earth. Arjuna, too, who
had disapproved from the first, was loud in his denuncia-
tions. Indeed he could not withhold his tears as he
bewailed the base and cowardly murder of their former

teacher and friend, and said that he would have to go to
hell for his share in so great an act of wickedness. This
strong language roused the anger of his brother Bhīma,
who told him that he was a Brāhmin and not a member
of the warrior caste. He seemed to be ignorant of the
duties of his order, and ought to give up fighting entirely,
and live as a hermit in the forest. He would be much
more at home if he retired to a hermitage, where he could
preach as much as he liked on the laws of morality. These
angry words led to a bitter discussion in which others
also joined, and for a time it seemed as if they would
come to blows. It is worthy of remark that Krishna,
who had advised the method of Drona's slaughter, took
no part in the debate and maintained a discreet silence.

The battle raged for some days more, but eventually
the whole of the Kurus were slain with the exception of
Duryodhana, the oldest of the Kuru princes, and three
others who took refuge in flight. The Pāndus were very
anxious to secure Duryodhana. But though they made a
thorough search in all directions, he was nowhere to be
found. At last he was discovered hiding in the waters
of a lake which he was able by his illusory powers to change
into a solid mass. Standing on the side of the lake, the
Pāndus taunted him with cowardice and challenged him
to come out and fight. The Kuru replied that his fighting
days were done. He had decided to devote the rest of
his days to the practice of asceticism, and the Pāndus
were welcome to rule the empty earth for whose depopula-
tion they were jointly responsible. In the end, Duryodhana
becoming uncomfortable at the taunts which were cast
at him, said that he had no weapons and no friends. He
couldn't be expected to fight them all at once. But he
was willing to come out if they would fight him one by
one and lend him a weapon. In his eagerness, Yudhisthira was so foolish as to say, " Come out and fight any

one of us you choose and with any weapon you choose. If you win, I shall give you back the kingdom." Duryodhana was quick to accept the offer, and said he would fight with a mace, a mode of warfare at which he was an expert, and with any one of the five Pāndus that they cared to choose. Krishna was very angry when he heard Yudhisthira's foolish offer. He said the prince was staking his kingdom on what was little better than a game of chance. Besides that, Duryodhana had no equal in the use of the mace, and if his opponent fought according to the rules, he was certain to be defeated. Bhīma was the champion chosen by the Pāndus, and he declared himself confident of victory; but when the duel began, it was very soon manifest that Bhīma would not be able to slay his opponent unless he took refuge in some trick forbidden by the laws of honourable warfare. And once more Krishna proceeded to give expression to his views. The gods had used deceit in their many battles with the demons on more than one occasion, and what the gods did, men were permitted to do. At his instigation therefore, Arjuna made a sign to his brother to strike his opponent " below the navel." Bhīma was quick to take the hint, and, smiting his enemy on a place that was forbidden by the rules of battle, brought poor Duryodhana to the ground.

On this occasion it was Yudhisthira who expressed his indignation at such an unworthy trick being played. But the chief critic was Balarāma, who arrived on the scene at the critical moment. Now Balarāma was the brother of Krishna, and like him an incarnation of the god Vishnu. He declared that Bhīma's action was contrary to all the laws and regulations of the warrior caste, and would have struck him if Krishna had not interfered. " It is our duty to kill our enemies," said Krishna, " and I don't see that Bhīma has done anything wrong. He

took an oath that he would kill Duryodhana, and he just
had to do it. Besides, he is our blood relation, the son
of our father's sister. I know that you are devoted to
righteousness, but you must remember that the evil age
is at hand. Warriors owe a debt to their foes and must
carry out their promise." Balarāma, however, refused
to listen to this "fallacious argument." He said that
men broke the laws of morality at their peril, and whatever Krishna might say, public opinion would maintain
that Bhīma had been guilty of an unworthy deed. " That
may be," said Krishna, " but if I had not adopted wily
and deceitful ways during the last eighteen days, the
Pāndus would not now be in possession of their ancient
kingdom. I had to use my illusory powers over and
over again. And in any case, the way the gods have
travelled may surely be used by mortal men, and we know
that the gods would never have conquered the demons
if they had not made use of deceit." Nevertheless, the
celestials seem to have approved of Balarāma's sentiments in opposition to those of Krishna, because a great
shower of sweet-smelling flowers fell from heaven on the
wounded man, and the spectators heard the heavenly
choirs singing his praise.

Mahābhārata, viii. 191, ix. 58.

NOTE.—It is said that 1660 millions of persons were killed in this
eighteen days' war; while the Kurus had only four survivors, the Pāndus
had 15,000; but, as we shall see, they were all slain with the exception of
the five brothers, the god Krishna and one other.

XXVI.

THE POWER OF SACRIFICE.

" By means of the sacrifice, the gods obtained that supreme authority
which they now wield."—*Shatapatha Brāhmana*, 3. 1, 4. 3.
" The sun would not rise were the priest not to make his offering;
that is why he performs the offering."—*Shatapatha Brāhmana*, 2. 3, 1. 5.

THE Kurus were now reduced to three unwounded men.
The leader of these three was Ashwatthāman, the false
report of whose death had such a baleful effect on the
issue of the fight.   Thirsting for revenge, this hero resolved
that if courage and prayers could achieve his purpose, he
would secure the destruction of those who yet remained
of his foes.   His plan was to visit their camp as they lay
asleep exhausted with the toils of battle.   Accompanied
by his two friends, who at first condemned his proposal
as immoral, and at the dead of night, he stealthily approached the camp of the sleeping enemy.   But as he drew
near to the gate of the camp, he was met by a mysterious
being of tremendous size, very terrible to look at, with a
thousand eyes, a gaping mouth and widely distended
nostrils.   From mouth and eyes and nose great flames of
fire blazed forth, and in the midst of the fire were seen
hundreds and thousands of divine forms; the forms of
the god Vishnu.   Nevertheless, the hero was not afraid.
He fitted endless arrows to his bow, and launched them
against the mysterious being who stood barring his way.
But the arrows either fell harmless to the ground, or were

swallowed by the terrible spectre. The same results
followed when he drew his sword and wielded his mace
and discharged his dart. They were all more or less celestial
weapons. But his opponent absorbed them all, even as
fire drinks up the ocean. When all his weapons were
exhausted and Ashwatthāman stood helpless and unarmed,
he looked up and saw the heavens filled to overflowing with
images of Vishnu, who in his incarnation as Krishna had
befriended and helped the Pāndus all through the battle.
It was only then that he realised the sin of which he had
been guilty, in seeking to slay men as they lay asleep.
He remembered, too, the words of Scripture, and how it
is written that one ought not to kill Brāhmins, cows and
women, persons who are asleep, intoxicated, or off their
guard.

But even as he made these pious observations and
reflected on the vanity of human effort, he resolved that
he would seek the help of Shiva, the god who is adorned
with a necklace of human skulls, the god who caused such
havoc at the sacrifice of Daksha, and plucked out Bhaga's
eyes. For, as he said, there is no god like Shiva, he is
the greatest of them all, their superior, not only in power,
but in the fervour of his asceticism. He accordingly
began a long hymn in praise of that mighty deity, calling
him the creator of the universe, the refuge of hermits, the
friend of ghosts, the dweller at burning ghats. As he thus
spoke, a golden altar came into view, and on it a blazing
fire that filled the whole sky with brightness. An innumerable host of fearful creatures also appeared on the scene.
They were of all shapes and sizes. They had the faces of
cows and bears, sharks, whales, pigeons, elephants, camels
and jackals, cats and tigers, snakes and ducks. Some
were fat, some were lean; some were bald, others had
great heads of hair, and they danced and sang, crying
aloud in the most hideous manner. It was an awful sight,

yet Ashwatthāman was not afraid, as he watched the
followers of Shiva drinking the blood and eating the flesh
and entrails of their victims. And we know that Shiva
himself never ceases to wonder and rejoice as he beholds
them, for does he not regard them as his own children in
thought, word and deed. Manifestly they already knew
that Shiva had resolved to fulfil the hero's hopes, and did
not wish to miss the slaughter which they expected would
ensue. But Ashwatthāman had not yet secured the
favour of the god. The altar and its burning fire awaited
their victim, and Ashwatthāman had determined that he
would offer himself. And so with dreadful rites he prayed
to Shiva, the doer of dreadful deeds, offering himself in
the hour of his distress and asking the god to receive him.
" All creatures exist in thee," he cried ; " thou dost exist
in all creatures. Thou art the refuge of all. I cannot
secure the defeat of my enemies and therefore I come to
thee." As he stood thus praying, prepared to ascend the
altar and cast himself into the fire, Shiva appeared in person
and most graciously said that Krishna had always paid
him due respect and worship ; worshipped him with truth,
purity, ascetic practices and forgiveness. There was no
one he loved more than Krishna, and it was out of respect
to Krishna that he had cast the shield of his protection
over the Pāndus, and given them the victory. But he
would protect them no longer. Their hour had come
when they must die. When he had said this, Shiva entered
the body of Ashwatthāman and placed in his hand a great
shining sword. In virtue of this twofold endowment the
hero had been rendered invincible. Attended by Shiva's
followers, he passed within the camp of the Pāndus. At the
gate he left his two companions with the command to
kill all who might try to escape. It is a gruesome tale
that follows. Ashwatthāman killed many with his own
hand. But in the panic that ensued, and the panic was

enhanced by the darkness, the Pāndus began to kill one another, while Shiva's attendants also seem to have joined in the slaughter. At least we are told that evil spirits of various kinds were to be seen on every hand, drinking the blood and gorging themselves on the flesh of the slain. In their glee they called to one another to come and taste what they were eating. It was so delightful and pleasing. Before half the night was over, there was not one man left alive.

By good fortune the five Pāndu princes, the god Krishna, and one other person were absent from the camp that night. And next day when they learned the awful news that the last remnant of their army had been slain, the princes asked Krishna how it had been possible for three men to kill so many thousands. The incarnation of Vishnu explained that Shiva had been their helper, and Shiva was the greatest of all the gods. In proof of that assertion Krishna told his cousins of what happened at the very beginning of the world, when Shiva quarrelled with Brahmā because he did not wait for his assistance, and went off to live the life of an ascetic among the mountains.[1] On a later occasion, also, when the gods were celebrating a great sacrifice in accordance with Vedic ordinances, they had been so foolish as not to invite Shiva.[2] They had neither proposed that he should assist them nor share in the offerings. When Shiva heard what they were about, he came, wearing the garb of a devotee and with a bow in his hand. The gods were filled with terror as he approached, The wind ceased to blow, fire would not burn. The sun, moon and stars were darkened in the heavens. Assuming the form of a deer, the sacrifice took refuge in flight, and she was followed by the god of fire. It was on this occasion that Shiva broke Savitar's arms, plucked out the

[1] What happened on this occasion is not fit for publication.
[2] The sacrifice of Daksha, doubtless, but his name is not given.

eyes of Bhaga, and drove the teeth of Pushan down his throat. Happily the gods were able to pacify the offended deity. They promised that they would never fail to invite him to be present at every sacrifice, and guaranteed that he would always get the clarified butter as his share. In proof that he accepted these offers, Shiva cast his anger into the water, with the result that under the form of fire it has been consuming water ever since. No one knows what would have happened if the god had not been appeased. But certainly the world was saved from destruction. " From what I have told you," added Krishna, " you can see that it is a very serious matter for any who happens to offend Shiva. And conversely, it is of the first importance to secure his favour. That is what Ashwatthāman did, and as a result, he was able to destroy these many thousands of men."

Mahābhārata, x.

XXVII.

THE DEATH OF KRISHNA.

"The whole universe moves at the will of its creator, but it moves under the controlling influence of Fate. It is not free."—*Mahābhārata*, ii. 57. 4.

"Destiny and Human Effort depend upon each other. The high-minded perform good and great deeds. It is only eunuchs who worship Fate."—*Mahābhārata*, xii. 139. 81.

"Destiny thwarts not the man who has acquired virtue and righteousness. The man who does not exert himself is never contented, nor can Destiny change the course of a man who has gone wrong. There is no power inherent in Destiny."—*Mahābhārata*, xiii. 6, 29, 47.

THREE eminent sages one day paid a visit to Dwāraka, the home of Krishna and his brother Balarāma. Soon after their arrival some of the younger members of the royal house, when in a state of intoxication, dressed up Krishna's son Shamva as a woman, and took their disguised companion to the holy men. "This female," they said, "is very anxious to give birth to a son. We believe you are able and willing to help her. Tell us, pray, when the child will be born, and what kind of person he will become." Now these sages were far too wise and far too holy to be deceived by such a foolish procedure, and they were very angry as well. They therefore sternly answered, "Yes, this young man will be seized with the pangs of labour as you desire, but it will not be a child to which he will give birth. Within twenty-four hours he will be delivered of an iron bolt which will destroy you

and every man belonging to the Yadu race." Nor did the
sages make any attempt to conceal their prophecy, for
they set out at once for Krishna's palace, and told him of
the curse they had pronounced against the members of
his house. Krishna received this information very quietly.
Though lord of the universe and able to alter all things,
able even to annul a Brāhmin's curse, he did not choose
to do so. He is the eternal, the sinless cowherd, the god
of unfading glory, but he did not wish that the word of a
Brāhmin should be proved untrue.

The very next day Krishna's son gave birth to a thunderbolt, as the sages had foretold. In the hope that he might
somehow avert the impending catastrophe, the king of
Dwāraka caused the bolt to be ground to powder and the
ashes cast into the sea. Aware also that the young men
were in a state of intoxication when they insulted the
rishis, the king forbade the manufacture of strong drink,
and announced that any one who evaded this proclamation in any way would be put to death. But these precautions were of no avail. Death roamed the streets of
Dwāraka and peered into every dwelling. He was pursued
by thousands of bowmen, but their arrows did not even
graze his skin, and fell harmless to the ground. Awful
portents, too, were seen. The sun was darkened at midday. The headless trunks of human beings were seen
against the sky. The streets and houses were overrun by
rats and mice, which gnawed at the nails and hair of men
and women as they lay asleep. Cows gave birth to asses,
and mules to elephants. Goats howled like jackals, and
storks hooted like owls. On the freshest and most carefully cooked food, worms and insects crawled. These
various portents soon began to tell upon the nerves of the
population, and realising that nothing could stay their
fate, they gave the rein to their passions and indulged
in all kinds of wickedness. Husbands and wives forsook

their marriage vows. Men spoke disrespectfully to their teachers and elders. They ceased to worship the gods and the spirits of the dead. They treated Brāhmins with contempt.

Anxious to hasten the inevitable end, Krishna proposed that they should go with their women folk to the sea-shore and bathe in the ocean. But the night before they started, both men and women were haunted by terrible dreams, and, worst of all, as they journeyed towards the sea, the discus which Krishna always carried was swept up into the sky, while his chariot and horses were seen to disappear across the ocean. Judging by what is said later, many thousands must have taken part in this excursion, but the text at this point speaks as if it were little more than a picnic party. During the days they spent at the sea-shore they were well supplied with every kind of food, and the regulations forbidding the use of liquor were in abeyance. And before long, scenes of wild intoxication ensued. In their madness, the princes mingled wine with the food that had been prepared and set aside for Brāhmins, and gave it to monkeys. From drunkennes˙ they passed to quarrelling and blows. Balarāma, the brother of Krishna, shared in the carousals. Among the fighters, Krishna's son, the youth who had been dressed up as a woman, took a leading part, and eventually was slain. When he saw his son fall, Krishna plucked a handful of grass and it was transformed into a weapon, with which he slew every one who approached him. This example was speedily followed by others. They, too, plucked handfuls of grass, and found, as Krishna had done, that the grass was changed into iron weapons. A frightful carnage followed. Sons killed their fathers; fathers killed their sons. They were so drunk that they did not know what they were doing. At that fatal picnic on the shores of the ocean, five hundred thousand were slain. Krishna and Balarāma, with two

others alone survived, and the text from which this tale is
taken does not fail to remind its readers more than once
that the curse of the Brāhmins was the prevailing cause.

When the slaughter had ceased, Balarāma retired to a
neighbouring forest, where he gave himself up to the
practice of *yoga*. But Krishna returned to Dwāraka and
to his father's house. He knew that his own end was
approaching, and his wish was to bid his father farewell.
But he had also decided to send one of the two other
survivors to his cousins in the Panjab, and request that
one of them should come and take charge of the widows
and children of the slain. When these two duties were
accomplished, he set off for the forest, intending to join
his brother. But when he got to the place where Balarāma
was, he saw a great snake issuing from his mouth. With
a thousand heads and as big as a mountain, this vast
creature glided swiftly away in the direction of the ocean,
where it was met and welcomed by a great company of
gods and other more or less divine beings, many of them
members of the snake race. In accordance with custom,
they asked after his welfare, they brought water to bathe
his feet, and presented those offerings which should always
be set before a guest. It was in this wonderful way that
the spirit of Balarāma, who like Krishna was the incarnation of a hair of Vishnu, departed from the earth and
resumed his rightful place in heaven. For a brief while
Krishna, plunged in thought, wandered here and there in
the forest. But he soon resolved that he also would
submit himself to the will of Destiny. Many years before,
he had offended the sage Durvāsa, and that bad-tempered
saint had cursed him to die of a wound in his foot. He
would now permit the curse to take effect. If he failed
to do so, the foundations of the three worlds would be
shaken. Men must be made to see that every act bore
its appropriate fruit. And so he, who is the lord of the

universe and the god of gods, sat down upon the bare
earth in the attitude of *yoga*. By so doing he exposed
the sole of his left foot, the only part of his body which
was vulnerable, owing to the sage's curse. He had not
long to wait. A hunter approached and, mistaking
Krishna for a deer, shot an arrow which smote him on the
foot. The hunter was deeply distressed when he realised
his blunder, but Krishna told him not to grieve or to be
afraid. These words of consolation were Krishna's last
words on earth. His soul parted from his body and rose
up to heaven. The inhabitants of the celestial world were
waiting to receive him. They bowed before him in adoration and praise, saying that he was Lord of the universe,
Vishnu Nārāyana of dreadful energy, the Creator and
Destroyer of all. Thus welcomed and adored, he passed
to his own peculiar abode, which is beyond the knowledge
or understanding of man.

When the messenger reached the Panjab [1] and told of
the great disaster that had befallen the race of Yadu,
Arjuna, one of Krishna's cousins, set off without delay
to carry succour to the widows and children of the slain.
On his arrival he found that Krishna's father was at the
point of death, and his first task was to perform the funeral
ceremonies for that aged hero and his two sons. Four
of the old man's wives performed Sati, and ascended
the funeral pyre, but Krishna's sixteen thousand wives
do not appear to have coveted that honour. In any case
they and the wives and children of the dead, to the number
of many millions, began their long and wearisome journey
towards the north under the escort of Arjuna. The
inhabitants of the city and surrounding country were
also with him, and in contradiction to what is said pre-

[1] Spoken of as the land of the five rivers. The cousins were the
Pāndus, whom Krishna had assisted by acting as Arjuna's charioteer
in battle (XXV.).

viously, vast multitudes of warriors are now spoken of as having survived the slaughter and sharing in the exile. When the procession started another terrible portent filled their minds with fresh forebodings. The waters of the ocean rushed in, devouring the land behind the very footsteps of the fugitives. And yet they travelled with great comfort until they reached the borders of the Panjab. There, however, they were attacked by robbers. The warriors of the Yadu race made a very poor fight. The assailants said that they saw only one man among them, and that was Arjuna. And even he found that Destiny was a power against which it was impossible to prevail. In former days it was for him an easy task to overcome a whole army by his single strength. But now he found that his hand had lost its cunning, and he could not even string his famous bow. He had once been able to call to his aid certain miraculous weapons, which came and went in obedience to his summons. On this occasion, when he called them, they failed to appear. Stricken with shame, Arjuna saw the robbers carry away thousands of the chief ladies of the Yadu race. Others, still more wretched, went of their own accord. It was with great difficulty and accompanied by but a poor remnant of the mighty host that had set out from Dwāraka, that Arjuna at last reached his own country. When they arrived, five of Krishna's queens expressed the desire to perform Sati. The others, at least those who survived of Krishna's sixteen thousand wives, adopted the forest life, resolved to pass the rest of their days in works of piety and devotion.

In connection with the funeral ceremonies which Krishna's cousins performed in honour of the dead, the Brāhmins were loaded with sumptuous gifts of gold and gems, clothes and villages, horses and cars, as well as hundreds of thousands of female slaves.

Mahābhārata, xvi.

XXVIII.

VISHNU'S INCARNATION AS BUDDHA.

" Withered are the garlands of the gods, and their glory is departed."
—*Mahābhārata,* i. 30, 37.

" There is no heaven, no final liberation, nor any soul in any other
world. . . . The three authors of the Vedas were buffoons, knaves and
demons."—The *Chārvākas,* quoted in *Sarva Darshana Sangraha.*

THE gods and demons were often at war. As a rule the
celestials were victorious. But one disastrous engage-
ment, which lasted for three hundred and sixty years,
ended in the overthrow of the celestials. The discomfited
deities took refuge on the farther shore of the Sea of Milk.
In their distress they gave themselves up to the practice
of austerities, and called upon Vishnu to come to their aid.
In the prayer which they addressed to that mighty god,
they said that the whole creation, visible and invisible, was
his body; that he was Brahmā, Indra, the Vasus and a
great many more deities, including themselves; that he
was at one with blessed saints, wicked demons, cruel
serpents, brute beasts and men; at one with piety, which
gives rewards for virtuous deeds; at one with Rudra,
who dances with delight after devouring all beings—gods
and men.

When their prayer had come to a conclusion, Vishnu
appeared in person. He was riding on the great bird
Garuda, and bore in his hands the shell, the discus and
the mace. The advent of the god called forth fresh

adoration, and a special appeal that he would save them from the power of the demons. The celestials did not indicate that they had been themselves remiss in the practice of devotion. But it was manifest that the demons had faithfully adhered to the teaching of the Vedas, and were so strengthened by asceticism that the gods could not destroy them. Indeed, the three worlds were now in their hands, and they were appropriating the offerings which really belonged to the gods. They therefore begged Vishnu to tell them what they ought to do for the recovery of their lost inheritance. Manifestly the only thing to do was to persuade the demons to abandon the study of the Vedas, and the practice of the rites and ceremonies which the Vedas enjoin. And this was the plan which Vishnu in his wisdom decreed. He produced from himself an illusory form and gave it to the gods. He added the explanation that this illusory form would deceive the demons and persuade them to forsake the Vedas, with the result that destruction would come upon them. Because, as he said, no god, demon or man can hope to prosper who becomes hostile to or forsakes these holy books.

The scene now changes to the banks of the river Narmadā, where we find the demons engaged in penance. The illusory form of Vishnu appears in their midst. He came as a naked mendicant (*digambara*), with shaven head and carrying a bunch of peacock feathers. Addressing the demons, the beggar asked them what purpose they hoped to serve by indulging in asceticism. The demons replied that they were seeking a reward in the life to come. " If that is so," said their interrogator, " I shall explain to you the great secret. You look as if you were worthy to have it revealed to you." Thus persuaded and cajoled, the demons turned an attentive ear to their new instructor, and before he was done with them they had abandoned the teaching and rites of the Vedas, believing " that the same thing might be for the sake of virtue and of vice; might be and might not be; might or might not contribute to liberation; might be the supreme object and not be the supreme object; might be effect and not be effect, might be manifest and not be manifest." Thus it came to pass that the demons put their trust in a series of contradictions and procured for themselves the name of *Arhata*.[1]

But the work of the illusionary form of Vishnu was not yet complete. Putting on red garments, assuming a benevolent aspect and speaking in soft and agreeable tones, he approached other members of the demon race and told them if they wished to secure either heaven or final liberation (*nirvāna*) they must abandon the cruel practice of offering animal sacrifices. His principal teaching, however, was to the effect that "this world subsists without support." The upshot was that these demons also were induced to abandon their religious rites and practices. And when their deceiver said to them "Know" (*Budhyadhwam*), they answered "It is known" (*Budhyate*).[2] In this way Vishnu deceived one gathering of demons after another, until he finally persuaded the whole demon race, not only to abandon the Vedas, but to speak against the gods, abuse the Brāhmins and treat the sacrifices with contempt. And so these beguiled creatures went about saying that it was wrong to take the lives of animals, and silly to imagine that any sort of merit could be acquired by casting butter into a fire. Here is how they argued. If Indra, who was made a god for the many sacrifices he offered, can be nourished by

---

[1] This is manifestly a reference to the Jain religion. One of its sects is known as *digambaras* (sky clad), because they go naked. They still employ the term *Arhat*.

[2] Here again the other great heresy is referred to, namely, Buddhism. The teaching of this Purāna still holds in India, and Buddha ranks as one of the ten descents of Vishnu.

the wood used as fuel in the holy fire, he is lower in the
scale of creation than a brute beast which at least feeds
on leaves. If it is true that the animal slaughtered in a
sacrifice goes to heaven, why don't you kill your own
father and thus secure him a place in that happy region ?
If the food eaten at a funeral feast really goes to nourish
the spirits of the dead, why do people setting out on a
journey take any food with them ? You who remain
behind can arrange to feed them in their absence by means
of food oblations. Think of what we say. Is it not
worthy of acceptation ? We don't believe that words of
authority come down from heaven. The only sacred text
that we acknowledge is reason, and reason alone.[1] The
upshot of this teaching was that not a single demon
acknowledged the authority of the Vedas.

The opportunity of the gods had come at last, and
they were not slow to seize it. Hostilities were renewed.
But the demons had weakened themselves hopelessly.
They had forsaken the path of truth. They had spoken
with scorn of the sacred books, and poured contempt on
asceticism and the other rites of religion. And so because
they cast aside the armour of righteousness which had
given them strength, stripped off the garment of the
Vedas that covered their nakedness, they were defeated
and slain. And he who tells this tale, does not fail to
point the moral for the benefit of ordinary men. Take
good heed, he cries; that you also are not deceived. Don't
look at those who teach such wicked doctrines. Even
to look at one of them is a very great sin—a sin which
can only be expiated by gazing at the sun. If you happen
to touch one of them, you must bathe with your clothes

---

[1] We have here a reference to another school of heretics, the Chārvākas.
In the *Sarva Darshana Sangraha* of Mādhava Āchārya, the author
quotes the words of Brihaspati as a summary of the teaching of this
school. The Purāna has used them to some extent.

on. Think of it, these wicked creatures do not worship the gods, make no offerings to the spirits of the dead, pay no respect to *rishis*. Don't eat with them, don't sit in their houses. They are robbers of the dead, robbers of the gods, for both the gods and the spirits of the dead depend on you and me for their daily nourishment, and their curse falls on those who rob them of the food they need.

Vishnu Purāna, iii. 17.

XXIX.

THE SIN OF SPEAKING TO A HERETIC.

"If you think that this world does not exist, and that there is no world beyond, the devils in hell will soon change your ideas on that subject."—*Mahābhārata*, xii. 150. 19.

"The spirit does not die. In death it simply changes its abode. The soul goes to another body, and this change of body is called death."—*Mahābhārata*, iii. 208. 26.

IN corroboration of the previous legend, listen to what happened to a king because he spoke to a heretic. He was of a very gentle and pious disposition. By prayers and fasting, by gifts and oblations, he showed how genuine was his piety and devotion. And yet one day as he and his wife came out of the river Ganges, in which they had been bathing, they happened to meet one of these heretics, and with the most disastrous results. The heretic happened to be a friend of the king's instructor in archery, and out of courtesy the monarch engaged shortly in conversation. But the queen was wiser. Remembering that she was fasting, she turned her eyes away from the heretic and fixed them on the sun. As far as this life is concerned, nothing happened. Indeed, it is said that in the lapse of time the king died victorious over his foes, and the queen ascended the funeral pyre of her husband.

But because of the sin he had committed, that is, speaking to an unbeliever, the king was, in his next life, born as a dog, while the queen who, very properly, had turned her eyes away, was born as the daughter of the king of Benares. The princess was able not only to remember what had happened to her in her previous lives, but, endowed with "the eye of divine intelligence," she knew that her husband had been born as a dog in the town of Vaidishā. In her desire to see her former husband, she made a visit to that city and immediately recognised him. For some time her father had tried to arrange her marriage, but she always resisted his efforts. And now that she had found her husband, although in the form of a dog, she solemnly "placed upon his neck a bridal garland." She also fed the dog with food and sweetmeats, much to his delight. But when she spoke to the dog and reminded him of the sinful act of which he had been guilty in a former life, the whole past was recalled to his mind, and he left the town in a mood of deep dejection. Retiring to the forest, the dog died not long after of a broken heart, to be born within a year as a jackal. Once more the princess in virtue of her divine intelligence was able to discover where her husband was. She found him this time on a mountain side, and spoke to him, as she had spoken to the dog, "Do you remember how I told you, when you were a dog, of the sin you committed when you were a king?" As on the former occasion, the question was enough. The jackal remembered his former lives and his former sin; gave up the use of food and died. The next birth he took was that of a wolf, and in that guise also the princess found him and reminded him of the past with a result similar to what had happened before. In short, the king was thereafter successively born as a vulture, as a crow, and as a peacock, and each time his wife was able to discover his whereabouts and reveal to him the secret of his birth. It is not explained how she got possession of the peacock, but the text tells us that she fed it and petted it continually.

In course of time, when her father was celebrating a horse sacrifice, the princess seized the opportunity and caused the peacock to be bathed. When the ceremony was over, she told the animal who he really was, and reminded him of the various births through which he had passed. As on former occasions, the peacock was grieved to the heart, and almost immediately thereafter died, but the sorrows of the princess had come to an end. In his next birth, he who had been king, dog, jackal, wolf, vulture, crow and peacock, was born as the son of the great king Janaka. The princess no longer resisted proposals for her marriage, and when her father held a *maiden's choice* which was attended by many candidates for her hand, she chose from among the suitors her former husband. They lived happily together for many years. As king of Videha in succession to his father-in-law, the prince offered many sacrifices, gave many gifts, was the father of sons and overcame his enemies. On his death, which took place on the field of battle, the queen once more ascended the funeral pyre, and they passed to heaven where they enjoyed a conjugal bliss as unusual as it was complete.

From this story you will see how great a sin it is even to speak to a heretic. And you will also observe what benefits result from bathing at a horse sacrifice. See to it, then, that you never speak to, never come into contact with, never entertain one of these wicked men. They have abandoned the Vedas and deny their truth. They put their trust in reason and do forbidden things. They make no offerings of food to gods, *rishis*, spirits and men. For them there is no place at the sacrifice offered to the dead. You will go to hell if you have any truck with them, those hypocrites of the twisted hair and shaven crown.

Vishnu Purāna, iii. 18.

PART TWO.

XXX.

SHAKUNTALĀ.

"The man who fails to protect his wife earns great infamy here, and goes to hell afterwards."—*Mahābhārata*, xiv. 90. 48.

THE practice of asceticism was a constant source of worry to the gods. By means of it both demons and men were able to wring from reluctant deities the things that they desired. Indra, in particular, was always trembling for his throne, and afraid lest some fresh ascetic would deprive him of his place and power as king of heaven. No one gave him more trouble than Vishvāmitra, the royal sage, and many were the plots that he contrived to rob him of the merit he had won. And none of them was more successful than the sending of Menakā, one of the celestial nymphs, with the order to beguile the ascetic from the paths of virtue. Menakā was very unwilling to undertake such a dangerous task. She reminded the god of the great power which Vishvāmitra enjoyed. Had Indra never heard how the ascetic had destroyed the hundred sons of Vashistha. He had once been a member of the warrior caste, and a great mónarch. But by the strength of his asceticism he had acquired the rank and the dignity of a Brāhmin. You know also, she said, that he created a river for no other purpose than that he might be able to

bathe in it, and the river is still running. And once when
he was angry with the gods, he made a new world with
stars all complete. He can uproot the highest mountains
and throw them to a great distance. When he stamps
his foot the earth trembles. If he chose, he could burn
up the universe with his glory. Have you never seen him ?
his eyes are like the sun and moon ; his mouth looks like
a blazing fire ; his tongue is as fearful as the lord of death.
The gods are afraid of him. What am I, a poor frail
woman, to stand before so great and holy a sage ? But
Indra would take no denial, and the maiden had to go.
And as Indra had hoped, the ascetic fell a victim to her
charms. Forgetful of his vows, he kept her in his company
for many years, and a daughter was born to them. But
when the child was born and the mother saw that she
had achieved her purpose, she abandoned both lover and
and child and went back to heaven. The father was
equally indifferent, and the helpless babe would have
perished had some vultures not placed her under their
protection.

By great good fortune a kind-hearted ascetic, whose
name was Kanwa, found the child surrounded by her
strange protectors, and took her home to his hermitage,
where he cared for and loved her as if she had been his
own daughter. And because he had found her under the
protection of birds (*shakuntas*), he gave to her the name of
Shakuntalā. In her foster-father's home she passed the
years of childhood and youth, growing more and more
beautiful every day, attending to his needs and sharing
in his ascetic toil. But one day Dushmanta, a king of
the lunar race, on a hunting expedition, came to the
hermitage when the ascetic was absent, and was so struck
with the maiden's beauty that he proposed immediate
marriage. Shakuntalā told the monarch the story of her
birth and upbringing, and begged him to wait till her

foster-father came home. The impatient monarch, however, would take no denial, and what is known as the
Gandharva ceremony—a declaration of mutual acceptance
—made them husband and wife. Shakuntalā made one
condition. She demanded that should a son be born, he
must be recognised as the heir apparent. Very soon after,
Dushmanta set out for his capital, promising to return
and take her with him to his palace. But he never came
back. In course of time a boy was born, of wonderful
strength and beauty. When he was three years of age
he was able to kill lions ; when he was six, he could seize
elephants and tigers and bind them to the trees surrounding
the hermitage ; and when he wanted exercise, he would
jump on their backs and go careering through the forest.
After the lapse of some more years the *rishi* advised his
adopted daughter to make a journey to the capital and
claim the immediate recognition of her son. In any case,
it was not proper for a wife to be too long absent from her
husband's home. When Shakuntalā, accompanied by her
son, reached the palace, the monarch at once recognised
her, but nevertheless denied all knowledge of her claims.
" You are," he said, " a very wicked woman. I never
saw you before. What do you mean by saying that you
and I were married in the hermitage of Kanwa ? " Shakuntalā was overwhelmed with grief and shame as she listened
to these cruel words. It was with the greatest difficulty
that she suppressed her anger and spoke to him instead in
the accents of pity and appeal. " Oh king, why do you
say that you know nothing ? Your own heart knows that
I speak the truth. Why rob yourself of all honour by the
practice of falsehood and deceit ? You think that you
alone know what you did. Do you not know that the great
Omniscient One dwells in your heart ? He knows all your
sins. He knows that you are sinning now. How foolish
men are. They think that no one sees them when they

sin. But the gods see them, and the god who dwells in every heart sees them. Here is your son. I have brought him to you, and you know that a son rescues his ancestors from hell. And here am I, your wife, your true and faithful wife. A wife is a man's other half; a wife is a husband's best friend. When he dies, she goes with him to the land of death. If she dies before him, she waits for him there. No man, even when he is angry, should do anything that causes sorrow to his wife, because both his happiness and virtue depend on her. Why should you refuse to recognise this child who is both yours and mine? What greater happiness is there on earth than that which a father feels when his son runs to him and clasps his knees with his little arms, even though his body is covered with dust and dirt? Surely I must have committed some great sin in a previous life when I have been abandoned twice, first by my father and mother, and then by you."

When Shakuntalā spoke of her parents, the king laughed and said, "Once more I repeat, I don't believe you. This boy is not mine. Women are in the habit of telling lies. Nobody will believe you. But you seem to be like your parents; you say you are the daughter of Menakā, that wicked woman. She must have been destitute entirely of natural affection when she forsook you so soon after you were born. And your father was no better; that vain, presumptuous, evil-minded man, with his foolish ambition to be made a Brāhmin." With these cruel words Dushmanta ordered his wife to leave his presence and come back no more. But Shakuntalā was not to be silenced so easily. "Oh, great king," she said, "you can see the faults of others, though they may be as small as the mustard seed; but you cannot see your own, though they are as big as the vilwa fruit.[1] My birth is better

[1] Cf. Matt. vii. 3.

than yours. You are only a mortal, but I claim kinship
with the gods ; my mother's home is heaven. You will
excuse me for repeating it, but I must remind you of the
proverb, ' The ugly man thinks himself more beautiful
than other people until he sees himself in a glass.' He who
is really handsome does not boast. You may put a pig
in a flower garden, but even there it will search for filth.
Set evil and good before a wicked man and he will choose
the evil. Mix milk and water and place them before a
goose ; she takes the milk and rejects the water. The
wise man is like her ; he chooses the good and rejects the
evil. Honest men always feel pain to speak ill of others,
and refuse to injure even those who have done them
wrong. I beg you then to speak the truth. Truth is
heavier than a hundred horse sacrifices. It is equal to
the study of all the Vedas and ablution at all the sacred
places. There is no virtue greater than truth. There is
no sin greater than falsehood. But if you will not listen,
then I tell you what will happen. You may refuse to
recognise your son, but when you are dead he shall obtain
the sovereignty of your empire, and become the monarch
of the world. The very day that he was born I heard a
voice from heaven which told me he would perform the
horse sacrifice not less than a hundred times." When she
had spoken thus, Shakuntalā turned her back upon the
king and was about to leave the palace. But once again
a heavenly voice was heard speaking clearly from the
skies. And this is what it said. "Dushmanta, why do
you insult your wife, and say what your heart knows to
be untrue ? Give her public recognition and confess that
you were married in the hermitage of Kanwa. Acknowledge also that this boy is your son, and do not forget that
by his birth he has saved you from the power of hell. If
you do not listen to my words, and give them instant obedience, great misfortune and distress will come upon you."

The monarch was more than content to give obedience
to this celestial injunction. Indeed, he told his ministers
and other attendants who had been witnesses from the
beginning of the scene between him and his wife, that he
had waited for the divine command, and that he had
been afraid to acknowledge Shakuntalā without it. The
marriage ceremony had been performed in secret, and men
might have doubted the legitimacy of his son and heir.
He also made a somewhat half-hearted apology to his wife
by saying that, all through, his one anxiety had been how
best to establish the purity of their offspring's birth ;
while he graciously added that he forgave her for the strong
language of reproach with which, in her anger, she had
ventured to address him. When in course of time Dushmanta died, his son became ruler of the whole earth, as
his mother had foretold, and was known as a *Chakravartin*,
or universal empéror. He gave great gifts to Brāhmins,
and with their co-operation offered many sacrifices, including that of the cow.

Mahābhārata, i. 69–74.

NOTE.—In describing the conversation between Shakuntalā and her
husband, a free use has been made of Mr. Dutt's translation.

XXXI.

LOVE CONQUERS DEATH.

" The woman who lives even for a moment after being separated from
her husband, lives in great misery."—*Mahābhārata*, i. 121. 27.
" In childhood a female must be subject to her father, in youth to her
husband ; when her lord is dead, to her sons ; a woman is never fit for
independence."—*Laws of Manu*, v. 148.

THERE was a king in Northern India renowned far and
wide for his benevolence and piety. He performed many
sacrifices, and gave much thought to the comfort of both
man and beast within his realm. But year after year
passed and he remained childless. Realising that old age
was fast approaching, this noble prince resolved to devote
himself to one particular deity, whom he worshipped ex-
clusively for the space of eighteen years. At the end of
that time the god appeared and said that his eldest queen
would soon become the mother of a female child. And
so it came to pass. The child was named Sāvitrī, in
honour of the celestial to whom her father had made his
special appeal, and when she grew up she was known all
over India for her beauty and goodness. Indeed, she was
so beautiful and so good that the princes of the land were
afraid of her, and none of them had the courage to ask
for her hand in marriage. Now in those days it was the
custom for princesses to choose their own husbands. And
when her father saw that his daughter had reached womanhood, he sent for her and said that he desired her to make

her own choice, and say whom she would like to marry. He pointed out that fathers who did not arrange for their daughters' settlement in life were blamed by both gods and men. Sāvitrī modestly agreed to do as her father suggested, and she proposed that she should make a tour of the various places of pilgrimage, and in particular visit those hermitages where kings and other members of the warrior caste were living the forest life. And so the princess set out upon her journey. She travelled in a golden chariot, and had as escort several of her father's ministers.

After some time had elapsed, she returned with the report that she had seen the person she would like to marry. His name was Satyavān, the son of a king who, because of his blindness, had been driven from his kingdom and compelled to take refuge in a forest. When the maiden was making her report, a very eminent *rishi* happened to be present, and her father asked the holy man if he could tell them anything about the character and disposition of the prince. The *rishi* replied that the young man was endowed with every virtue. He was exceedingly handsome. He was very strong and courageous, generous and truthful, and of an eminently wise, patient and forgiving disposition. He was also very clever with his hands, and as a child had learned to make pretty little horses of wood which he covered with paint of various colours. "But has he not any vices?" said the king. "Is there no defect of any kind about him?" "Yes," said the *rishi*, "there is a defect, a very serious defect, which eclipses all his good qualities. In twelve months from this very day he is destined to die, and nothing can avert his fate." When her father heard this awful prophecy, he begged his daughter to think of someone else. But she refused absolutely. "I have made my choice," she said, "and I will choose no other."

Realising that he could not bend her purpose, the king set out and interviewed the young man's father in the forest. The marriage took place very soon after, and Sāvitrī, of course, lived the same life as her husband and his parents. She ceased to wear her ornaments and jewels, and put on the ascetic garb. Her father-in-law was much gratified by the way in which she worshipped him as a god, while her mother-in-law was equally pleased because she was of a meek and docile spirit, always ready to minister to her needs. But Sāvitrī, happy though she was in many ways, could not for a moment forget, by night or by day, that her husband's life was quickly passing. She counted the months, the weeks and days. When the last week arrived she gave herself up to fasting and prayer. As they watched her at her devotions, little realising how her mind was burdened, the other ascetics who lived in the hermitage prayed that she might never become a widow. Her father-in-law urged her not to waste her strength. But it was all to no purpose. At length the morning of the fatal day arrived, and her husband announced that he must go to the forest to gather fruit and cut down wood for their altar fire. Sāvitrī at once declared that she would go with him. A year had passed, she said, since she came to the hermitage, and she had never once been in the forest. This was all the more reason, her husband thought, why she should not go now, weakened as she was by days of fasting. But once again she would not listen to advice, and so the two set out together. The beauty of the woods lay before them, and Satyavān bade his wife give heed to the loveliness of the scene before her, the streams and flowers, and watch the peacocks as they flashed among the trees. But nature and its beauties were nothing to her that day. She could not give an intelligent answer to her husband's questions and appeals. The dreaded hour was fast

approaching. In a few moments her husband would be
lying dead upon the ground. At last they came to a spot
where the prince began to fill a bag he had brought with
fruit and flowers, and when that task was accomplished,
to cut down branches from the trees. But all at once he
stopped and said, " I can't go on any longer. Every
bone in my body is aching, and I have a fearful headache.
I shall lie on the ground for a little and try to sleep. Let
me place my head on your lap." The prince lay down
with his head resting on Sāvitrī's lap. " Alas ! " she
cried in her soul, " my husband is about to die. Can I
do nothing to save him ? " As she thus pondered in her
heart, there appeared before her a person of a gigantic
size, clothed in red garments, with a crown on his head.
He was shining like the sun, and had great red eyes. He
carried a noose in one of his hands. The princess recognised that she was in the presence of a god. She therefore
gently placed her husband's head on the ground and
with her hands joined together in worship, asked who he
was, and why he had come. " I am Yama," he answered,
" Yama, the god of Death. I have come for your husband's
soul. His years are numbered, and he cannot stay a
moment longer. But I have heard of his many virtues,
and instead of sending one of my messengers, as I usually
do, I came for him myself." As he made this reply, the
god of Death stooped down and drew out the soul of
Satyavān. It was about the size of a thumb. Whenever
the soul had been withdrawn, an immediate change took
place in the appearance of the prince, and Sāvitrī knew
that she was looking at the body of a dead man. Having
bound the soul with his noose, the god of Death told the
princess to attend to her husband's funeral rites, and set
off for the lower world. But Sāvitrī was resolved not to
leave her husband. She said, " Where he goes, I will go."
And despite the protests of the god, she continued to

follow him. As she did so, she spoke in praise of the life
of the householder, declaring that it was the most meritorious of all lives. It obtained greater rewards, and was more
efficacious in securing righteousness than either celibacy
or renunciation of the world. She also talked at length
on the duty of exercising mercy and benevolence, even
to an enemy, and said that people should devote themselves to the welfare of others, without expecting any
return. The earth was upheld by the asceticism of pious
men, while their loyalty to truth preserved the sun from
wrong and kept him steadfast in his course across the
heavens. Nor did the princess fail to sing the praises
of the god himself. She dwelt on his evenhanded justice,
and the benefit she was acquiring from travelling in the
society of one so virtuous as he was. The god was so
pleased with her piety and wisdom, so flattered and moved
by her words of praise, that he stopped on four separate
occasions and told her to ask any boon except that of her
husband's life. She took advantage of each of these four
offers, and asked first, that her father-in-law, who was
blind, might receive his sight; next, that his kingdom
might be restored; thirdly, that she and Satyavān might
have a hundred sons; and lastly, that her own father might
have a similar boon. Having granted these four boons,
Yama begged the lady to go away and not to trouble
him any more. But she began to address him in more
pious and persuasive strains than before, with the result
that he told her she could ask for one further boon. And
on this occasion he put no limit to her asking. Sāvitrī's
opportunity had come at last. She pointed out that she
and her husband could not have a hundred sons unless
the prince was made alive again, and so she insisted on
that incomparable boon. To this appeal Yama cheer-
fully agreed, and set Satyavān's soul free. When Sāvitrī
returned to where she had left her husband's dead body,

she was rejoiced to find that the soul had arrived before her. Her husband was now not dead but sleeping. By this time darkness had begun to fall, and husband and wife hurried home as fast as they could.

When Sāvitrī told the story of her successful pleading with the god of Death to the *rishis* and ascetics gathered there, they could not say enough in her praise. And in after days, when any one wished to pay a wife the highest compliment in his power, he said she was like Sāvitrī, who brought back her husband's soul from the gates of the lower world. Of course, all the other boons that Yama had promised were realised, one after the other, in due course, while Sāvitrī and Satyavān lived happily together for four hundred years.

Mahābhārata, iii. 292–297.

XXXII.

THE STORY OF NALA AND DAMAYANTI.

"Gambling is the root of all misery."—*Mahābhārata*, ii. 58. 11.

"Women, gambling, hunting and drink have been designated as the four evils by which people are deprived of prosperity."—*Mahābhārata*, iii. 13. 7.

NALA, king of the Nishāda, was possessed of every virtue and beauty, deeply versed in the Vedas, and a brave warrior. He had, however, one vice, a love of gambling. Damayanti was the only daughter of the king of Berār. She was more beautiful than any of the celestials. These two had so often heard of each other's beauty that they fell deeply in love. Nala was so overcome by his passion that he became gloomy and sad, spending much of his time alone in the gardens of his palace. One day he caught a swan with golden wings. The swan told the prince that if he would set it free, it would go to Damayanti and speak of him in such a way that the princess would never think with love of any other person as long as she lived. The prince set the bird free, and it at once flew to the capital of Berār. Finding Damayanti in a solitary place, the bird began to praise Nala for his beauty and goodness, telling her that she must be married to him. Having sent back a message to Nala, the princess became as afflicted with anxiety as he was. She grew pale and thin, refusing to take rest either night or day. When the king heard of his daughter's condition, he realised that she had now reached puberty and decided to arrange for her marriage. He accordingly sent out messengers, inviting the kings of the earth to attend his daughter's Svayamvara.[1] So many princes came that the world was filled with the sound caused by the clatter of their cars and the neighing of their horses.

The news of the approaching Svayamvara was carried to heaven by the *rishi* Nārada. The gods were so much excited by the account given of Damayanti's beauty, that Indra and three others decided to go and be candidates for the hand of such a lovely maiden. Getting into their celestial cars, the gods set off for the land of Berār. On the way they met Nala and asked him if he would render them a service. When Nala agreed, he was told that he must carry a message to Damayanti to say that four of the celestials wished to be present at her Svayamvara, and that she must choose one of them as her husband. To this Nala protested that they should send some one else, as he was going there with the same purpose in view for himself. But he was told that he must keep his promise. Again, when he asked how he could get into the presence of a maiden so jealously guarded,[2] Indra told him that he would see to that. Thus bound by his promise, Nala continued his journey, and when he got to the palace, gained admission (it is not explained in what way) to the presence of Damayanti. His beauty filled Damayanti with still greater desire, and when he told her that he had come in obedience to the command of the gods, she declared that her heart was his, and that she would wed none of the celestials. Nala, anxious to do his duty as a faithful messenger, pointed out the advantages of marrying a god. He reminded her, too, that, by offending them, she might suffer from their wrath. The maiden, however, replied

---

[1] Svayamvara is the maiden's choice of a bridegroom.
[2] This illustrates the existence of the Purda system.

that, while she paid all honour to the gods, it was Nala
and Nala only that she was prepared to marry.   If he
would not have her, she would kill herself by poison or by
fire.   When Nala pleaded that as the god's messenger he
could no longer look to his own interest, Damayanti replied
that she would herself choose him as her husband from
among all the candidates, whether they were gods or men,
and thus he would be free from all blame.

When the day of the Svayamvara arrived, and the
kings and princes had taken their places on the seats
appointed for them, Damayanti entered the amphitheatre.
But, alas ! when she looked for Nala, she saw not one,
but five Nalas exactly alike in every respect.   The four
gods had changed themselves into Nala's likeness.   Greatly
perplexed, she resolved to appeal to their compassion, and
briefly told them of how she had learned to love Nala, and
had resolved to have him only as her husband.   Accordingly
she begged the gods to assume their proper forms.   The
gods listened to her prayer, and as a result she at once
recognised them, because they did not perspire like mortals,
and were able to sit without touching the ground.   Damayanti then advanced to Nala and put round his neck the
garland by which she signified her choice.   In his joy,
Nala declared that as long as he lived he would always be
ready to obey his wife's commands.

On their way back to heaven, the gods met Kali-Yuga,
one of the four ages.   When asked where he was going,
Kali said he was going to the Svayamvara of Damayanti.
Indra smiled and said that he was somewhat late.   The
Svayamvara was over, and a mortal had been chosen, in
the very presence of the gods.   Kali could not take this
insult to the celestials as easily as Indra did, and he resolved
upon revenge.   His plan was to enter into Nala and dis-
possess him of his kingdom.   But the problem was how to
secure an entrance.   Nala was free from fault and stain

of any kind. After waiting and watching for twelve years, Kali found that, before performing the ceremony of evening worship, Nala had neglected to wash his feet. This was enough, a flaw had been detected, and the evil spirit entered the prince. Having accomplished thus much, Kali then began to tempt Pushkara, the prince's brother. He filled his mind with haughty thoughts of sovereignty, and told him to challenge his brother to play at dice, saying he would be certain to win, and in the end secure the whole kingdom. When Nala was challenged to play by his brother, he could not refuse, and a game began which lasted for months, in which Nala, day after day, lost some of his wealth. Realising what the end would be, Damayanti sent her two children to her father's house.

At last the crisis came, and having staked all his wealth and his kingdom, and lost, Nala and Damayanti, each wearing nothing but a single cloth to cover their nakedness, were driven from the city by the command of Pushkara, who proclaimed that no one must offer them food or clothing or shelter. The unhappy pair spent three nights outside the city. Oppressed with hunger, Nala tried to catch some birds with his cloth. But the birds seized the cloth and carried it up into the sky, crying out, as they did so, that they were the dice that had ruined him, and they would not be content till they had robbed him of his cloth also. Nala then tried to persuade his wife to leave him and go to her father's house, but she steadfastly refused, declaring that in all kinds of misery there is no medicine equal to a wife. She pleaded, however, that they should both take refuge with her father, but for shame he would not go.

Exhausted with hunger and thirst, they came on the fourth night, after many wanderings, to a rude hut. There they lay down upon the bare ground and Damayanti fell asleep. By this time Nala had resolved that the

wisest plan was to abandon his wife, persuaded that when
left alone she would be sure to seek her father's protection. He therefore divided her single garment in two
and set off. But time after time he came back to look
at her, lamenting his foolishness, and torn by the anguish
of parting. After he had finally gone, Damayanti awoke
to find that her husband had deserted her. Crying to
the beasts and mountains to tell her whither he had gone,
the distracted woman was met and swallowed by a snake.
Fortunately a hunter saw what had happened and delivered
her by tearing the snake in two. But the hunter was so
captivated by her beauty that he sought to bend her to
his desire. Appealing to her own chastity to save her
and to destroy the hunter, if she ever had thought of
any man but her husband, her cry was heard, and the
hunter fell dead to the ground. After other adventures
Damayanti at last came to the kingdom of Chedi, where
the queen mother took pity on her and made her hand-
maid to her own daughter, promising to care for her and
keep her from the presence of men.

When Damayanti's father heard of how his daughter,
with her husband, had been driven from their kingdom,
he sent out Brāhmins in every direction to search for them.
One of these came to Chedi, where Damayanti was, and
recognised her, despite her disguise. Getting near her,
he told her who he was, and why he had come. Her joy
was great when she heard that her parents and children
were well. After explanations had been made to the
queen mother, who proved to be Damayanti's aunt, she
set off for her father's capital, attended by a strong
escort.

Very soon after Nala had abandoned his wife, he saw a
great fire in the forest where he was, and heard a voice
crying for help. When he approached the fire he saw a
huge snake lying on the ground. The snake told him,

that because of a curse passed on him by the *rishi* Nārada,
he was unable to move, and that if Nala did not help him
he would be consumed by the fire. Nala accordingly
lifted him up, to remove him to a place of safety. Whenever Nala took him up, the snake contracted to the size
of a thumb. They had not gone ten steps when the
snake bit his benefactor, and Nala at once was transformed into an ugly dwarf. The snake, however, explained that he had done what he did, not from enmity,
but from friendship. When Nārada had cursed him he
had told him that the curse would be removed when Nala
came to his help. He added that his change of form
would enable him to live free from recognition till he
should be reunited with his wife. He also explained that
the poison had not entered his own body, but the body
of Kali-Yuga, the evil spirit that possessed him, and
would continue to plague Kali-Yuga till he was driven
out in desperation. By the snake's advice Nala directed
his steps to the kingdom of Ayodhyā, where, under an
assumed name, he entered the service of the king. He
served in the double capacity of cook and trainer of horses.

Meanwhile the Brāhmins continued their search for
Nala. By Damayanti's order, they cried aloud, in every
city, " Oh, beloved gambler ! where have you gone,
deserting your beloved wife as she lay asleep in the forest."
After a long search, one of the Brāhmins returned with
the news that he had seen in Ayodhyā a dwarf who,
when he heard the proclamation of Damayanti, was not
able to conceal his emotion, and began to weep. He
had also spoken some words in defence of Nala's conduct.
The messenger was sure that the dwarf must be Nala.
Damayanti at once sent messengers to Ayodhyā, announc-
ing that, as her husband appeared to be dead, she had
resolved to hold a second Svayamvara.[1] When the king

[1] Evidently widow remarriage was not illegal.

heard of this, he resolved to be present at the Svayamvara, but on inquiry he learned that the ceremony was to take place the very next day. As the capital of Berār was seven hundred miles away, he called for the dwarf, his trainer of horses, and asked him if he could accomplish that distance in twenty-four hours. The dwarf, who, of course, was Nala, was as anxious to go as the king, and to reproach his wife for her unfaithfulness. He accordingly told the king that he would take him there in time. A wonderful description is given of the journey. The horses, yoked to the chariot, looked weak and thin. But after Nala had spoken to them, and under his skilful guidance, they renewed their vigour and, spurning the earth, mounted up into the sky. Now the king was remarkable for his proficiency in gambling, and very proud of his capacity for making rapid calculations. This latter gift he proved on the journey by telling Nala how many leaves had fallen from a tree, and how many still clung to the branches. Nala was so interested that he stopped the chariot, cut down the tree, and, by counting the leaves, found that the monarch's forecast was true. This action of his must have been prompted by a desire to acquire the king's proficiency in gambling. But the king was also moving in a similar direction. To be an expert charioteer was the ambition of his life. The result was that he exchanged his skill in gambling for Nala's gift in driving horses. Whenever the exchange was made, Kali-Yuga, the evil spirit, came out of Nala's body, vomiting the poison of the snake that had bitten him.

When the king of Ayodhyā and Nala reached their destination, they were surprised to find that no preparations had been made for the Svayamvara, and they both waited with anxiety to see what would happen. Having thus brought her husband within reach, as she had hoped, Damayanti sent a female messenger to the charioteer to

14

ask why he had come and who he was. The charioteer
evaded her questions, but when the messenger repeated
the words, " Oh beloved gambler, where have you gone ? "
he began to weep, and said, " Good women never become
angry, and hold their lives protected by the armour of
good character, even though deserted by their husbands."
When Damayanti heard this account from her messenger,
she was convinced that the dwarf must be her husband.
To make absolutely certain, she sent the woman back
more than once. She also procured some of the food which
the dwarf had cooked for his master, and the taste of it
also showed that it must have been prepared by Nala.
Finally, she sent her two children to him. The dwarf at
once took them on his knees and began to weep. Unable
to restrain herself longer, and with the consent of her
parents, Damayanti had the charioteer brought to the
palace. Calling him by his assumed name, she asked him
if he had ever heard of a man who abandoned his wife as
Nala had done. To this the dwarf replied by asking why
Damayanti had appointed a second Svayamvara. Her
explanation, that it was only a device to bring Nala to her
side, led to further revelations. But reconciliation was
not complete until Damayanti had appealed to the gods
to testify to her purity, and the truth of what she said.
In response to her appeal the wind god told Nala that
what she said was true. The drums of heaven, too, began
to play, and flowers fell from the sky. Nala then resumed
his true form, and after four years of cruel separation, was
reunited to his wife.

After staying a short time at Berār, Nala went to his
brother, Pushkara, and challenged him to play again.
The stakes, strange to say, included not only Pushkara's
kingdom, but Damayanti as well. At a single throw,
Nala won back all that he had lost. But he treated his
brother very generously. Indeed, he said that he loved

him as much as ever, endowed him with a large stretch
of territory, and excused his fault by putting all the blame
on Kali-Yuga, the evil spirit who had tempted them both.
As for Nala and Damayanti, they passed the rest of their
days in great happiness and prosperity, as blessed as the
gods in the garden of Indra.   And they continued to show
how genuine was their piety by the number of their sacrifices
and the largeness of the gifts they made to Brāhmins.

Those who listen to this beautiful old story never suffer
from any kind of calamity.   They get all their desires
fulfilled.   They obtain wealth, sons and grandsons, cattle
and an honourable position in life, health and gladness.

Mahābhārata, iii. 52–79.

XXXIII.

THE FOWLER AND THE PIGEONS.

"A person should never do to others what he does not like others to
do to him, knowing how painful it is to himself."—*Mahābhārata*, xii. 259.
19.

ONCE upon a time there was a very wicked fowler, shunned
and detested by all because of his occupation. And how
could it be otherwise ? He earned his livelihood by destroying the lives of other creatures and selling their flesh
for food. And yet this sinful man lived for many years
without ever realising what an evil occupation his was.
But one day when in the forest snaring and destroying
birds as was his practice, a great storm arose. Dense
masses of clouds covered the sky. Indra poured down
rain to such an extent that the whole world seemed to be
flooded. The tempest wrought great havoc among the
trees, and many beasts and birds were killed. Absolutely
bewildered and stricken by fear, the fowler wandered hither
and thither, plunging through the water looking for some
raised piece of ground on which he might find refuge.
While in this condition he chanced to find a female pigeon
lying on the ground, paralysed with cold ; and quite forgetful of the fact that the poor creature was the victim of
misfortune as much as he was, he picked her up and put
her into a cage that he was carrying. Even at that hour
the wicked fowler had no pity for a fellow sufferer !

Now just at that moment the fowler saw in front of him

a great tree on whose mighty branches many birds and
beasts had taken refuge. It looked as if the Creator
himself had planted it there to be a protection in their
extremity to the creatures he had made. The fowler
hastened to seek its shelter as quickly as he could, and
soon after the sky began to clear. Hungry and cold, he
realised that he had wandered far from home, and that he
must spend the night underneath the tree. Resolved to
make the best of it, he chose a stone for his pillow and lay
down to sleep. But before he did so, he prayed to the
spirit of the tree to grant him protection. Now it so
happened that the fowler had brought the female pigeon
to the very tree which was her home. That morning she
had gone out to look for food, and her husband was exceedingly anxious at her failure to return, and giving relief
to his feelings by bewailing his sad fate. " Oh, my dear,"
he cried, " what a dreadful storm for you to be exposed
to. I fear some calamity has befallen you. How shall I
ever be able to live, deprived of your presence ? What is
home without a wife ? It may be filled with sons and
grandsons, with daughters-in-law and servants, but it is
empty and desolate without a wife. And what an ideal
wife she is ; so beautiful to look at with her many-coloured
feathers and lovely eyes and gentle voice. She never
thinks of eating till I have been satisfied ; she never bathes
till I have bathed ; she never sits when I am standing ;
she never seeks repose till I have lain down. She rejoices
when I rejoice ; she is sad when I am sad. When I am
absent she always feels lonely. When I get angry she
does all she can to calm my wrath. She puts all her trust
in me ; she does what I ask her to do, and has no will but
mine. There is no companion like a wife. She is her
husband's richest treasure ; she is his best medicine in
sickness and pain."

The female pigeon was very much uplifted when she

heard her husband talk about her in this way, and she
told herself that she was a very happy and blessed pigeon
to have a husband who thought so much of her. It was
now her turn to moralise on a wife's duties, and she dwelt
on the fact that ever since they had been wedded she had
looked upon her husband as her highest god. These
observations she made, as it were, to herself, but she now
raised her voice and thus addressed her lord. " My dear
husband, I am here, and I wish to ask you a favour. As
you are well aware, there is no greater virtue than hearing
the cry of the suppliant. No more pressing duty than the
exercise of hospitality. Look at this wretched fowler,
lying as it were at the door of your house, perishing of cold
and hunger. You must exercise the rites of hospitality
and offer him some food. If you allow him to die, you
will be guilty of as great a sin as if you had killed a cow
or a Brāhmin. You are a householder ; perform the duties
of a householder. Offer him hospitality, and as a reward
you will secure unending happiness in heaven. Children
have been already born to you. If it be necessary, you
should be willing to surrender life itself rather than see
him suffer. Don't worry about me ; if you continue to
live, you can get other wives."

The pigeon was greatly delighted to find that his wife
was alive and able to address him in such pious strains.
Indeed he was so overcome with happiness that he shed
tears of joy. And in obedience to her advice he at once
addressed the fowler and said he was glad to see him. It
would be a great favour if he would say what service he
could render. It was both a duty and a pleasure to offer
hospitality even to an enemy. The tree does not refuse
its shelter to the woodman who is about to cut it down.
In reply, the fowler said that he was benumbed with cold
and would be grateful if the pigeon would collect material
and make a fire. This the pigeon immediately did. He

collected a large quantity of dry leaves, put a light to them, and the guest was soon sitting before a cheerful blaze. As the fowler warmed himself and eased his weary limbs, he turned to the pigeon and said : " I should now like some food ; I am very hungry indeed." " I am sorry," said his host, " that I cannot help you in the matter of food. We pigeons never keep anything in store. We live from day to day on what we are able to pick up, and never think of the morrow. Such is our mode of life." But even as he said this, the pigeon grew pale. For he remembered that if he had no food in store he could give his own flesh to appease the fowler's hunger. And so he added, " Yes, I can help you in this matter also. I can supply you with food, the very food you are in the habit of selling to your customers. I can give you myself." And without a moment's hesitation the noble-hearted bird, when he had walked three times round the fire, stepped into the flames.

This great act of self-sacrifice wrought an immediate change in the heart of the fowler. Stricken with grief, he cried out, " What is this that I have done ? My sin can never be wiped out, and yet, after all, I am only reaping the fruit of an evil life. I once had an honourable occupation, but I gave it up to become a fowler, snaring birds and selling their flesh, and now this pigeon gives his life for me. However, it is not even now too late to make amends. I shall abandon my wife and children and spend the rest of my days in this forest. By the practice of asceticism, I shall deprive myself of every comfort. I shall endure hunger and thirst and cold. By rigid fasts I shall so emaciate my body that it will be possible to count my veins." As he made this resolve, the fowler opened the cage in which the female pigeon was imprisoned and set her free. He threw away his nets and traps and springs, and disappearing in the depths of the forest, gave himself up to a life of devotion, resolved to imitate, as well as he could, the noble example of self-sacrifice that had been set before him.

The female pigeon, now left a widow, was filled with overwhelming sorrow. She declared that never once had her husband done her the smallest wrong. He had been her constant stay and shelter. He had shown her unvarying respect and honour. Their life had been one of unsullied happiness, but these joys were gone for ever, never to return. His conversation, too, had been most instructive and sweet. No, she could not think of living alone. A widow's life, even when she had sons to care for her, as she had, was not to be endured. She was an object of pity always, and sometimes of contempt. No pure-hearted woman would venture to go on bearing the burden of life alone. Her husband had loaded her with innumerable blessings, and no wife worthy of the name would fail to worship him as a god. There was only one course open to her. She would follow her husband to the other world. As she said this, she cast herself upon the fire in which her lord and master had offered up his life. But in the very hour of death their reunion was accomplished. Her husband appeared, seated in a heavenly car. Indeed, the sky was filled with celestial chariots, and in them were vast numbers of glorified saints, who, like him, had done meritorious deeds when they were on earth. Escorted by these noble spirits, husband and wife passed on to enjoy the bliss and happiness of heaven.

Not long after, the fowler was privileged to get a glimpse of their heavenly glory, and the sight of it made him redouble his austerities in the hope that he would obtain a station as lofty as theirs. And before many days had passed, he secured his reward.

This is a very ancient story. The man who reads it every day is never overtaken by any evil, and will be sure to go to heaven, purged of distress and sin. It has a special lesson for wives also. If they imitate the female pigeon and follow their lords as she did, they will most certainly reach the upper world. And it has a lesson for householders also. To hear the cry of the suppliant is a virtue so outstanding and full of merit that you will be cleansed of your sin, even if you have killed a cow, and there is no greater crime than that.

Mahābhārata, xii. 143–149.

XXXIV.

AN INDIAN JOB AND HIS WIFE

"The movements of creatures are determined by what they have done, be it good or bad, in a former life."—*Rāmāyana*, vii. 119.

"In his new existence, a man's good and evil acts follow him like his shadow, and the consequences thereof make his life either pleasant or painful."—*Mahābhārata*, iii. 183. 78.

YUDHISTHIRA ruled over a great empire in Northern India. His wealth and power excited the jealousy of his cousins, who on more than one occasion challenged him to play at dice. Despite the fact that he was a very poor player, Yudhisthira was exceedingly fond of the game, and he foolishly accepted the challenge. His friends did their best to dissuade him, but he was too proud to refuse, and excused himself by saying that it was the will of Fate that he should play. Many high stakes were proposed, but the last and highest was the most absurd of all. It was that in the event of defeat, Yudhisthira should surrender not only his wealth and dominions, but consent to thirteen years of exile in a forest with his brothers and Draupadi, their wife. Thanks to the dishonest play of which his opponents were guilty, Yudhisthira was the loser every time, and the princes, stripped of all their property, were driven into exile. Some of the brothers, at least, were very unwilling to submit, but none of them protested more violently than Draupadi, and she bitterly reproached her husband for showing so meek and forgiving a disposition. She was greatly surprised at the calmness with which he accepted the situation, and gave no expression to his anger. How was it possible, she asked, when he contrasted their present with their former state ? Did he not remember how they used to sit on thrones of ivory, thrones that were studded with pearls ? Did he not remember how they ate the choicest food from plates of gold, and wore garments of the finest silk ? And now they were compelled to sit and to sleep on the ground, eat the plainest food, and wear garments made of bark. When she thought of all that they had lost, she was beside herself with grief, and what was the reason of it all ? He had given a foolish pledge, which he should have refused to keep. Here were four brothers, one of whom at least could, with his single arm, put both gods and men to flight. Were they to be bound by a promise and act contrary to the spirit and practice of the warrior caste ? Who ever saw a member of their caste, so devoid of anger as he was, submitting so meekly to an unjust demand ? Why should he forgive his enemies in such a generous fashion ? There were times and occasions, no doubt, when one ought to forgive, but this was neither the time nor the occasion. Nobody listened to and nobody paid any respect to the man who was always forgiving others their sins. His servants and friends, his wife and children, took advantage of him. If we never punished people we only did them harm. It was the man who knew when to forgive and when to be angry who inherited the earth. And she hoped that he would put forth his strength and smite his enemies. If he failed to do so, he would lose all honour and respect.

To these arguments Yudhisthira could only reply that anger never helped anybody. No one ever got any profit out of anger. It did nothing but destroy. It warped a man's judgment and caused untold evil, leading us to injure those whom we ought to help, and to help those who ought to be punished. Nor did he agree with her scornful references to forgiveness. The wise man did not seek to give pain to those who caused him pain; he did not abuse those who abused him; and he was confident that in another world that man would reap his reward. Truth was better than falsehood; pity was better than cruelty—and so also forgiveness was better than wrath. To refuse to exercise forgiveness, to manifest a spirit of anger and strife, meant the spread of irreligion, and would bring the world to ruin. She must not say that forgiveness was a sign of weakness. It was forgiveness which was strong, and crowned our lives with victory. Had she never heard the ancient hymn which the father of the race had taught them to sing? It said that forgiveness was the support and sustainer of the world; it was equal to sacrifice and asceticism; it was equal to truth and purity; equal to Brahmā himself. Why then should any one think that he was willing to forego a virtue which was calculated to secure for him such high rewards. This world belongs to the forgiving; the other world belongs to the forgiving; they obtain honour here and holy blessedness hereafter. He hoped that his cousins would eventually relent and give them back their kingdom. But if they did not, they would be the chief sufferers in the end. Destruction would come upon them. As for himself, however, he would not surrender that which was the highest virtue. He would continue both to pity and to forgive.

Draupadi declared that such lofty language only bewildered her. She wondered what his father and grandfather would have said in reply to such talk. Men didn't succeed in this world by practising pity and forgiveness. "But what is the use of talking?" she cried. "You will never abandon righteousness. You are willing to abandon

your wife. You are willing to abandon your brothers,
your wealth and empire, but you will not abandon
righteousness. The sages are reported to have said that
righteousness cared for the righteous, but it does not
seem to care for you. And you are a righteous man.
Think of the sacrifices you have offered, the horse sacrifice
and the cow sacrifice and many others. Think of the
Brāhmins and ascetics whom you have fed from plates
of gold. I remember it well, for I served them with my
own hands. Think of the gifts you gave to these holy
men, and never withheld anything. Nay, we were content
to wait till they had eaten, and take what was left over.
And now what is our state? Why was it that one so
virtuous, so modest and truthful, ever ventured to gamble?
Alas! it is very manifest that God plays with men as a
child plays with her doll, and makes them dance according
to His will. God pervades men's spirits like an atmosphere,
and awards them joy and sorrow as He pleases. They
are not free. Like a bullock with a rope in his nose, like
bits of wood swept by the current, like straws before the
wind, they are not masters of themselves, not even for a
moment. How great is the power of God's illusion. He
fills all things, He is the doer of all that is done, whether
it be good or evil, and yet no eye has even seen Him or
been able to say, 'This is God.' Man's body is the field
of His activities, and He who is the Creator beguiles His
creatures to their destruction, causing them to slay and
to be slain. For He does not love men as parents love
their children. He treats them as if they were His enemies,
giving happiness and prosperity to the wicked, and plunging the righteous into perplexity and grief. That is why
I reproach God. I see Him doing such perverse things.
I wonder what benefit the Creator expects to get from all
this. Does He imagine that our cousins are going to
satiate Him with sacrifices and gifts? It is said that

we enjoy or suffer the fruits of what we have done in a former birth. If that is so, then God ought to be stained with the consequence of our evil deeds. But He is all-powerful, and human actions do not touch Him, while man in his weakness and poverty has to bear the whole burden."

In reply to these strong assertions, Yudhisthira acknowledged that his wife had put her case very well, but nevertheless she was talking like an atheist. As far as he himself was concerned, he never cultivated virtue because it paid. He offered sacrifices and gave gifts because it was his duty to do so, and he performed the obligations of a householder without asking whether he was going to be rewarded or not. He supposed he had a natural inclination to righteousness, but he could not conceive anything more obnoxious than the man who made a trade of piety. And it was quite certain that those who tried to milk virtue would find their efforts all in vain. They would secure nothing either here or hereafter. Nevertheless, he went on to assert that virtue had very real rewards, and pointed to the sages, with most of whom they were personally acquainted, who showed what one could achieve by a persistent adherence to righteous deeds. Their asceticism in particular had made them able both to curse and to bless, and raised them to a position more exalted than that of the gods. And did she think that these worthy men, so gifted with divine insight, so deeply versed in the Vedas, would have continued their efforts if they had known that a virtuous life had no reward? It was the same with the gods and with the demons. They knew that the practice of virtue yielded fruit both here and hereafter. Were it otherwise, gods and men would have ceased to strive. There would have been no desire to accumulate wealth and knowledge, no desire to secure emancipation, and the race would have been reduced to the level of the beasts. There were those he knew who argued very cleverly, and who thought themselves very wise. They cast doubts on religion and spoke contemptuously of righteousness. He did not mean to say that life was free from mystery. There were many things which were beyond the understanding even of the celestials. But she must resolve never to speak as she had done, and utter reproaches against God. It was not right to doubt religion or the celestials because we did not get what we want, and our worship seemed to be in vain. There is no other way to secure salvation ; no other raft by which we can travel across life's ocean. Think of what has been your own experience since birth. Dispel your doubts and fears. Humble yourself before God, learn to know Him, and don't allow your understanding to be darkened. For why should you blaspheme the Creator of all, through whose kindness the faithful obtain immortal life.

Draupadi appears to have been moved by this touching appeal. At least she said that she had never wished to speak disrespectfully of God. She would not dare to do so. But he must, nevertheless, bear with her a little longer, as there was one other matter on which she felt she must say something or her heart would break. It was on the subject of human effort. Manifestly she thought that Yudhisthira was too easy-going, and wished to sit down for their thirteen years of exile and do nothing. And so she prefaced her remarks by dwelling on the general opinion that men reap in this life the fruits of what they did in a previous existence. The result was that many were inclined to explain anything that happened to them by referring it to Destiny. She had no patience with such persons. This life was given to them as a sphere of action. And those who blamed Chance and Destiny were positively wicked. They were cracked pitchers that could never hold any water. They never made any progress or achieved any success. She did not deny that there was always a threefold influence at work—divine action, destiny and *Karma* (that is, the effect of what we have done in our previous lives), and if this influence were not always present, nothing that we did would ever fail.[1] But the great lawgiver, Manu, had said that the man who did not make an effort was always defeated, and her own experience showed that idle people were never prosperous, while it often happened that when we did exert ourselves our misfortune and difficulties melted away.

One of the brothers now intervened, but his argument was on a much lower plane. He objected to the way in which Yudhisthira was always harping on virtue. They must choose a less ideal course. He would rather die than forgive his cousins. The safest rule for warriors and kings was to keep what they had got with a strong hand. They had been listening to opinions which were good enough for Brāhmins, but they would not work in ordinary life. The gods themselves had cheated the demons, who were their elder brothers, and deprived them of the sovereignty of the worlds which they had once enjoyed, and he did not see why they should be more virtuous than the gods. Members of the warrior caste were by nature crooked in mind, and if it was wrong for them to break the promise they had given, and to make war before the thirteen years had expired, they would always be able to wipe away the sin by offering sacrifices to the gods and making gifts to Brāhmins. Yudhisthira, however, refused to be persuaded. And he closed the discussion by asking

[1] *Karma* (acts, product, effect) represents the totality of what we have done in our previous lives. We begin our present existence either hampered or helped by our *karma*. It is responsible for the condition or state in which we begin our present existence. But it lies with each of us to make our present and also our future life better than our past. And that is where *human effort* has its opportunity. The great epic often emphasises this truth.

his brother what five men and one woman, without
arms and without friends, could do against the powerful
forces which their cousins would be able to bring into the
field.

Mahābhārata, iii. 27–36.

XXXV.

FIFTY SISTERS MARRIED TO ONE MAN.

"Neither the happiness derived from the gratification of the senses, nor the great happiness one may enjoy in heaven, is equal to a sixteenth part of the happiness which comes from the destruction of all desire."— *Mahābhārata*, xii. 174. 48.

MĀNDHĀTRI, king of Ayodhyā, had fifty daughters whose matrimonial experiences were very remarkable, in that they were all married to one man. The circumstances which led to this strange event were as follows: There was a very eminent *rishi* of the name of Saubhari, who lived immersed in water. This he had done for a period of twelve years, during which time he formed a friendship with the king of the fishes who lived in the lake where the *rishi* had made his home. This fish had a very large family of sons and daughters, who were happily married and had children of their own. The sage was often disturbed by these frolicsome creatures, and found it difficult in consequence to concentrate his thoughts on spiritual things. Finally, envy arose in his breast as he watched his friend, born, though he was, in the low condition of a fish, with his children and grandchildren swimming on all sides of him. He watched with growing envy till he could watch no longer. For he got up out of the water, determined that he, too, would be a householder, taste the joys of family life, and play among his children. It was to king Māndhātri's palace that the sage directed his steps. Whenever the monarch heard of the great honour he was about to receive, he descended from his throne, hastened to meet the sage, and received him with the greatest reverence. But when Saubhari, who by this time was old and frail, broken by years of asceticism, explained that he wanted to marry one of the king's daughters, Māndhātri did not know what to say. He was afraid that if he refused to grant the sage's request, the holy man would blast him with a curse. And so he held down his head and remained silent. After waiting some time, the sage asked why he was so reluctant to answer. Did he not know that by gratifying the desires of the eminent person who stood before him, he would be able to secure anything he wanted ? Realising that some sort of reply must be made, Māndhātri reminded his visitor that the ancient practice of their royal house was to allow princesses to choose their own husbands, and it was impossible therefore for him to make any promise. The girls must choose for themselves, and no action could be taken until they had been consulted.

The sage was too clever to be deceived by this excuse. He knew that the king was confident none of his daughters would consent to marry so old and unattractive a person as he appeared to be. But he concealed his knowledge, and merely suggested that in the circumstances the best plan would be for the young ladies to see him, and he would marry the one who was willing to have him. If they all happened to refuse, then the blame must be attributed to the burden of his years. With evident reluctance, Māndhātri ordered a eunuch to escort the sage to the inner chambers of the palace. But as the sage advanced, a wonderful change took place in his appearance. His beauty became so wonderful that there was no one in earth or heaven to be compared to him. And when the eunuch had explained the purpose of the sage's

coming, the fifty sisters eagerly competed with each other
in their desire to win him as their lord. Indeed, they
quarrelled violently with one another over the matter,
each of them asserting that Brahmā had specially created
her for no other purpose than to marry so extremely
attractive and beautiful a bridegroom. When the super-
intendent of the zenana informed the king of what had
happened, he came to the conclusion that the only way
out of the difficulty was to marry the whole fifty to the
holy man.

When the marriages had been celebrated, the sage
commanded the architect of the gods to build for each
of his wives a crystal palace. The beauty of these build-
ings seems to have passed belief, and it is said that wealth
personified took up its abode in each of them. Their
furniture was equally gorgeous, and they were surrounded
by gardens and woods and lakes, where water birds played
among the lotus beds. The ladies, too, exercised un-
bounded hospitality, in which both guests and attendants
shared. After some time had passed, king Māndhātri,
naturally anxious to see how his daughters were, paid a
visit to what he imagined would be the hermitage of
their husband. What was his surprise, when he arrived
at the place, to find a mighty row of gorgeous palaces,
each standing in its own grounds, and surrounded, as has
been said, by woods and gardens and lakes of water.
Entering the first palace and greeting the daughter he
found there, he learned that she was supremely happy.
She could not say enough in praise of her husband, nor
could she be tempted to express any feeling of home-
sickness. Indeed, she asked how any one could yearn
for home, surrounded as she was by every luxury that
wealth could give, and the wife of a husband so loving
and attentive, that day or night he never left her side.
It was in that connection that she betrayed the one feeling

of anxiety that troubled her. She sometimes wondered
if her sisters were not jealous. They must be bitter at
the thought that their husband never went near them in
his consuming love for her alone. But, strange to say,
when Māndhātri passed on to the next palace and interviewed his second daughter, he found, after the usual
inquiries, that she was as happy as the sister whom their
father had just left, and that the one cause of anxiety,
in her case also, was the fear that her sisters would be
jealous, as he never left her by night or day. And as the
king went from palace to palace—for he did not fail to
visit every one of his fifty daughters—he was told the
same story. His daughters were all equally happy, and
all of them more or less afraid lest her sisters were broken-
hearted by their husband's neglect. Māndhātri was overwhelmed with wonder as he listened to the words of his
daughters and, when his visits had been completed, sought
the presence of the sage. Bowing low before him, he
gave expression to his feelings, and said that he had never
seen or heard of such miraculous power before. It was
very manifest his son-in-law was reaping a rich reward
for his long years of asceticism.

But doubt was beginning to perturb the mind of Saubhari. In course of time his wives made him the father of
no less than one hundred and fifty sons. And as the days
passed, their father became more and more devoted to
them. He pictured in his mind how they would learn to
speak, learn to walk, how they would reach manhood, get
married and have children of their own, and how these
grandchildren in turn would occupy his thoughts and his
affection. And thinking of these things, the saint realised
that one desire gives place to another, and that, in short,
there is no end to the desires that spring up within the
mind of man, even were he to live for a hundred thousand
years. Then casting his mind back to the days when he

lived immersed in water, he remembered how desire had first arisen in his heart as he watched his friend the king of the fishes sporting with his offspring. This first desire was the beginning of evil, and he realised at last that the only hope of liberation lay in separation from the world. But it was not yet too late. He would break the chain which bound him to material things. He would not allow wealth or luxury or offspring to rob him of salvation. He would renew his former devotions. He would regain the favour of Vishnu by the practice of asceticism, and thus be freed from sin. Having formed this pious resolve, Saubhari lost no time in acting upon it. Leaving his wealth and children behind him, the sage, accompanied by his wives, took refuge in the forest and devoted his nights and days to the practice of asceticism. In the end, he obtained his reward and was born no more.

Those who read this story of Saubhari and of his marrying Māndhātri's fifty daughters, will not be afflicted by selfish attachments or wicked deeds, for eight successive births.

Vishnu Purāna, iv. 2.

XXXVI.

THE BIRD-CATCHER.

"That man is a strict vegetarian who never eats the flesh of animals other than those killed for sacrifice."—*Mahābhārata*, xii. 221. 12.

THERE was once a Brāhmin held in high repute for his piety and virtue. He had made a thorough study of the Vedas and other sacred books. But one day, as he was seated under a tree, a female crane chanced to let some droppings fall on his head. This filthy act roused the anger of the holy man, and as a result of his curse the creature fell lifeless to the ground. When he saw the bird lying dead, the Brāhmin felt sorry for what he had done, and said to himself that he had undoubtedly been guilty of grievous sin in giving such free vent to his wrath. Very soon after, he got up from where he was sitting and proceeded to a neighbouring village. He made the round of several houses, begging for food, as was his custom. The last house he came to was one to which he had often gone before. As he stood at the door, he uttered the one word *give*. But the mistress of the house was equally abrupt and merely replied *wait*. The Brāhmin said nothing, and almost immediately thereafter the woman's husband arrived very hungry and clamorous for food. His wife at once placed a seat for him to sit on, brought water to rinse his mouth, and bathed his feet. When these preliminary tasks were over, she set before him savoury dishes of various

kinds and meekly attended to all his wants. It was only
when her husband had thoroughly appeased his hunger
that the woman ventured to take any food herself.

Now all this time the Brāhmin was being quite ignored.
At last he could restrain himself no longer. " May I ask
you what you mean," he said, " by such treatment ? Do
you realise who and what I am, when you treat me with
such disrespect ? Don't you know that we Brāhmins
have no superiors in either earth or heaven ? Has no
wise old man ever told you that if we cared we could burn
up the world in a week ? Indra is the king of heaven,
and even he is afraid of us." " Yes," said the lady, " I
have heard all that and more. I know that Brāhmins
are equal to the gods, and that it was they who by their
curses made the sea undrinkable. I know, too, how one
of the greatest of Brāhmins drank up the ocean. But I
must request you not to be angry with me. I have no intention of showing disrespect to you or any other Brāhmin
at any time. I have been performing what is a woman's
highest duty, attending to the needs of my husband, and
my husband comes before either you or any of the celestials.
I look upon him as my chief deity, and I shall acquire more
merit by serving him faithfully than by any other method.
So please do not think I am a female crane, to be blasted
by your anger. Besides, she added, anger is man's worst
enemy, and you ought to keep it under control. You call
yourself a Brāhmin, and so you are by birth. But in the
eyes of the gods the real Brāhmin is the man who does
not lose his temper, who does not pay back an injury, who
is truthful and generous with his means, who keeps his
passions under control, who offers sacrifices, who studies
the Vedas and teaches it to others. In fact," she added,
" you don't know what real piety and virtue are. But
I'll tell you what you ought to do. There is a bird-catcher
in the town of Mithilā ; if you are willing to be advised

by a woman, go and see him; he will tell you how to live."

The Brāhmin took this rebuke very meekly, and after a good deal of heart-searching, decided that he would go and see the fowler. When he arrived in the capital, he got another shock to find that the fowler kept a butcher's shop. Indeed, the shop was surrounded by a great crowd of people buying venison and buffalo flesh. But his confidence was somewhat restored when the fowler addressed him by name and said he had been expecting him for some time. "Expecting me!" cried the Brāhmin. "What do you know about me? Who told you I was coming? I did not know it myself till the last moment." "I knew you were coming all the same," replied the fowler. "A woman told you to come and see me. Besides, I know where you have secured lodgings, and I don't think it is a suitable place for you to stay. You must come home with me." And so, closing his shop, the low-caste fowler took the Brāhmin to his dwelling. In spite of these wonderful happenings, the Brāhmin, nevertheless, had the courage to observe that he did not like the fowler's occupation, and said that he ought to give it up. "Why should I give it up?" answered the fowler. "It is the occupation of my caste, the trade to which I was born by the appointment of the Creator. My father was a bird-catcher and my grandfather was a bird-catcher. I belong to the Shūdra caste, and it is the duty of the Shūdra caste to serve the other three. You say it is a cruel occupation. Perhaps it is. But how can any one strive with Destiny? I am the victim of my own past deeds, of the sins I committed in a former birth. As it so happens, I don't kill the animals whose flesh I sell. But animals are always being killed for food, and their flesh is one of the foods that have been appointed for all creatures. Brāhmins, too, offer animals in sacrifice. We feed the gods, the

spirits of the dead, and our guests with animal food. You
have heard surely of how the famous king, Ratnideva,
caused two thousand cows to be killed every day for the
entertainment of his guests, while the Scriptures declare
that animals offered in sacrifice acquire a great deal of
merit thereby, and go to heaven. It is all very well for
people to say, don't kill, but those who say so don't know
the real facts. It is quite impossible to refrain from taking
life. Fruits and vegetables are full of living organisms.
When farmers plough the ground, they destroy a great
many lives. It is the same with the woodman who cuts
down a tree. Whether awake or asleep we are always
killing some creature, in the air we breathe, in the water
we drink, or concealed unknown to ourselves in the food
we eat. It is impossible to go for a walk without trampling
some insect under foot. The best that can be said of any
one person is that he has killed fewer animals than other
people. As I said before, I only buy carcases, I am not
a butcher by trade. And I may add, that personally I
am a vegetarian. But all the same, the safe rule is to
stick to the precepts and practice of your own caste. Once
you break away you don't know how far you will travel.
It doesn't matter what one does, however, there will always
be somebody ready to find fault and say you are wrong."

The fowler then began to speak of personal conduct,
and he said that for himself he tried to be truthful and
charitable. The great thing was to avoid all malice and
falsehood, to be full of patience and self-control. Nor
was it wise to be too uplifted when successful, or too
depressed when exposed to suffering. Was it only the
well-to-do and the comfortable who were followers of
virtue ? Our aim in life should be to seek the happiness
of others, and not to exact revenge when any one did
us an injury. The really virtuous man did good, hoping
for no reward. There are wicked people who laugh at

the righteous, who mock at what is pure and good. But we should not worry about them. They are nothing but bags of wind, and their days are numbered. The sinful man is his own worst enemy. He is the murderer of his own soul. He doesn't deserve to be called a man. On the other hand, repentance purges the heart. Whenever you say, I shall not be guilty of that sin again, you have made a resolve that gives you strength. The knowledge of self is the highest knowledge that a man can acquire. The secret of communion with the Eternal Spirit cannot be explained by any earthly teacher. At best he can give us no more than a hint. It is the system of *yoga* that reveals the true wisdom. By the practice of austerities, by the exercise of self-control, by breaking the fetters which bind us to the world, one is eventually able to obtain absorption in Brahm. As the fowler proceeded in his discourse, he spoke more of the mysteries of life, of the doctrine of rebirth, and the diversities of man's earthly lot. He also answered a number of questions bearing on pyschology and physiology. In connection with the doctrine of rebirth he referred to those who abused the gods for causing them so much suffering, when they ought to blame themselves and remember that they were reaping the fruit of the evil they had done in a former life.

In conclusion, the fowler invited the Brāhmin to go and have a talk with his old father and mother. When they entered the beautifully furnished room where these two aged persons were seated, the son was greeted with great affection. They told him that in thought, word and deed he never had wronged them, that he was the joy of their hearts, and that there was not a god in heaven more deserving of worship than he. The son repaid this compliment by telling the Brāhmin that he looked upon his parents as the chief objects of his devotion. He knew

that people worshipped the thirty-three million gods.
But he preferred to worship his father and mother, and
if they asked him to do what was wrong, he would do it
rather than offend them. It was not without an object
that the fowler thus enlarged on the duty of filial piety.
The Brāhmin, it would appear, in his zeal for the Vedas
and their study, had been guilty of neglecting his parents.
And he was told to go home and look after them. Old
and helpless, they had wept their eyes out sorrowing for
their son. And he would be very much better employed
attending to their needs than studying even the books of
revelation. If he wished to acquire the highest virtue,
he must learn to honour his father and mother.

Once more the Brāhmin showed that he had the root
of the matter in him. He thanked the bird-catcher for
his advice, and said he would act upon it. There was
not a shadow of doubt that he had been providentially
guided to come to Mithilā. The fowler had saved him
from falling into hell. But before he went, he would like
to ask one question more. It was very difficult for a man
of low birth to acquire a knowledge of the divine mysteries.
And he could not believe that the fowler really belonged
to the base-born Shūdra caste. Would he tell him how
it had all happened? The fowler graciously assented.
And this is what he said. In a previous birth he had
been a learned Brāhmin, deeply versed in the Vedas and
other books cognate thereto. But owing to a friendship
he had formed with a king, he had become very fond of
hunting, and was in the habit of going with him to the
forest. One day they had been specially successful in
their sport. As ill luck would have it, he happened to
aim an arrow at what he thought was a deer. But it
wasn't a deer; it was a *rishi* whom he struck. The holy
man raised a cry of pain. Greatly distressed and alarmed,
the Brāhmin rushed forward and begged the *rishi* to

forgive him. His apologies and explanations failed to avert the wrath of the sage. "You have wounded me without cause," he said, "and in punishment I curse you to be born in your next life as a cruel fowler, in the Shūdra caste. When the Brāhmin continued to plead for at least some mitigation of the curse, the *rishi* so far relented as to say that while the curse could not be annulled, he would promise that his victim would be a virtuous Shūdra, distinguished for his devotion to his father and mother, that he would be endowed with a knowledge of his previous existence, and after death obtain entrance to heaven.

Mahābhārata, iii. 205–215.

XXXVII.

THE KING AND THE PIGEON.

"The protection of a suppliant is a great act of merit. By following this duty even the killer of a cow may be cleansed of sin."—*Mahābhārata*, xii. 149. 18.

THERE was a king of Benares whose name was Shivi. One day when seated on his throne, a pigeon, pursued by a hawk, took refuge in his bosom. "Have mercy on me," cried the pigeon, "and save me from my cruel enemy!" The king replied that the pigeon need have no fear. To refuse to hear the cry of a suppliant was quite as great a sin as to strike a cow or a Brāhmin. He would surrender his kingdom rather than close his ears to the appeal of those who were in need. The man who was guilty of that offence was struck by lightning, his children died, the gods refused to accept his offerings, and his ancestors went to hell. By this time the hawk had appeared on the scene, and remarked that such observations were all very well in their own way. But he would like to know who had appointed the king of Benares monarch of the skies. He acknowledged that he was, as king on earth, ordained to govern men and administer justice among them. Who had given him authority over birds, and to interfere with their affairs? And apart from that, to come to what he had said about suppliants, it was no doubt very nice to protect those who appealed to you; but problems of conduct were many-sided, and ought to be considered not merely from one point of view. "And so I would point out to you," said the hawk, "that while you are helping the pigeon and casting over him the shield of your protection, you are doing me an injury. You are robbing me of my natural and appointed food. Nobody can live without food. If I don't get food, I shall die. That means you save the pigeon's life and you kill me. And if I die, who is to look after my wife and child? They will die, if I am not here to look after them. And that means three lives lost, because you have made up your mind to save one. As I say, you must look at moral questions from an impartial point of view; look at them all round, and see to it that the course you have resolved to pursue does not involve you in an injustice to somebody else. True piety and virtue should be free from such contradictions. But when you find that contradictions insist in presenting themselves, it is your business to weigh the two conflicting duties, one against the other, and choose that which is the more weighty. In this case, which is the more weighty, to save three lives or one?"

To this powerful argument the king at once replied by saying that he recognised its force. The hawk was a perfect ocean of wisdom and knowledge. He surely was not an ordinary hawk. He must be Garuda, the king of birds, travelling in disguise. And his language was most beautiful, the purest Sanskrit, and so well expressed. He had never heard anything like it. He would not therefore presume to argue with him. But he would like to say just one thing, and it was that the hawk was in no danger of dying. There was a great variety of other food which he would gladly place at the hawk's disposal. Would he be good enough to say which sort he would prefer—buffalo, ox, wild-pig or deer? Yes, he would order his servants to kill and roast an ox whole, cooked with rice, too, and take it

to any place the hawk chose to appoint. They would bring
the whole animal, not a bone or sinew would be lacking,
and he could eat it at his leisure. " But I don't want any
one of these animals," said the hawk. " I don't like their
flesh. I never eat it. I eat pigeon, and I like pigeon ;
that is the kind of flesh the gods have ordained that hawks
should eat. And I am not going to transgress the divine
ordinance, merely to please you. So be good enough to
release the pigeon and thereby enable me to comply with
the regulations which belong to my species and which have
come down from ancient days. And furthermore, I should
like to observe that you are putting forward a very poor
argument when you suggest that I should eat cow or deer,
when my natural food is pigeon. You make me think of a
man trying to climb a plantain tree which can never bear
his weight." " That may be so," answered the king.
" But despite the poverty of my argument, I decline to
surrender the pigeon. You can have my wealth. You
can have my kingdom. Anything I possess, I shall willingly give you, but not a suppliant whom I have promised
to protect." " All right," said the hawk ; " I take you at
your word. If I may have anything of yours that I choose,
cut off a piece of your own flesh, equal to the weight of the
pigeon. I shall accept that as a satisfactory substitute."
" Thank you," said the king, " I shall do so with pleasure."
He therefore bade a servant bring a pair of scales and cut
off from one of his thighs a piece of flesh large enough, as
he thought, to place against the pigeon. But when the
bird and the piece of flesh were set against one another in
the balance, the pigeon weighed the heavier. The king
was thus compelled to cut off another piece of his flesh,
and, strange to say, the two pieces combined proved to be
lighter than the bird. By this time the news had spread to
the zenana precincts and to every corner of the palace, that
the king was hacking himself to pieces, in obedience to a

promise which he had made to a hawk. His queen, his ministers and attendants came hurrying to the scene. They implored him to stay his hand. But he refused to listen. By this time, king Shivi had placed not one but many portions of his flesh into the scale, and notwithstanding, the pigeon continued to outweigh them all. When at last he had cast all his flesh into the balance and there was nothing left of him except bones, he made the supreme sacrifice and himself stepped into the scale.

This heroic deed excited so much wonder in heaven that the gods came to look on. The drums of heaven began to beat, while nectar bathed the limbs and garlands crowned the head of the royal sage. The celestial nymphs and choristers also appeared and danced and sang around the hero, just as they are in the habit of doing up in heaven. When every one was waiting to see what would happen next, and how the hawk would act in the face of such a unique situation, the bird flew high up into the air and disappeared from view. But the spectators could hear him calling out, " Saved! Saved ! " The monarch, as we have seen, had his doubts as to the hawk's identity, and addressing the pigeon he said, " Who is this hawk from whom I have been able to save you ? " And then the pigeon had a confession to make. " You were quite right when you said he was not an ordinary hawk. He is not a bird at all. He is Indra, the king of the celestials. And I am not a pigeon ; I am Agni, the god of fire. There was some talk in heaven about your steadfast piety, and the suggestion was made that Indra and I should come and find out how thorough and genuine you really were. And you have proved beyond the shadow of doubt that there is nobody like you in all the world. Your name will be handed down to future generations, and ages yet unborn will sing your praise." We are not told how the mutilated portions of Shivi's body were restored to their proper

16

place. But they must have been, somehow, because **Agni**, before returning to heaven, conferred on him a very unusual boon. He promised that the monarch would give birth to a son. And this duly came to pass, when a child emerged from his side.

This, however, is not the only remarkable incident in the career of the king of Benares. Because on another occasion he showed that he was as resolved to pay due and fitting respect to Brāhmins, as he was determined to hear the cry of a suppliant. It is recorded that one day a Brāhmin came to the royal palace and said that he wished to see the king. When Shivi appeared and, after the usual salutations, asked the holy man what he would like to eat, the Brāhmin answered, " I should like to eat your son. Kill him yourself and prepare his flesh with your own hands. When everything is ready, come and tell me." Without a moment's hesitation, Shivi killed and cooked his son. And when the meal was ready, he went in search of the Brāhmin to summon him to his horrid repast. At the palace gate he met some of his servants, who told him that the Brāhmin had set the palace on fire and that the female apartments and the stables, in which his horses and elephants were kept, had been burned to the ground. Shivi listened to this heart-rending report with the utmost calmness. He showed not the least signs of anger. He didn't even change colour. At that very moment the Brāhmin appeared. No word of reproach, no sign of impatience, indicated that the monarch was in the least annoyed. He merely said, " Sir, your food is ready. Will you do me the honour of coming to the guest-chamber ? " The Brāhmin accordingly accompanied his host to the room where the food had been set forth. But he did not sit down, or make any attempt to begin. Instead, he turned to the king and said, " I do not want any of this food. It is you who must eat the meal you have prepared." And even this command the

monarch was prepared to obey, because it was the command
of a Brāhmin. He therefore sat down before the dish containing his own son's flesh and was about to eat it, when the
Brāhmin seized his hand. "Of a truth," he exclaimed,
"there is nobody like you. I have tried you and tested you.
I ordered you to kill your son and to cook his flesh. I have
burned down your palace, your zenana and your stables.
You have obeyed my every injunction. You have not
shown the least anger or resentment. What a difficult
thing I asked you to do, and yet you did it, because a
Brāhmin told you to do it. You are manifestly willing to
give anything to Brāhmins."

As he listened to the Brāhmin's words of commendation,
Shivi happened to look up and saw his son, whom he had
killed and cooked, standing before him. The prince had
never looked so beautiful. There was about him an
ampler, a more divine appearance than belongs to mortals.
When the father took his son in his arms, the Brāhmin
disappeared. But those who tell the tale say he was not
an ordinary Brāhmin, but the creator himself, who came
in mortal guise to put the monarch to a searching proof,
more testing even than that by which Indra and Agni
had tried him and failed.

By this time the ministers and attendants of the king
were crowding round with words of admiration and praise.
"How was it, O king," they cried, "that you were able
to achieve such an impossible task? How did you persuade
yourself to kill and cook the heir to your throne?" To
this question Shivi replied: "I did it, not for the sake of
wealth or fame. I did it, not for the sake of happiness.
I did it, because it was the right thing to do, and it has
always been my earnest resolve to do what is right."

Mahābhārata, iii. 131, 197, xiii. 32.

XXXVIII.

THE FEAR OF LIFE AND DEATH.

" Do that to-day which you would keep for to-morrow. Do that in
the forenoon which you would keep for the afternoon. Death does not
wait for any one to see whether he has or has not performed his task."—
Mahābhārata, xii. 322. 73.

WHEN the battle between the Pāndus and Kurus, which
is described on an earlier page,[1] was over, Yudhisthira was
so overwhelmed with sorrow at the thought of having been
the cause of the deaths of so many brave men, that he
announced his intention of retiring to the forest. He
declared that the whole warrior caste was accursed. Might
and valour and wrath had always been their bane. They
had fought like dogs over a piece of meat, and now as the
victorious dog he had no pleasure in what he had won.
This lust for earthly things could only be crushed out by
a life of renunciation, by fasts and sacrifices and vows, in
the forest. There, freed from action and desire, he would
purify his soul. His brothers protested violently, asking
why they had fought if this was to be the result. He was
like a man who begins to dig a well and stops just before
he gets to the water. He was neglecting the duties of his
order, which were to fight with other kings and protect
his own subjects. They told him a story about Indra
appearing in the guise of a bird and sending back to their
homes some young men who had gone to the forest, with

---

[1] See XXV. and XXVI.

the words that the life of a householder was the truest
renunciation. They quoted the Vedas also to the same
effect, that the householder's mode of life was equal to
the other three put together, on the condition, of course,
that a man gave away the wealth he had acquired to the
Brāhmins.[1] As for killing one's enemies, it was no sin
to kill them. The gods had killed the Asuras, their elder
brothers. The beasts were constantly killing one another.
Even ascetics could not live without killing some living
creature. Some animals were so minute that the moving
of the eyelids killed them. The gods that were most
worshipped were all destroyers, and remorseless. Time
came to all and carried all away. So let him fight his foes
as other warriors did. Worship the gods and offer sacrifices
with many gifts to the Brāhmins. That was the teaching
of the wise. Besides, it was not possible to kill the soul.
So one could not be said to kill anybody. The soul passed
from body to body like a man moving to a new house.
They told him, too, of a king whose wife, by her wise words,
persuaded him from becoming a forest-dweller. She said
it was only a poor man, abandoned by his friends, who
could find happiness in the shaven head and the brown
robe of the ascetic. It was not for a king who had fed
thousands of Brāhmins to go and ask these very men for
a handful of grain. If all men became beggars, who would
be left to feed them ? Men thought they became free from
desire because they wandered about with the beggar's bowl,
but they were still in bondage to desire ; were it desire
for a handful of barley and nothing more, it would still be
desire. He could remain a king, and yet break the fetters
of the world. If he did that, he would really be a liberated
man, and in the end reach the regions of the blessed.

[1] The four modes or stages of life through which all Brāhmins at least
were supposed to pass : (1) Student of Vedas ; (2) Householder ;
(3) Forest-dweller ; (4) Religious mendicant.

Yudhisthira was not persuaded. He admitted that the
Vedas were conflicting in their teaching. Sometimes they
preached action, sometimes they bade men refrain from
acts. For himself, he thought their praise of wealth was
quite wrong, and he was certain that men reached a higher
state of bliss by way of renunciation. The practice of
yoga, without a doubt, procured salvation, though in these
days, he confessed, there were men going about giving
lectures to large numbers of people, denying the existence
of the soul, and speaking against the doctrine of liberation.
They were very learned men, well versed in logic, but they
were wicked men and fools for all that.

Certain sages then took part in the discussion. They
advised him to do his duty as a king for the present, and
afterwards he could go to the forest. The four modes of
life should be followed in turn. What would happen to
the sacrifices if there were no wealth ? He must not
speak so disparagingly of wealth. Let him give gifts, and
rule the earth righteously for the good of Brāhmins and
cows, and he would be rewarded in the end. It was the
business of Brāhmins to indulge in penance, sacrifice,
forgiveness, living in solitude and contentment. A fourth
part only of a Brāhmin's virtue was expected from a member
of the warrior caste, and the life of a good householder
was really the most difficult of all, especially for a king,
who had to bear the burden of his kingdom. One of the
rishis in particular urged him not to indulge in useless
grief. There was a mean in all things. It was only the
fool who was ever really happy and content ; the fool and
the man with all his passions under control. But to be
ever thinking about others' sorrows, would rob him of
happiness entirely. Let him remember that Time carried
all men away. We met with one another, even our dearest,
like travellers meeting at an inn. There was nothing we
could call our own. Our fathers were dead and we too

would die. Death and Disease, like a pair of wolves, were ceaselessly devouring all. Destiny was a wonderful thing. The rich man died in his strength and youth ; the poor man dragged on his miserable life for a hundred years. The rich had no appetite, while the poor were able to digest pieces of wood. People asked if the Supreme Being was responsible, or man. Some spoke of chance, and others of destiny. If one man suffered for the sins due to another's action, then we should put all the responsibility on God. On the other hand, if a man was the real agent of all his acts, good and evil, he did not think there was room for God at all, and what a man had done could bring no evil effects upon him. What happened, in his opinion, happened because it was ordained, and from destiny no one could escape. Destiny was the result of one's deeds in a former life, and for that no sin attached as far as this life was concerned. Man's acts, be they good or bad, were revolving unceasingly as on a wheel, and the fruits of these acts man unceasingly reaped. The sum of the whole matter was, to do his duty as a member of the warrior caste, and at the same time perform those acts of expiation and sacrifice which would cleanse him of all his sins.[1]

Yudhisthira, however, was not content, and when he visited his dying friend, the illustrious Bhīshma, and asked his counsel on these and other matters, the aged hero showed by his replies that many had begun to doubt if sacrifice and other religious rites conferred any lasting benefit on the soul. By way of an illustration, he gave an account of a discussion which had taken place between an old man and his son. The father was an orthodox

---

[1] There is a curious list given of the sins that require expiation. They are set down together, as if on the same level. The student who rises before the sun ; the man with a rotten nail or black teeth ; the man who marries before his elder brother ; the man who kills a Brāhmin ; the man who speaks evil of others, etc.

believer, putting his trust in the teaching and rites of
the Vedas, while the son had adopted the doctrines of
Liberation. " Tell me, father," said the young man,
" what I ought to do. Life is passing very quickly. Tell
me what is the best way to acquire virtue." The father
replied in the usual fashion. " You know what has been
appointed. The four stages through which we must all
travel. There is first the life of the student, when you
read the Vedas and practise the duties connected there-
with. When that stage is over, you must become a
householder, marry and have children. If you don't do
that, your ancestors cannot hope to escape from hell.
Having fulfilled the duties of a householder, lighted the
family fire and performed the sacrifices which belong to
that mode of life, you will spend the rest of your days,
first as a forest-dweller, and last of all as a religious
mendicant."

To the father's amazement, the youth had nothing but
scorn for such an easy-going scheme. He was deeply
impressed by the sorrow of life, and he could not understand how his father could talk so calmly, when he knew
that the world was surrounded on all sides by implacable
foes. When he said this, the father intervened : " I don't
understand what you are saying, my son. Are you trying
to frighten me ? Who is attacking the world ? Who has
surrounded it on every side ? " " Have you never heard
of Death, father ? How can you be so happy," said the
youth, " when you think of Disease, old age and Death."
And then he began to dwell on the universality of Disease,
old age and Death ; and on how Death comes to all, the
wise and the ignorant, the weak and the strong, the happy
and the sad ; came, too, when they did not expect him,
breaking in upon their schemes and hopes and joys, like
a tiger carrying off a sleeping deer. It was truth alone
that could conquer Death. Immortality dwelt with

Truth. With Truth in his possession, he would escape
from Death, and become like one of the immortals. By
controlling his senses and refraining from injury to all
creatures in thought, word and deed, he would perform
the sacrifice of peace. He could not possibly take part
in an animal sacrifice. It was not only full of cruelty,
but it produced very uncertain rewards. Nor did he need
children to rescue him from hell.[1] He would rest on his
own self. There was no reward like knowledge ; no
penance like truth ; no sorrow like attachment to the
world ; no happiness except in renunciation.

Bhīshma continued the discussion by quoting the teaching of various eminent sages, all of which went to show
that life itself was the root of all sorrow, and that man's
one desire was to be freed from the burden of rebirth.
" The river of life," he said, " is full of dread, and the
soul has to pass endless ages of time before it can be set
free. As a goldsmith purifies gold of its dross, so has the
individual soul to purify itself by means of countless
rebirths. Think of thousands of lakes and of immense
size ; think of men trying to dry them up by taking out
each day as much water as would cling to a single hair,
and you will realise the length of time required by one
created soul to pass from its beginning to the hour when
it ceases to be. During its many million stages of existence, the soul may have to suffer in hell for many thousands
of Kalpas, and a Kalpa lasts for 4320 million years.
On the other hand, the soul may go to the upper world
and live as a god. But until the soul is emancipated,
heaven is just a sort of hell. Because, even in heaven,
no one can live for ever. Time after time the soul has
to come back to earth. Time after time it will have to
revisit either heaven or hell. When the dissolution of all

---

[1] A son is necessary to offer sacrifices to his deceased ancestors. They
cannot escape from hell otherwise.

things takes place at the end of a Kalpa, it is only the man who has been able to destroy his gross body by means of *yoga* discipline, who enters Brahm. But all others, be they gods or men, with an unspent capital of merit, take the position in the new universe that they occupied in the old. The gods who have nothing to their credit, must descend to earth and be born as men. It is only when a man's soul becomes white that he does not return."

In another passage, Bhīshma, by drawing on his stock of wise saws and instances, showed how some people had foolishly imagined that liberation was the same as annihilation. It was the consummation, not the extinction, of life. Just as smaller rivers fall into larger rivers and lose their old forms and names ; just as these larger rivers again fall into the ocean and lose their separate existence in the sea, in the same way takes place that form of extinction which is called liberation, when the individual soul is lost in Brahm.

Mahābhārata, xii. 7. 30. 219. 277–280.

XXXIX.

THE OLD AND THE NEW.

"The red garment, the shaven head, the triple staff and the water-pot are only external modes of life. They do not help us to secure Liberation."—*Mahābhārata*, xii. 321. 47.

A CELESTIAL one day came to visit king Nahusha. In accordance with the " true, ancient and eternal injunction of the Vedas," the monarch was about to slay a cow in honour of his guest.[1] But Kapila,[2] the philosopher, happened to be present, and with the piety and firmness which always characterised him he cried out, " Oh, ye Vedas ! " Now there was another sage also present who did not at all approve of Kapila's sentiments in this matter, and to make the protest more effective he entered into the body of the cow, and, using the cow as his mouthpiece, sternly told Kapila to be silent. It was very wrong indeed to speak disrespectfully of the Vedas which, as every one knew, were the very words of God. The retort led to a long discussion in which Kapila, by way of introduction, said he had no wish to speak lightly of the sacred writings. He acknowledged that they prescribed a great many rules and regulations for the guidance of mankind, and the acts which they told us to perform undoubtedly led to heaven. He also knew that the four modes of

---

[1] The Sanskrit word for guest is *goghna*, cow-killer.

[2] Kapila was the founder of the Sānkhya philosophy. He destroyed the 60,000 sons of Sagara with his frown (VIII.).

life—the student, the householder, the hermit and the religious mendicant—had each and all of them their own separate duties which conferred on each their own characteristic rewards. But while the Vedas said we were to perform acts, it also said we were to refrain from acts. And from that he inferred that if there was merit in abstention, there must be demerit in performance. He would therefore be grateful if the cow would advise him. He confessed it was a very difficult question indeed, but could she prove from Scripture that there was any higher religion than the religion of *harmlessness*?

To this the inspired cow replied, that not only was the flesh of sheep and goats, cows and horses, used as food, but these animals, as well as grains of various kinds, were offered in sacrifice. It was an ordinance of Brahmā that both gods and men should offer sacrifices, and it was a very ancient ordinance. She had never heard before of any learned person who refrained from taking part in them. Indeed, the whole world depended for its security on the due performance of sacrificial rites, and the man who adhered to this ancient ordinance and repeated the sacred syllables OM and Vashat, had nothing to fear about what would happen to him after death. Besides that, the animals he sacrificed shared in the reward, because both the sacrificer and the animals he killed went to heaven together. When that was the case, it was absurd to speak of cruelty being shown to an animal that was both grateful and pleased that it had been used in such a way. The cow then went on to say that she knew what Kapila was aiming at. He was evidently a follower of the doctrine of Liberation, but she was of the opinion that these new ideas about obtaining absorption in Brahm, what they called Emancipation, were destructive of the real teaching of the Vedas. They were the invention of clever men who had failed in life and were too lazy to work. It was by practising the rule laid down in scripture that we overcame the power of sin, and nobody who failed to perform these rules could ever attain to Brahm.

To these arguments, Kapila replied that the performance of acts could only secure a temporary reward. He did not deny that the life of the householder, with its sacrifices and gifts, produced a certain amount of merit, but he wanted something more permanent than that. Even the gods had got confused and helpless in trying to find out the new path. The true path, however, could be found, and when it was found the householder would discover that he did not require to perform the duties of the householder. What that path was, he would explain. Acts and their performance no doubt helped to purify the body, but knowledge is the *highest end*. This knowledge can only be acquired by self-control and the practices of *yoga*. What these practices of *yoga* were, he did not say ; but in speaking of self-control he emphasised the need of forgiveness, benevolence, mercy and truth, and said that the four doors of the body, the hands and feet, the tongue, the stomach and desire, must be made the servants and not the masters of the soul. But it is evident that Kapila's chief object was to secure correct knowledge, and to see himself at one with the Universal Soul. For that is the goal, the supreme bliss of emancipation ; and here is the final verdict of scripture, that this universe exists and does not exist.

The sage concluded his observations by saying, possibly by way of concession to the orthodox, " He who is master of the Vedas knows everything, because everything is established in the Vedas. The present, the past and the future all exist in the Vedas." But he could not avoid the parting jibe, that the man who is not thoroughly acquainted with the Vedas is only a bag of wind.

Mahābhārata, xii. 268–270.

XL.

THE FRIEND OF ALL THE WORLD.

" For the weak as well as for the strong, forgiveness is an ornament. What can a wicked man do to him who has the sword of peace in his hand ? "—Mahābhārata, v. 33. 54.

JĀJALI was a very eminent ascetic. He had a thorough knowledge of the Vedas, and attended to the sacrificial fire. He observed long fasts. During the rainy season he slept under the open sky by night and lay in water by day. In the hot weather he scorned to seek protection from either the burning sun or scorching wind. He made for himself the most uncomfortable beds. He smeared his body and unkempt locks with filth and clay. If he wore any garments at all, they were made of rags and skins. He travelled over the whole earth ; dwelt in the forests, made his home among the mountains or by the shores of the ocean. On one occasion when he was beside the ocean he resolved to conceal himself beneath its waters. He was able to do so by virtue of the ascetic merit which he had acquired. Indeed, he could do much more than that, for he could project his mind in every direction and make himself acquainted with all that was happening beyond the farthest stars. As he thus lay at the bottom of the ocean, thinking of how his mind could travel everywhere, pride filled his heart, and he told himself that there was nobody like him in all the universe. As he made this boast, a voice spoke in his ear. It was the voice of certain evil spirits who had been watching him. " You should not have made that boast, most noble Brāhmin. There is a shopkeeper of our acquaintance, a very virtuous man. He lives in Benares and earns his livelihood by buying and selling. But we don't think that even he would be entitled to say of himself what you have said about yourself." " A shopkeeper ! " said the ascetic. " I should like very much to see this wonderful shopkeeper. Tell me where he lives, and how to get there." In obedience to this request, the evil spirits lifted the ascetic out of the water and gave him directions as to the way he ought to travel.

Jājali, very much perturbed in mind, set out for Benares. But on the way he came to a forest, where he stayed his course and gave himself afresh to a prolonged period of asceticism. For many days he abstained entirely from food, and, in particular, stood absolutely motionless and still. He never moved a muscle, and to all appearance was much more like a wooden pillar than a man, with his great mass of filthy and dishevelled hair on top. And it was not long before two birds, in search of a place to build their nest, decided that no better spot could be found anywhere than the ascetic's head. And so they built their nest among his hair, making use of straw and leaves. The nest contained a full clutch of eggs in due course, but the ascetic never moved. Indeed, by this time pity would have prevented him from doing so. Eventually the eggs were hatched, the young birds were born. Days passed, and their feathers grew. More days passed, and they learned to fly. As their courage increased, the young birds would go off with their parents for a few hours and eventually for a whole day, in search of food. One should have thought that the ascetic had fulfilled any obligation that might be supposed to rest upon him. But no ! He would not disappoint his guests. Once they were absent for a whole week, but he waited to see if they came back.

When they did come back he was there, waiting for them, as motionless as ever, resolved that he would not, by any movement of his, make them afraid. Finally, he waited a month, and when they did not return he decided that they had abandoned their nest for ever, and that he was at liberty to move. Unfortunately, Jājali felt very puffed up as he thought of his noble conduct. Once more he said to himself, " There is nobody like me in all the wide world. I have acquired a very large store of merit by this unselfish act." Indeed, he felt so pleased with himself that he slapped his arms in his joy, and shouted out loud, " There is nobody my equal anywhere." And once more he heard a voice. This time it was a voice from heaven : " Jājali ! don't say that. You are not as good a man as the shop-keeper in Benares, and even he would not dare to boast as you have done."

When the evil spirits quoted the shopkeeper to him, the ascetic felt very depressed. This time his heart was filled with anger, and he decided that he would go to Benares without further delay and see the wonderful shopkeeper who had twice been cast in his teeth. But before he set out he bathed in a river, poured libations on the sacred fire, and worshipped the rising sun. At length he came to Benares, and one of the first persons he saw was the shop-keeper busily engaged in his shop, buying and selling. Whenever the shopkeeper saw him he called out a welcome. " I have been expecting you, oh most noble Brāhmin, for quite a long time. I know all about your great asceticism, of how you lived immersed in the ocean, and of what you have done since, allowing the birds to build a nest in your hair. I know, too, how proud you were of that, and of how a voice from heaven rebuked you. You were angry with the heavenly voice, and that is why you came here. You wish to see me. Tell me what you want. I shall do my best to help you."

To these observations the Brāhmin ascetic replied : " You are a shopkeeper, my friend, and the son of a shopkeeper. How is it that a person like you, who spend your days buying and selling, has acquired so much knowledge and so much wisdom ? Where did you get it ? That is the question I wish to ask." In answer, the shopkeeper said : " My knowledge and wisdom consist in nothing but this. I follow after and obey that *ancient morality* which everybody knows and which consists of universal friendliness and kindness to man and beast.[1] I earn my livelihood by trade (and he specified the things that he bought and sold, consisting chiefly of scents and juices extracted from the lotus and other plants). But I never trade in intoxicants of any kind. My scales are always just, and I never cheat any one, because I seek to be the friend of all creatures, and I never injure any one in thought, word or deed. In fact, I treat all with whom I come in contact with absolute impartiality. I quarrel with no one, I fear no one, I love no one, I hate no one, I praise no one, I censure no one, and I desire nothing. A clod of earth, a stone, and a piece of gold are all the same to me. I follow the example of good men before me, who, with their sons and grandsons, have observed the rules laid down in scripture. And I am convinced that the life I live is the life that secures prosperity and heaven quite as surely as the life that is devoted to penance and sacrifice, to the making of gifts and truth." As he proceeded in his talk, the shopkeeper became more assertive, using language hardly consistent with what he had said about his abstention from either praise or blame. He not only condemned the killing

---

[1] " ancient morality " (*sanātan dharma*), Mr. Dutt translates it. *Dharma* means the prescribed course of conduct, duty, anything right, proper or just, virtue, morality, merit, good works, usage, practice, religion, piety. See Monier Williams, *Sanskrit Dictionary*. " *course of conduct prescribed from ancient times* " may be better.

of animals, but expressed his disapproval of agriculture, because the plough gives pain to the earth and causes the death of many minute creatures buried in the soil, apart from the unwilling labour it extracted from bullocks and slaves. As for animal sacrifices, especially of the cow, he expressed his great abhorrence, and said they had been initiated by greedy priests. The true sacrifice was the sacrifice performed by the mind, and if they had sacrifices at all, people should use herbs, and fruits, and balls of rice. Nor did he believe in pilgrimages. There was no need to wander over the earth, visiting sacred rivers and mountains. There was no place so holy as the soul itself.

These animadversions roused the indignation of the ascetic, and he told the holder of scales, as he called him, that he was an atheist. How were men to live if they did not plough the ground? Where would they get food? And as for sacrifices, the world would come to an end if we gave them up. But the shopkeeper asserted that he believed in sacrifice, the true kind of sacrifice, and he was sorry to think that Brāhmins had so far forgotten themselves as to practise a class of sacrifice that belonged to the warrior and not to the priestly caste. And he was sure that if only men could go back to the real teaching of the Vedas, they would find that they did not need to plough the ground. In ancient days the earth spontaneously yielded all that was required. The blessing of the sages had such a wonderful effect that herbs and plants grew of themselves. The shopkeeper ended his discourse (it looks like an interpolation) by advising the ascetic to engage in the practice of *yoga*, and to meditate on the sacred syllable OM. It was the only way to secure absorption in Brahm. But he had yet another surprise for his guest, for he summoned to his presence the very birds that had built their nest in Jājali's hair, and what was still more wonderful, the shopkeeper invited them to confirm the teaching about harmlessness which he had imparted to their benefactor. This the birds proceeded to do, even quoting scripture in support of the arguments which they put forward, and introducing a new doctrine, the doctrine of faith, which they advised him to cultivate without further delay.

Despite the wealth and variety of the arguments which had been poured upon him, it does not seem as if the ascetic was convinced, because we are told that both he and the shopkeeper died very soon after, and that they went to the particular heaven which they had each acquired as a result of their own very different modes of life.

Mahābhārata, xii. 261–264.

XLI.

I AND THOU.

"A man may obtain heaven by asceticism; he may secure objects of enjoyment by making gifts; he may destroy all his sins by bathing at the holy places : but complete emancipation cannot be obtained without knowledge."—*Mahābhārata*, iii. 199. 118.

MORE than two thousand million years ago there was a king of India whose name was Bharata. Like his father and grandfather before him, he spent his declining years in the practice of asceticism. In order that he might do so with perfect devotion, he resigned his empire into the hands of his son and retired to the forest. Now one might have thought that his devotion to Vishnu, as well as the sacredness of Sālagrām, his place of retirement, would have secured for him final liberation from the burden of rebirth. But he failed in his object and was born again, first as a deer and then as a Brāhmin, before he achieved that blessed goal. How this delay occurred the following narrative will explain.

When the monarch first retired to Sālagrām he did nothing but repeat the names of Vishnu. Not even in his dreams did any other name present itself to his mind. And on these names he meditated night and day. In fact, apart from accepting fuel, flowers and sacred grass for the worship of that god, he performed no other religious rites of any kind, so absorbed was he in his devotion to the sacred names. But it so chanced that one day he

went to bathe in a certain river. When he was in the
water a deer that had come to drink was so alarmed by
the roar of a lion that she gave sudden birth to her young.
Unfortunately she died in the act of parturition, and her
offspring fell into the stream. Had the king not gone
to the rescue, the poor little creature would have been
drowned. But Bharata plunged into the water, brought
it safe to land and carried it to his hermitage. As the
days passed he grew fonder and fonder of the creature he
had saved. It played about his cell, or grazed on the
grass outside the hermitage. Gradually he became so
devoted to it that he could think of nothing else, and if
it chanced to stray into the forest, or was longer away
than usual, his anxiety became acute, and he wondered
if some wild beast had destroyed it. And thus it came
to pass that the monarch who had abandoned home and
children, wealth and power, could think of nothing but
his four-footed companion. And when, in course of time,
he died, it was not Vishnu who occupied his thoughts.
In the moment of death, both eyes and thoughts were
turned to the creature that he loved. Final liberation
was therefore not possible for one who had gone so far
astray. And because his last thoughts had been centred
on a deer, it was as a deer that Bharata was born in his
next birth. But happily he was able to remember who
he had been in his former life, able to remember also the
foolishness of which he had been guilty. He therefore
abandoned his mother not long after he was born, and
made once more for Sālagrām, the scene of his past efforts
and failures. By living on grass and leaves he was able
to atone for what he had done, with the result that in
his next life he was born as a Brāhmin in a family noted
for its piety and asceticism. And once more he was able
to remember what had happened to him in his former
births. We are not told how he acquired it, but it is

said that Bharata was endowed with all true wisdom,
though he never studied the Vedas or performed any
religious ceremonies. Indeed his manner of treating those
with whom he came in contact led them to believe that he
was an ignorant and stupid Brāhmin. He replied in a
rude and ungrammatical way when any one spoke to him,
and he added to the delusion by wearing dirty clothes,
never washing his body, and letting saliva dribble from
his mouth. But Bharata didn't worry about what people
said concerning him. Because, if you are anxious to retain
the respect of men, you won't make progress in piety.
The more they despise you, the more likely you are to
attain your end. That at least is what philosophers tell
you, and for that reason Bharata assumed the appearance
of a crazy idiot in the eye of the world.

But when his father died, Bharata's brothers and cousins
took advantage of his simplicity. They sent him to work
in the fields, and the only recompense he received was
the coarsest and most unsavoury food. Others also
shared in the exploiting of the poor simpleton, and because
he was strong and vigorous in body, he was at the disposal
of every one who chose to bend him to their needs. At
last he was commandeered by a king's steward to assist
in carrying the royal palanquin. One day this king set
out to visit the famous sage Kapila, and the Brāhmin
was one of those who were compelled to carry the palanquin. None of the bearers were paid for their work, but
while the others marched sturdily on, Bharata, plunged in
thought, lagged behind his companions. Remembering
his former lives and the sins of which he had been guilty,
he was glad to think that by bearing burdens he was
able to do something by way of atonement. His slower
movements, however, caused the palanquin to jolt badly,
and the king several times ordered the bearers to keep
step. When he had protested more than once without

getting any satisfaction, one of the bearers at last replied that it was the Brāhmin's fault, not theirs. "How is this?" said the king. "You look strong and hearty; are you so very tired that you cannot keep step with the others and bear your proper share?" To these remonstrances Bharata replied by a series of questions relating to the distinction between *I* and *Thou*. "You say that I look strong and hearty. You say that you see me and that I am not bearing my proper share. What do you mean by *I* and *Thou*? What part of *me* have you seen? The feet rest on the ground, the feet support the legs, the legs the thighs, and so on up to the shoulders, and the shoulders support the palanquin. How then can it be said that the palanquin is my burden?" And so, pointing to the king's body, he said, "This body, which is seated in the palanquin, is defined as *Thou*. Tell me what is *I* and what is *Thou*, or for that matter, tell me what *others* are. Acted on by the three qualities, the elements, of which I and Thou and Others are composed, assume bodily shape. They have different names, god or demon, man or beast, bird or tree; and they are what they are, because of the acts that ignorance has accumulated. But there is one Supreme Soul, devoid of all qualities, present in them all." With much more of the same kind Bharata closed his observations by saying that the substance of the palanquin was the substance of the king, the substance of himself and the substance of all others. This flow of wisdom was too much for the king. He came tumbling out of his litter and fell at the Brāhmin's feet. "Have mercy upon me," he cried, "and tell me who you are. You look like a fool; but I feel sure that you must be Kapila, the great sage, to whose hermitage we are now travelling." This led to further discourse, when the Brāhmin, not unnaturally in view of what he had already said, replied that it was impossible to say who

he was. Because when one has arrived at a knowledge
of the truth, how can one speak of his own individuality
and say, " This is I."

The king, greatly impressed by this fresh outburst of
wisdom, declared that it was unnecessary for him to travel
any farther. Every one knew that Kapila was a portion
of Vishnu himself, and he was confident that that venerable
person had taken compassion upon him, and was now standing before him in the person of the Brāhmin. The object
of his journey had been to ask what was the best and most
excellent object on which a man could set his heart, and
he hoped the Brāhmin would be good enough to tell him
what it was. This fresh question produced another lengthy
reply. As the Brāhmin pointed out, the king was asking
what was *the best*, when he ought to be asking what was the
supreme and final truth. No doubt when men worshipped
the gods, hoping thereby to obtain offspring, power or
wealth or happiness in heaven, they were seeking what
they thought was *the best*. But none of these was man's
chief end. How could wealth be called man's chief end,
when it was surrendered for the sake of virtue, or more
commonly spent in gratifying our material desires ? Nor
could offspring be reckoned as the supreme and final
truth, because the son who was *the best* in his father's eyes,
began to hope for a son who would be *the best* to him.
Reference had been made to religious rites and ceremonies.
They were very good in their own way. But how could
things like fuel, clarified butter and sacrificial grass,
things that perished in the using, serve more than a
temporary purpose ? It was quite certain that no form
of worship could achieve for us eternal truth. Even
meditation, in which we sought to achieve union with
the Supreme, was not efficacious ; because the very act
of seeking implied that the seeker was making a distinction that did not exist, meditating on a difference

when there was no difference, trying to unite what was already *one*.

As the king had said, it was not necessary to go to Kapila, when he had such a competent instructor near at hand. And he profited greatly by what he heard. He learned to recognise that there is no other than Vishnu, and to say, " He is I, he is thou, he is all ! this universe is his form." Bharata himself, as we can see, had already acquired the true wisdom in all its fulness, and in consequence was never born any more, being freed from the burden of future lives.

Vishnu Purāna, ii. 13, 14.

XLII.

STRIVING AFTER UNITY.

" Freed from both merit and demerit, the individual soul enters the
Supreme Soul which is shorn of all attributes . . . and does not return."
—Mahābhārata, xii. 302. 97.

THE god Brahmā had a son called Ribhu, famous for his
piety and profoundly versed in the doctrine of unity.
Among his many disciples was a nephew of his own, a
youth named Nidāgha.   When his course of instruction was
over, this youth returned to his father's home in a distant
city.   But though his disciple was far away, his old instructor had not forgotten him, and at the end of three
hundred and sixty thousand years he resolved to go and
see what progress he was making in his studies.   Nidāgha
was standing at the door of his house when his spiritual
teacher drew near.   After the usual greetings were over and
the hands and feet of the honoured guest had been duly
washed, Ribhu, when asked to eat, said he had no liking
for ordinary and indifferent food.   Indeed he declined to
eat the plain rice, barley and pulse that were set before
him, and said he would have nothing but the very best ;
rice boiled with sugar, wheaten cakes and milk, curds,
fruit and molasses.   When this sweet and savoury food
had been consumed, the disciple asked his master if he
had had enough, and was satisfied with its quality and taste.
He also asked Ribhu where he was living, where he was
going, and from whence he had come.   To this Ribhu

replied by telling his disciple not to ask so many foolish questions. It was a stupid thing to say, "Where are you going? where have you come from? and so on." The soul of man went everywhere. He was neither going nor coming, nor was he dwelling in any one place. He added, "Nor are you, you; nor are others, others; nor am I, I." As for his hunger, of course, a hungry man's hunger was satisfied when he had finished his meal, and one was pleased when hunger and thirst were removed. That was all. Probably his disciple wondered why, if that was the case, he made so strong a demand for special food. He would explain. There was really no difference between sweetened and unsweetened food. They were both the same. If you would only think a thing to be sweet, it would become sweet; while sweet things cease to be sweet, as the sense of repletion grows. No food was equally delightful at the beginning, middle and end of a meal. Just as a house is strengthened by applying fresh plaster, so is a man's body maintained by earthly atoms. Barley, wheat, butter, oil, milk, treacle, fruits and the like are made of earthly atoms, and it is their function to support and strengthen the human frame. Ribhu ended this very irrelevant explanation by saying he hoped his pupil had understood what was sweet and what was not sweet. If he would grasp the truths he had expounded to him and allow his mind to be possessed by the notion of identity, he would at length secure final liberation. Nidāgha said he was quite overwhelmed by the wisdom that had dropped from his master's lips, and that the infatuation of his mind had been entirely removed. After a few more observations on the undivided nature of the Supreme Spirit which is Vishnu, Ribhu went away.

At the end of another period of three hundred and sixty thousand years, Ribhu resolved to pay a second visit to the town in which his favourite disciple dwelt, and impart still

further wisdom. As he drew near the city gate he saw
his pupil. He looked very starved and emaciated. On his
head was a bundle of fuel and sacrificial grass which he
had brought from the forest. And he was standing apart
to avoid a great crowd of people watching their king as
he entered the town riding on an elephant. Approaching Nidāgha, Ribhu asked him who among the crowd
was the king, and who were the others. Nidāgha replied
that the person seated on the elephant was the king,
and the others were his attendants. "You have pointed
out to me the king and the elephant," said Ribhu, "but
will you be good enough to explain which is the elephant
and which is the king ?" "The elephant is beneath, and
the king is above," was Nidāgha's reply. "Such an
answer," said Ribhu, "explains nothing. You must first
tell me what you mean by *beneath* and *above*." This was
too much for the victim of these many questions. And
so, dropping his bundle of grass and fuel, he jumped on
the top of his interrogator with the cry, "I am *above* like
the rajah and you are *beneath* like the elephant. I hope
you understand now." But Ribhu was not to be silenced,
for, as he panted beneath the weight of his assailant, he
was able to say, "That is all very well ; but please answer
this question also. It seems that I am like the elephant
and you are like the rajah ; but which of us two, pray,
is you and which of us is I." At last Nidāgha's eyes were
opened. He fell at Ribhu's feet with the words, "You
must be my old teacher. There is no other person alive
so deeply impressed with the doctrines and principles of
unity." It is not said what happened to Ribhu, but his
disciple, we are told, was so impressed by this practical and
final lesson of his master, that he learned the supreme secret.
He saw that himself and all others were one, not many, and
that this *one* is Vishnu, from whom nothing is distinct.

Vishnu Purāna, ii. 16.

XLIII.

WHAT HAPPENS AFTER DEATH.

" Acquire that wealth which has no fear from either kings or thieves and which we have not to renounce, even at death.   Except our good and evil deeds, nothing follows us to the other world."—*Mahābhārata*, xii. 322. 46. 51.

" It is either by the divine will, or by Destiny, or as the result of their own acts (*karma*), that men attain to happiness or misery."—*Mahābhārata*, iii. 183. 86.

THERE was once a Brāhmin who sought to win the favour of the gods by presenting to the priests certain cows, the only wealth he had. As he looked at the cows, which seemed to be poor creatures, the Brāhmin's son said to himself, " My father won't acquire much merit by surrendering these." And so, seized by a sudden impulse, he turned to his father and said : " You are giving away all your wealth. To whom are you going to give *me* ? " But the father made no reply. The son waited for a little and put the question again. And once more the father was silent. When he asked the same question a third time, however, the Brāhmin lost his temper and cried, " To whom shall I give *you* ? I give you to Death."

In consequence of this reply, which was equivalent to an imprecation, the youth descended to the lower world. But Yama, the lord of death, was absent when he arrived there, and did not appear till three days had passed. Now, it is a very grievous sin to be wanting in hospitality

to Brāhmins. It is an omission which may involve the
loss of children and cattle, as well as the merit one has
acquired by sacrifices and other meritorious deeds.
Accordingly when Yama returned to his home and found
that the youth had been in his kingdom for three days
without receiving any entertainment, he was very much
distressed and told his guest, by way of compensation, to
ask for three boons. The first boon the young man asked
was that he might return to the upper world and be reconciled to his father, and the second was that he might
obtain such a knowledge of a particular sacrifice, which
he specified, as would bring him safe to heaven. Both
these requests the lord of death readily granted. But
when the youth announced his third boon, Yama was
most unwilling to grant it. It was as follows : " Tell me
what happens to people when they die. There is a great
diversity of opinion on that question. Some say that
the soul continues to exist, but others say that it doesn't.
Which is true ? Nobody can answer that question better
than you." " You are putting a very difficult question ;
one that is not at all easy to answer or to understand,"
said Death. " Even the gods had many doubts concerning it in former days. And I beg you not to insist
on an answer. Ask me for something else. Ask for
length of days for yourself ; ask for sons and grandsons
who will live till they are a hundred years old ; ask for
horses, elephants and cattle ; ask for wealth ; I will make
you one of the great ones of the earth ; whatever is
difficult to obtain, ask for it, and it is yours ; heavenly
nymphs even will be at your disposal, the like of whom
no mortal man has ever seen. But do not ask me what
happens after death."

The young Brāhmin, however, would not take a refusal.
" None of the things you offer me, O Death, last for
ever. No matter how long I live, I must die sometime,

and old age is not an unmixed blessing. And how can
wealth afford permanent satisfaction. And it is the same
with the pleasures of the flesh. I want to know the
secret. I must obtain that which will abide for ever in
the midst of a changing world." When Death saw that
the youth was determined to have an answer to his
question, he complimented him on having so steadfastly
resolved to choose the better part. For a wide gulf
divided those who chose the pleasant from those who
chose the good. He was a wise man, indeed, who when
pleasure was offered to him scrutinised it carefully. It
was love of pleasure, love of wealth and what it could
procure, that caused the endless succession of rebirths
to which living creatures were exposed. And how very
few were able to guide the soul along the narrow path of
truth, sharp as a razor's edge, which led to liberation.
Ignorance was the root of all this evil, and there were
many blind guides, who led others as blind as themselves
hither and thither in an endless maze. Death thereupon
proceeded to enlarge on the true doctrine. Before any
one could achieve it, he must learn to deny himself and
cultivate the art of meditation. The best help of all was
the repetition of the sacred syllable OM, because by a
true knowledge of that syllable a man secured happiness
in the world of Brahm. The practice of *yoga* was also
essential. And yet the individual soul did not obtain a
knowledge of the Universal Soul by any effort of his own.
It was by the grace of the Creator. Nor was it by virtue
of any one's wisdom and learning that this was achieved.
The Universal Soul revealed himself to his own elect.
But those who were chosen must not be of evil life, or
lacking in tranquillity. The Universal Soul could not be
known by such as these.[1] The soul never dies and is

---

[1] This was in opposition to what Hume calls the unbridled licen-
tiousness of the earlier *Upanishads*, where the possession of some

never born; it lives for ever and passes from body to
body.

> "The smiter thinks that he can slay,
> The smitten fears that he is slain,
> The thoughts of both alike are vain,
> The soul survives the murderous fray." [1]

But the soul is equally deceived if it distinguishes
between itself and the world, or between itself and the
Universal Soul. The individual soul must learn to recognise itself as God, but the Universal Soul cannot be defined.
You can only say: It exists; it is *that*. " Higher than
the Person, there is nothing at all. That is the goal." [2]

When the youth had acquired this instruction and a
great deal more, and had duly practised the system of
yoga, he became free from desire; he was delivered from
the burden of rebirth and was absorbed in Brahm. And
what he accomplished is possible for others also, if they
follow his example.

Katha Upanishad.

metaphysical knowledge permits the knower unblushingly to continue
in what seems to be much evil. See *Thirteen Principal Upanishads*,
p. 60.

[1] Quoted from Muir's metrical version of the story. *O. S. T.*, vol. v.
p. 334.

[2] Hume, p. 352.

XLIV.

HOW TO PLEASE GOD.

" Bathing at all the holy places and kindness to all beings, these are
equal. Perhaps kindness is better."—*Mahābhārata*, v. 35. 2.
" Fasting and penance, however much they weaken the body, cannot
destroy sins."—*Mahābhārata*, iii. 199. 102.

WHEN any one dies, he goes down to the kingdom of
Yama, the god of death, and there he is subjected to the
most cruel punishments. But that is not the end. When
a certain period has elapsed the soul is released, but only
that it may return to one of the upper worlds, when it is
born again, it may be as a god, it may be as a man, or it
may be as one of the lower creatures.[1]

Such were the thoughts that perplexed the disciple of
one of the ancient sages, and he asked his master if there
was no course of action by which a man could free himself
from the grasp of Death. The sage said that his pupil
was standing on the borderland of a great mystery. But
he would repeat to him what he had once heard. He had
never heard any one speak of it before or since. It was
an account of a conversation which had taken place between
the god of the dead and one of his messengers. This
messenger was setting out for the upper world and he
carried in his hand the noose with which he binds the
spirits of the dead and takes them captive down to hell.

[1] Even Brahmā, the creator god, is not exempt. Long though his
life may be, there is a limit to his existence. Of Brahm, the spirit from
whom the universe proceeds and into whom it all dissolves, of him alone
can it be said that he is eternal.

" Remember," said Yama, " that you do not touch any of the worshippers of Vishnu. I am the lord of all creatures. Brahmā appointed me to act as judge over the deeds of men, but the worshippers of Vishnu are absolutely free from my control. Just as gold is always gold, whether it is made into bracelets or ear-rings or tiaras, so is Vishnu always Vishnu, whether he appears in the form of god or animal or man. The man who bows before Vishnu, whose lotus feet are held in reverence by the gods, is not subject to sin's fetters, and you must keep out of his way."

Yama's messenger not unnaturally asked how he was to recognise the devotees of Vishnu. To this question the god replied : " The worshipper of Vishnu never fails to perform the duties assigned to his caste. He looks on friend and foe with equal indifference. He finds no pleasure in either love or hatred. He never injures any one. He never beats or slays any creature that has life. He takes nothing that is not his own. He does not covet either the gold or the wife of another man. His heart is as pure as crystal, because Vishnu cannot dwell where envy, malice and other evil passions reign. His thoughts are centred on the eternal God, and he recognises that Vishnu, his worshipper and all the world are one. The man who is guilty of pride and malice, who is covetous, untruthful and cruel, who is unkind to his wife and children, to his parents and friends, is not a worshipper of Vishnu. He whose thoughts and deeds are evil is a beast and not a man, and in his heart Vishnu cannot dwell." When he had said this, the god of the dead repeated his original warning, and told his messenger to keep far away from all such worshippers of Vishnu. The noose of Yama had no power over those who, protected by the discus of that deity, were destined to escape the tortures to which others were subjected, and passed at once to heaven.

Vishnu Purāna, iii. 7.

XLV.

THE TRUE HEAVEN.

"Attachment to earthly objects produces evil. The silkworm constructs a cocoon round itself and is at last destroyed by its own deed. Renounce both virtue and vice, both truth and falsehood."—*Mahābhārata*, xii. 330. 29. 40.

ONCE upon a time there lived in Northern India a very pious and virtuous man, whose name was Mudgala. The only food he ever ate was grains of corn which he laboriously picked up from the ground, not with his fingers, but with his lips. This was a practice which had been adopted by others before him, and was known as the pigeon mode of life. And yet despite the toil involved, he was always able to entertain any number of guests, and to take a part in the customary sacrifices and other religious rites. Indeed it is said that he was able not only to support his wife and child, but also to entertain thousands of Brāhmins with the grains of corn which he gathered in this way. His sacrifices were even honoured by the gods, who came in person, and Mudgala never thought of eating till his guests had all been satisfied. Manifestly he was endowed with miraculous powers, for the more people he fed, the greater was his remaining store. The vessel in which he kept the grain was never so full as after a feast at which hundreds had been partakers.

In those days there was a *rishi* known far and wide for his wild and rude appearance. He never wore any clothes.

He looked like a madman, and he often acted like one. His temper, too, was most uncertain, and when he got angry, he used the most insulting words. Now this strange individual, whose name was Durvāsa, had heard of Mudgala's miraculous powers, and he came to his hermitage resolved to put them to the test. He did so, and found that they were real. When he had eaten all he could, the filthy creature smeared his body with what was over and went away. This rude conduct on the part of his brother ascetic did not disturb Mudgala in the least. And when Durvāsa came back later, he was as ready to feed him as he had been before. Six times in all did Durvāsa come and ask for entertainment, and on each occasion his wants were more than satisfied. On his final visit, Durvāsa could not restrain himself longer, and he said : " There is nobody like you in all the wide world. I have tested you six times. I have eaten up all your food, and left you hungry. But you have never uttered a word of complaint, never made an impatient gesture. Hunger makes other people bad-tempered, and they give way to wrong feelings and strong language. A starving man will do almost anything for food. But you are altogether different. In my opinion a person like you ought to be translated to heaven right away, just as you are, both body and soul."

Just as the *rishi* said this, a heavenly messenger appeared. He was seated in a car drawn by swans and cranes. It was a very handsome equipage, beautifully painted, and garnished with a number of bells. A most delightful fragrance emanated from it.

Addressing himself to Mudgala, the messenger from heaven said : " I have been sent for you. Get into the car. Your ascetic life has secured for you the bliss of heaven." Much to the celestial's surprise, however, Mudgala didn't get into the car. " Before going with you," he said, " I should like to hear what are the advantages I shall reap by going to heaven. What kind of people live there, and what do they do ? And in addition to telling me what are its advantages, I should like to know what are its defects." " I never heard of any one refusing such an offer before," replied the messenger. " You are surely a very simple-minded individual. However, I shall answer your questions. First, as to the people who go there. I have to say that they include those who have offered sacrifices, performed austerities or died in battle. The orthodox, the truthful, the self-restrained, the generous, and those who are charitable in thought and speech, are also there. They enjoy every kind of happiness, in a large variety of beautiful worlds, with lovely gardens, and they associate with the gods and other supernatural beings. They experience neither hunger nor thirst. They suffer from neither cold nor heat. Sorrow and sadness, old age and disease never distress them. There is nothing there to make them afraid, nothing that offends or disgusts. Their bodies never perspire or give forth unpleasant odours. They have no calls of nature to attend to. They have no work to do, and no sins to bewail. Dust never soils them, and their garments never grow old. If you come with me to heaven, you will be crowned with garlands that do not fade, and ride in a celestial car as beautiful as mine. The highest of the heavens I have tried to describe is the dwelling-place of Brahmā. But higher even than that is the region which is the best and most blessed of all. There live the Thirty-three gods, called Ribhus, who are worshipped by the gods who rule over the lower heavens. Their condition is so fortunate and happy that they are objects of envy even to the other celestials. These mighty beings do not require to be fed on man's oblations, nor do they drink nectar as the others do. They are a class apart. They are free from sexual desire,[1] and even at the dissolu-

[1] This cannot be said of the other gods, as many passages prove.

tion of a universe they continue to exist.   And one does not
speak of happiness there, just as one does not speak of
sorrow.   The inhabitants of that region are beyond both
joy and sorrow, anger and love.   And that blessed region
may be yours if you will come with me.   You have earned
it by your hospitality and your austerities.

"I have told you of the advantages.   But you wish to
hear also of the defects.   And the first and greatest is that
in heaven you cannot acquire any fresh merit.   You go
there that you may enjoy the fruits and the rewards of the
virtuous life you have lived on earth.   You reap the harvest
you have sown.   But in heaven there is no fresh sowing
possible.   That means that you gradually exhaust the stock
of merit which raised you to the skies, and the time inevi-
tably comes when, having exhausted the capital that lies
at your credit, you must go tumbling down to earth.   Now
when a man comes back to this lower world, he cannot
help being miserable.   He can't help thinking of the joys
he has lost.   And there is also the misery of anticipation.
As your period in heaven draws to a close, as you look at
your garland and see that its flowers have begun to fade,
your heart is filled with many conflicting thoughts and
fears."

When the messenger had concluded his statements,
Mudgala said in reply : "I thank you for your explanations
and have only this to say, I am not going.   I do not wish
to dwell in a place which has such serious defects ; whose
happiness is always darkened by the thought of future
grief.   I am resolved to seek a better country than that.
Tell me of some celestial region where there will never be
any cause for sorrow, regret or fear.   A region of which
you can say, that it has no defect, from which, once I
reach it, there shall be no return."   For this appeal also the
messenger had an answer ready.   "Yes, there is such a
region.   High above the heaven of Brahmā (and appa-

rently above the heaven of the Ribhus, though he does not say so) there is the highest sphere of all, the home of Vishnu, who is identified with Brahm, the eternal spirit. The sensual, the arrogant, the covetous, the wrathful, the ignorant, cannot go there. It is reserved for those who have brought their senses under control, who are indifferent to pleasure and pain, who are given to contemplation and the practice of *yoga*."

When he heard about the home of Vishnu, the dwelling-place of Brahm, Mudgala returned to his old life with the utmost content. And by profound contemplation and the practice of *yoga*, he so clarified his understanding that he gave no heed to either praise or blame. He held a clod of earth, a stone, and a piece of gold in equal estimation, and in consequence he achieved the supreme eternal emancipation which is called *nirvāna*.

Mahābhārata, iii. 259.

XLVI.

THE GREAT JOURNEY.

" You should not doubt religion or the gods because you do not see
the fruit. Let your scepticism yield to faith. Do not speak ill of God,
who is the lord of all creatures; learn to know Him and to bow before
Him. Never disregard that Supreme Being by whose mercy the mortals
become immortal."—*Mahābhārata*, iii. 31. 38.

THERE were five brothers who lived and reigned in Northern
India. They belonged to the lunar race of kings, and were
cousins of Krishna, one of the incarnations of the god
Vishnu. When these princes heard of their cousin's death,
they grew weary of the world and resolved that they would
set out on the last great journey, the journey from earth to
heaven.

The *Mahābhārata* tells how one of the five brothers had
already paid a visit to Indra's heaven. It does not, however, tell us how he got there. But with regard to this
undertaking, we are given comparatively full details. The
home of the gods was at the top of Mount Meru, and Mount
Meru lay far to the north, beyond the Himālayas. And
that means that the heroes were able to walk up to
heaven. Before setting out, they put on the garb of
ascetics, and as they did so, they felt as if they were putting
off all worldly cares. They were accompanied by their
wife, Draupadi, whom they held in common. Soon after
leaving the capital, a dog attached himself to their company, and never left them in all their travels. Though

heaven, they knew, lay towards the frozen north, it was not
their first objective. They had decided to make a circuit
of the earth. Accordingly they journeyed east, until they
reached the ocean. When they could go no farther in that
direction, they turned their faces to the south ; and
when there also farther progress was barred, they moved
west and north, till they came in sight of the Himālayas.
All through this long and wearisome pilgrimage the
travellers meditated with undivided thought on the
principles of *yoga*. When they had passed beyond the
Himālayas they came to a great desert of sand, and
beyond the desert, on its farthest verge, they saw Mount
Meru, the home of the gods, the goal of their journey.
But as they passed through this desert, Draupadi, the
wife of the five brothers, fell down. One of her husbands,
whose name was Bhīma, asked Yudhisthira, the eldest of
the five, why this had happened, because, so far as he
was aware, she had never committed a sin in all her life.
But his brother replied that in her attitude to her husbands
she had not been as impartial as she ought to have been,
and she was now reaping the fruit of her sin. Without
making any further comment or extending any help or
sympathy to their fallen wife, the five brothers, intent on
their meditation, passed quickly on. Yudhisthira walked
in front and the dog brought up the rear. But not long
after, three of the brothers, one after the other, fell to the
ground, even as Draupadi had done. They seem to have
fallen without a cry and without warning. Yudhisthira
and Bhīma were now left alone, except for the dog. When
Bhīma questioned his brother as to the cause of these
successive calamities, he was told that the first had
suffered because he was proud of his wisdom, the second,
because he was proud of his beauty, and the third, because
he boasted of his strength. These repeated lessons had
deeply grieved the hearts of the lessening band of survivors

with the exception of Yudhisthira, who remained un-
ruffled in his self-control and never once looked back.
And very soon thereafter, Bhīma also fell down. When
he saw that he was falling, Bhīma cried aloud: "Oh,
my brother, I too am falling. Tell me, you who love
me, tell me why I have fallen." "You were always a
glutton," replied Yudhisthira, "and in your greed you
never gave a thought to the needs of others." And
without once looking back, he continued his journey,
with the dog as his solitary companion. But he had not
gone far when heaven and earth resounded with the whir
of a celestial car. Looking up, he saw that he was in
the presence of the god Indra. "I have come for you,"
said Indra. "Seat yourself in the chariot, and come with
me to heaven." Yudhisthira by his answer made it
plain that he was not lacking in natural affection. "I
cannot go with you to heaven," he said, "and leave my
wife and brothers lying helpless on the ground. Take
us all with you and I shall go gladly, but I shall not go
alone." "But your brothers and Draupadi are there
already," said the god. "Like other mortals, they have
shed their mortal frames, and in their spiritual forms have
entered into rest. For you the gods have ordained that
you should enjoy a further privilege and go as you are,
both body and spirit." When Yudhisthira heard that
his brothers and Draupadi were already in the upper
world, he was greatly pleased. But he had another
condition to put forward before he would consent to enter
the car. "This dog," he said, "has been with us in all
our travels. He attached himself to us when we set out
from our capital, and has never left us since. I cannot
abandon him to his fate in this great sandy desert." "It
is quite impossible to let a dog enter heaven," said Indra.
"You will be guilty of no cruelty in leaving the animal
here. The presence of a dog at an earthly sacrifice makes

the sacrifice, as you know, unclean." "That may be so," said Yudhisthira, "but I should be guilty of a most dishonourable deed if I were to abandon my four-footed friend. To forsake a friend or refuse the appeal of a suppliant is as bad as killing a Brāhmin. I once made a vow that I would never betray a friend, or refuse help to any one in sorrow or distress. And even for the sake of procuring eternal bliss, I will not break that vow." "But you abandoned your wife and brothers," said Indra; "you left them lying on the ground, and continued to press on, when, one after the other, they fell helpless to the earth." "I left them lying on the ground," replied Yudhisthira, "because I could do nothing for them; because they were dead, and one can do nothing for the dead. Had they been alive, I should never have forsaken them."

While this debate was proceeding between Indra and the king, the dog had stood, meekly waiting, and never said a word. But at this point he intervened and spoke. And as he spoke, his form underwent a wonderful change. "I am Dharma, the god of duty," he said, "and I am greatly pleased, O Prince, with your faithfulness and devotion. Even when I came to you in the form of a dog, which men reckon as unclean, you would not forsake me, and called me friend. I have tried you in the past and never found you wanting. Now I know that you are prepared to surrender a place in heaven rather than be false to what is right."

Yudhisthira was now prepared to go to heaven, and took his place in Indra's car, accompanied by the transformed dog and a number of other deities. On his arrival in the upper world he was met by a great concourse of glorified saints and sages. One of these personages, acting as spokesman, congratulated him on the unique honour he had received in being permitted to enter

heaven in his bodily form. But the monarch paid little
heed to these flattering observations, and when the
address was finished, immediately remarked that his chief
anxiety was to see his brothers and Draupadi. His mind
could not be set at rest until he knew that they were safe
and well. "What do you mean by talking about your
wife and brothers?" said Indra. "You are now in heaven,
and in heaven the ties of earth are forgotten. As the
sage has said, you have received a most unusual honour
and been allowed to enter heaven in your bodily form,
and yet your only concern is about your wife and brothers."
But even Indra could not persuade the monarch to forget
those whom he had loved on earth, and so he merely
repeated his request : "Tell me where my brothers and
Draupadi are, that I may go and see them." While this
argument was proceeding, Yudhisthira happened to notice
a relative of his own among the crowd. Now this relative
had been a bitter enemy to Yudhisthira and his brothers
in former days. As a result of his wicked plottings, they
had been driven into exile ; they had been involved in a
long and bloody war in which many millions had been
slain. And the monarch's eyes blazed with anger as he
asked why such a scoundrel had been allowed to enter
heaven. But the sage, who had already acted as spokesman, again intervened, and told the monarch to control
his feelings. The loves and hates of earth had no place
in heaven. He must forget their ancient strife and speak
politely to his cousin. Because, whatever his sins might
have been, he had achieved his right of entrance in virtue
of the fact that he had died in battle with his face to the
foe. "Well," said Yudhisthira, "if heaven is the reward
of men of my cousin's character, please tell me in what
lofty regions my noble-hearted brothers now are. They
were men who always spoke the truth. They always kept
their promises, and were faithful to their vows. They

performed sacrifices ; they studied the Vedas and gave
gifts to Brāhmins. Where are they, and a great many
others whom I have known and heard of ? If these great
heroes were unfit to enter heaven, where are they ? I
don't wish to live here if they are absent. Where my
brothers are not, cannot be heaven to me."

Now Indra had already informed the monarch that his
brothers and Draupadi were in heaven, but when he made
this appeal, the celestials with one voice assured him
that they had no desire to keep him by force, and they
would willingly send a messenger to conduct him to the
place where his brothers and Draupadi were. Alas ! it
was a fearful road along which they had to travel, and
shrouded in thick darkness. On every side lay corpses
that polluted the air. They were in every stage of corrup-
tion, smeared with fat and blood. Vultures and other
beasts of prey, creatures with beaks of iron, as well as evil
spirits, worms and insects, fed upon the dead. They had
to cross high mountains, and a great river full of water
as hot as fire. They had to pass under trees whose leaves
were as sharp as razors, and through deserts full of burning
sand. It was the land of torture ordained by the gods
for sinful men. Unable to restrain his wonder any longer,
Yudhisthira demanded why he was being taken by such
a fearsome way. Was this one of the roads that led to
the celestial regions ? The messenger merely replied by
saying that he had been told to accompany the king thus
far and no farther. If he did not like the road, he was
welcome to retrace his steps. And so, unable to endure
the thick darkness, the horrid stench, the frightful
scenes of horror and pain any longer, Yudhisthira resolved to abandon his quest. But just as he was about
to return, he was assailed by loud cries, and he heard
the voices of his wife and brothers beseeching him not to
leave them. Poor souls, they said that with his coming

their hearts had been filled with joy. A cooling breeze had begun to blow. They had found untold comfort in his presence and had ceased to feel their pain. Perplexed and amazed beyond endurance, Yudhisthira began to hurl reproaches at the gods. He asked himself, "Have I gone mad? Am I sleeping or awake? How is it that men of sinful deeds are dwelling in heaven while my wife and brothers are enduring the tortures of hell?" And so, turning to the messenger of the gods, he told him to go back to his masters and say that Yudhisthira would stay where he was, to be a comfort and help to his brothers in their affliction. As he uttered these words the gods, with Indra at their head, suddenly appeared. The thick darkness was dispelled; the boiling river, the loathsome corpses, and all the other horrid sights vanished, while Indra stepped forward to explain that the gods had subjected the monarch to an illusion. They had wished to test his constancy and faith, and they begged to assure him that his wife and brothers were, as they had said at first, enjoying the happiness of heaven. By way of further explanation, the god added that all men had to endure the pains of hell sooner or later. It was the custom to let bad men have a brief period in heaven before sending them to hell, where they would reap the fruits of their evil deeds. Good men, on the other hand, were first sent to hell, and afterwards they enjoyed the bliss of heaven. The monarch, on one occasion, had been guilty of a sin, deceiving an enemy and telling him that his son was dead when he was really alive. It was necessary that he should receive some punishment for that evil deed. But by his brief stay in hell he was purged of every stain, and would dwell in Indra's own heaven, free from all disease, sorrow and pain, with celestial nymphs to wait upon him, and sharing the society of the most famous kings of old. Before returning to heaven, however, the gods took him

to the sources of the Ganges, and caused him to bathe
in her sacred stream. The result of these ablutions was
that he left behind him his mortal body, and, even as
others do, assumed a celestial frame, suited to the glorious
world which henceforth would be his home.

Mahābhārata, xvii., xviii.

NOTES.

NOTE A.

THE SACRED BOOKS OF INDIA.

VEDAS.—This general name is made to include three very distinct component parts very far removed from one another in time as well as in thought.

1. There are first the *Hymns*, the Vedas proper. These hymns also vary greatly in age and purpose. They are— (*a*) The *Rig-Veda*, the oldest, and to a very large extent the source from which the later collections of hymns are drawn. It is essentially a book of praise addressed to the nature gods of the early Aryans. (*b*) The *Sāma-Veda*, almost entirely composed of hymns drawn from the *Rig-Veda*. It was compiled for the use of priests at the great Soma sacrifice. (*c*) The *Yajur-Veda*. It also, though not to so great an extent, is based on the *Rig-Veda*, and was used by the priests who performed not only the Soma sacrifice, but others as well. These are the *three Vedas* of which the *Mahābhārata* so often speaks. They were in existence and recognised as "revelation" long before (*d*) the *Atharva-Veda* had been recognised or compiled. The *Atharva-Veda*, says Professor Macdonell, "only attained its present position after a long struggle. In spirit it is not only entirely different from the *Rig-Veda*, but though a later compilation, it represents a much more primitive stage of thought." It is a handbook of spells and cursings. It has to do with the gods of the lower world, and not with the kindly gods of the *Rig-Veda*, who are expected to bless their worshippers with children and cattle, health and happiness and length of days.

The Vedic period is believed to have begun as early as 1500 B.C., and the *Rig-Veda Sanhita* to have taken its present shape by 1000 B.C.

2. The second portion of the Vedas are the *Brāhmanas*, written in prose. Their purpose is to explain the significance of the sacrificial ritual. These explanations, however, do not stand alone. The *Brāhmanas* also contain a large number of legends, and for that reason are of great value as showing the changes which took place in the religious beliefs of the people of India.

It should be noted that the four sets of hymns have their corresponding *Brāhmanas*, while the dates assigned to them range from 800 to 500 B.C.

3. The *Upanishads* are reckoned as the third and final portion of the Vedas, hence the name which is sometimes given to them : *Vedānta*, or end of the Vedas. "The pantheistic groundwork of their doctrines was later developed into the Vedānta System, which is still the favourite philosophy of the modern Hindus. . . . They really represent a new religion. Their aim is no longer the obtaining of earthly happiness and afterwards bliss in the abode of Yama by sacrificing correctly to the gods, but release from mundane existence by the absorption of the individual soul in the world-soul through correct knowledge " (Macdonell's *Sanskrit Literature*, p. 218).

With the acceptance of pantheism and the belief that correct knowledge was the key to union with the world soul, went the theory of transmigration, which, according to the above-quoted authority, is to be found in the oldest *Upanishads*.

The *Upanishads* probably began to be written about 600 B.C. Some of them are very late. There is even a Mohammedan treatise which claims the name ! The three portions of the Vedas are all declared to be Revelation (*Shruti*), in contrast to other and later books which are termed Tradition (*Smriti*).

Hymns of the Vedas	.	.	.	1500 B.C.–
The Brāhmanas	.	.	.	800 B.C.–500 B.C.
The Upanishads	.	.	.	600 B.C.–

Though the later literature, which is detailed below in so far as it affects the subject-matter of this book, is only spoken of as tradition, these works claim for themselves verbal inspiration of the most emphatic kind. Vālmīki, the author of the *Rāmāyana*, was told by Brahmā that it would not contain one single word of falsehood. The creator also intervened in connection with the *Mahābhārata*, and arranged that the god Ganesha should act as scribe to its author. As for the *Laws of Manu*, it is said that the creator himself taught it to Manu alone at the beginning. In the case of the *Vishnu Purāna*, a mind-born son of Brahmā undertook to make its author acquainted with the true nature of the deities, with the result that he produced a book equal in sanctity to the Vedas. The *Mahābhārata* is spoken of as the fifth Veda.

Approximate dates are given for this post-Vedic literature:

Rāmāyana	.	.	.	500 B.C.–
Mahābhārata .	.	.	.	500 B.C.–400 A.D.
Laws of Manu	.	.	.	200 B.C.–200 A.D.
The Purānas .	.	.	.	400 A.D.–800 A.D.

NOTE B.

OTHER VIEWS ON WOMEN.

THE god Krishna said, "Women, gambling, hunting and drink are the four evils by which people are deprived of prosperity" (*M*. iii. 13. 7). He also advises the forcible abduction of his own sister, defends such action by quoting men learned in the precepts of religion, and says, "Who knows what may happen if it is left to the maiden's choice" (*M*. i. 221. 23). Another individual held in high honour for his wisdom says you should never trust a woman, a thief or an atheist, which he varies in another chapter by adding serpents and kings (*M*. v. 37. 39). But the lowest opinions are expressed by the dying warrior Bhīshma. To enhance the value of his observations it is said that Krishna entered his body and gave him the knowledge of the Past, the Present and the Future, and said that when he died knowledge of every kind would disappear from the earth. Some of these opinions have already been given in the Introduction, others are so frank that they cannot be quoted, but here are some : In the Vedas themselves one may read that women are false. There is nothing more sinful than women. They are the root of all evils and, even when of noble birth and possessed of protectors, are always seeking to transgress the restraints laid upon them. The creator himself is unable to keep them within proper limits. How can you expect that men can do so. When the world was first created there was no sin of any kind, with the result that men began to attain the rank of gods. This circumstance alarmed the celestials, and they invited the grandfather (Brahmā) to do something that would relieve such a grievous situation. In obedience to their request Brahmā created women of a sinful disposition and with one object in life (*M*. xiii. 19, 38–40).

The *Laws of Manu* have equally diverse teaching. They say in one chapter, " Day and night women must be kept in dependence by the males of their families. They must be carefully guarded. Even weak husbands must strive to guard their wives. It is a good plan to see to it that their time is fully occupied," though it is recognised that better than placing them under the supervision of servants, is when a wife keeps guard over herself. After another drop into base suspicions, the same chapter goes on to say that between wives who are destined to bear children, who secure many blessings, who are worthy of worship and irradiate their dwellings, and the goddess of fortune, there is no difference whatever (ix. 1, 26). This is a somewhat utilitarian note, but farther on we come to another passage which must not be ignored. It breathes that lofty morality which in place after place breaks through the teachings of Manu and illuminates the darkness. " Let mutual fidelity continue until death : this may be considered as the summary of the highest law for husband and wife. Let men and women united in marriage constantly exert themselves that they may not be disunited and may not violate their mutual fidelity " (ix. 101, 102). Manu, of course, repeats the teaching of the epics, that a woman's husband is her highest god, that apart from him she needs no rites, no vows, no fasts. By obeying her husband, and by that alone, she is raised to heaven. If she wishes to go to heaven, then she must never offend him, whether he be alive or dead. He may be devoid of every virtue. He may follow after other women, a faithful wife must continue to worship her lord. And when he dies she must never so much as mention another man's name. A virtuous woman never marries a second time, but it is lawful for a man to marry again (v. 147–169).

NOTES ON THE LEGENDS

NOTE TO LEGEND I.

THE GOLDEN AGE was the first of the four ages. We are living in the fourth or evil age. Taken together, they amount to more than four million years.

THE SEA OF MILK.—Beyond our earth and its surrounding ocean there are said to be six other encircling continents with their corresponding oceans; making in all seven island continents and seven seas. The Sea of Milk is the sixth ocean. Right in the centre of our earth stands Mount Meru, the home of the gods.

BRAHMĀ, THE CREATOR, had a number of mind-born sons, called Prajāpatis or lords of creatures. Kashyapa was one of them. He had eight wives. One of them, *Aditi*, became the mother of the *thirty-three gods* (twelve Adityas, eight Vasus, eleven Rudras and two Ashwins); another, *Diti*, was the mother of the demons (Daityas); a third, *Manu*, was the mother of men; while the rest were the mothers of beasts, birds and trees (*Rāmāyana*, iii. 14). Another tradition, while saying that Kashyapa was the father of all creatures, makes him the grandson, and not the son of Brahmā, and ascribes to his uncles, the mind-born sons of the creator, a share in populating the worlds; thus one of them was the father of demons, another of tigers and so on (*Mahābhārata*, i. 65). Brahmā, the creator, is frequently called grandfather or great father (*Pitā maha*), because he was the father of Kashyapa and the others, and therefore the grandfather of gods, demons, beasts and men. In the *Brāhmanas*, which are earlier than the epic poems, Prajāpati (in the singular), or lord of creatures, afterwards identified with Brahmā, is himself the fathe·

of gods, demons and men. "There are thirty-three gods, and Prajāpati is the thirty-fourth" (*Shatapatha Brāhmana*, iv. 5. 7). It adds, "Prajāpati is everything."

VISHNU was the youngest of the twelve *Adityas*; "the youngest and the best," says a later admirer. He eventually rose to an equality with the creator and ranked as the *preserver* god. The *tortoise incarnation* (*avatāra*, or descent) is only one of ten main incarnations attributed to Vishnu.

SHIVA was originally one of the eleven *Rudras*. He also was raised above his fellows, and, along with Vishnu and Brahmā, came to form the Hindu triad (*trimurti*). Another explanation of Shiva's blue throat is given in the *Mahābhārata* (xii.343), where it is said that Vishnu quarrelled with Shiva and seized him by the throat, with the result that it has had a blue mark ever since. When the fight took place the other gods were greatly alarmed, and Brahmā fell off his chair. In the sectarian literature devoted to Shiva, his adherents magnify the service he rendered by drinking the poison.

"Thou mad'st me Thine; didst fiery poison eat, pitying poor souls. That I might thine ambrosia taste—I, meanest one."

The epics, that is, the *Rāmāyana* and the *Mahābhārata*, which contain the origins of the story, however, place all the emphasis on Vishnu.

The THIRTY-THREE GODS are frequently referred to in the *Rig-Veda*, but that work does not suggest that Kashyapa was their father. A later mythology is responsible for this idea. *Ananta* (without end) is the great snake (*Shesha*) on which the world rests. He is a manifestation of Vishnu. *Lakshmi*, originally used to indicate good fortune (*Rig-Veda*), became the wife of Vishnu.

AMRITA (undying); compare the passage in Genesis iii. 24, "And he placed at the east of the garden of Eden Cherubims, and a flaming sword which turned every way, to keep the way of the tree of life." Other passages show that the Amrita did not save the gods from death. The time came when they too had to die and to be reborn.

RĀHU.—The belief that he tries to swallow the sun and moon at seasons of eclipse still prevails in India, and the

multitudes manifest their anxiety by beating drums and
bathing while the struggle is taking place.

NOTE TO LEGEND II.

INDRA.—One of the twelve Adityas. Originally standing
in the front rank of deities (*Rig-Veda*), he had to give place
to the triad Brahmā, Vishnu and Shiva; but both the
Rāmāyana and the *Mahābhārata* recognise him as king of
heaven. Many unsavoury stories are told about him and
also about Shiva. This is one of the most presentable.
The epics, however, record such legends without disapproval; though Brahmā on one occasion told Indra that
certain trying experiences through which he had passed
were due to his adultery with the wife of an eminent sage.
By the time of Tulsidās (sixteenth century), from whom
our headline is taken, the Vedic gods had ceased to be of
any real interest to Hindus, and the poet could express
himself freely.

SHE PUT HER FEET WHERE HER HEAD SHOULD HAVE
BEEN.—To make the slightest blunder in the ritual of a
sacrifice was sufficient to bring about results the very
opposite of what was desired. The most striking illustration of this is in *Sh. Br.* i. 6. 3, when, owing to the mis-
placing of an accent, an enemy of Indra produced from a
sacrifice a son who became not the *slayer of Indra*, but *the
slain of Indra*.

MARUTS.—Sanskrit, *ma rodih*, weep not.

NOTE TO LEGEND III.

VASISHTHA, according to the *Laws of Manu*, was one
of the *seven great rishis* or sages, and also one of the
Prajāpatis, or lords of creatures (Note I.). He is also
spoken of as having two fathers, the gods Varuna and
Mitra. Many of the *Rig-Veda* hymns are attributed to
him. He appears as a minister of Rāma and his royal
house for at least twenty-seven generations.

THERE ARE FOUR PRIMARY CASTES: the Brāhmins or
priests, the Kshatriyas or warriors, the Vaishyas or agricul-

tural and trading classes, and the Shūdras or servile class.
According to the strange statement in *R.* iii. 14, they were
the offspring of Manu, wife of Kashyapa. The Brāhmins
were born from her mouth, the warriors from her breast,
the Vaishyas from her thighs and the Shūdras from her
feet. The more usual explanation is that they originated
from those portions of the creator's body (*M.* xii. 297).
This legend is also referred to in the creation hymn, *Rig-
Veda*, x. 90, in which the universe, including gods, animals
and men, as well as the Vedas, are reckoned as parts of
Purusha, the primeval male. "When they divided
Purusha, how many portions did they make ? What did
they call his mouth, his arms ? What did they call his
thighs and feet ? The Brāhmin was his mouth, of both
his arms was the Rājanya made. His thighs became
the Vaishya, from his feet the Shūdra was produced "
(Griffith's translation).

The GREEKS (*Yavana*) no doubt refer to the Bactrian
Greeks, descendants of those whom Alexander the Great
left behind him and who carved out for themselves kingdoms on the borders of India. *Barbara* is the Greek word
barbaroi. The HUNS (*Huna*) and SCYTHIANS (*Shaka*) also
established themselves in India. The CHINESE (*Chinas*)
probably refer to a tribe on the north-east of India. The
PARTHIANS had control of Baluchistan and Khāndahār
in the first century A.D. Their prince, Gondophares, is
said to have been baptized by St. Thomas.

YAMA.—The god of the lower world and judge of the
dead. In the Vedas, spoken of as the first man who
died, he had nothing to do with the punishment of the
wicked. In the epics and *Purānas* the souls of the dead
appear before him and receive reward or punishment
according to their deeds.

NOTE TO LEGEND IV.

The nymph MENAKĀ became the mother of Shakuntalā,
whose subsequent career is described in Legend XXX.

This incident is supposed to have taken place in the
first age of the world. We shall find Vishvāmitra acting

as counsellor to Rāma (*R.* i.–vii.) at the end of the second age, one million years later. But his age was nothing to that of another of Rāma's ministers, who had witnessed many dissolutions of the universe, and yet looked like a young man of twenty-five (*M.* iii. 183).

PUSHKAR, India's most sacred lake, is a few miles distant from Ajmer, Rajputana. Many thousands of pilgrims bathe there at full moon in the month of November, when the waters are supposed to be particularly efficacious. There are only two temples to Brahmā in all India, and one of them is at Pushkar. To so low a depth has the creator fallen, while Vishnu and Shiva are everywhere supreme.

The theory, that a man is born into a particular caste as a reward or as a punishment for what he did in a former life, accounts for the rigidity of the caste system. Human equality and democracy are impossible so long as belief in caste and transmigration prevails in India.

NOTE TO LEGEND V.

TRISHANKU was an ancestor of Rāma, the incarnation of the god Vishnu. The solar race claims descent from Manu, who after the Flood repeopled heaven, earth and hell with gods, men and demons. Manu was the offspring of the Sun (see Note X.). His son, Ikshvāku, built Ayodhyā (*Oudh*).

The *Laws of Manu*, ascribed to this individual, are still quoted in the law courts of India.

Trishanku is identified with *Orion*.

THE *SEVEN RISHIS* are the Prajāpatis or mind-born sons of Brahmā (Note I.), and the progenitors of gods and demons, men, animals and trees. They are referred to very frequently. The different lists do not always agree. We even get lists of eight and nine. In the *Laws of Manu* again we read not of *rishis*, but of *Prajāpatis*, ten in number, while the *Rāmāyana* speaks of seventeen and the *Mahābhārata* of twenty-one. In addition to these *great rishis*, there are many other *rishis* or sages ; *e.g.* the authors of the hymns of the Vedas are so referred to.

MIXED MARRIAGES.—In the tenth chapter of the *Laws of Manu*, marriage between members of different castes is condemned, and the Chandāla is spoken of with special opprobrium. But in chapters three and nine it is said that a Brāhmin may marry, in addition to a wife from his own caste, one from each of the castes below. Another law-book says that, while a Brāhmin may marry wives from his own and from the second and third castes which are reckoned as twice-born, he may not marry a Shūdra. In the *Mahābhārata* we have the general statement that in addition to marrying a wife in his own caste a man can also marry in the castes below his own. That means that the Shūdra or lowest caste can only marry from his own caste. It is always reckoned as a great sin for a man to approach a woman of a higher caste. Hence the objection to the Chandāla. The epic recognises that there are many such outcastes. It also says that the sons of wives belonging to a lower caste are reckoned as members of their father's caste. As to marriage with a Shūdra woman, it says the practice is common, but scripture does not sanction it (xiii. 44). The laxity of the epics and the law-books filled the commentators of later days with pained amazement. Marriage is now only permitted within one's own caste. And there are several hundred castes and sub-castes.

NOTE TO LEGEND VI.

There are a number of references in the *Rig-Veda* (i. 24. 5. 2) to the efficacy of Shunashepha's prayers.

VARUNA was one of the most prominent and powerful of the Vedic gods. There was a distinctly moral element in his character which was lacking in his brother deities. By the time of the epics he had fallen from his high estate. He is often spoken of in association with Mitra, and sometimes in ways not to his credit, as in the legends of Urvasi, the celestial nymph, and of Manu's daughter.

The *Aitareya Brāhmana* is an earlier work than the *Rāmāyana*. If the reader will compare the names of the gods which appear in the two narratives, he will see how the situation had changed. *Prajāpati* the lord of creatures,

(Brahmā's predecessor), Agni the god of fire, Savitar the sun, Varuna, Vishvadevas (all the gods), Indra, the Ashwins (harbingers of dawn) and Ushas (the dawn) appear in the former narrative. In the later, only Agni and Indra remain, while the name of Vishnu is new. The sacrificial post to which the youth was bound is spoken of as Vishnu's.

MAN SACRIFICE.—In *Shatapatha Brāhmana*, i. 2, 3, 6, we read that at first the gods offered up a man. When he was offered up, the sacrificial essence went out of him and entered into a horse. They offered up the horse, and the sacrificial essence entered into the ox. When the ox was offered up, the essence went out of it and entered the sheep. The same process was again gone through, a goat becoming the substitute of the sheep. From the sacrifice of the goat the essence entered into the earth. When the gods dug for it there, they found it in rice and barley. The comment is : " As much efficacy as all these sacrificial victims would have for him, so much efficacy has this oblation (of rice, etc.) for him who knows this." Here, no doubt, is the history of the process when less cruel and less costly sacrifices were shown to be as efficacious as those formerly practised.

NOTE TO LEGEND VII.

AGASTYA is credited with having two fathers, the gods Mitra and Varuna, and the story of his birth is one of the most repulsive in Hindu legend. Further reference to his miraculous power will be found in Legend XVIII.

Mention is made of Vishnu's incarnation as a BOAR, as a MAN-LION and as a DWARF. (1) In the *Mahābhārata* (iii. 142) it is said that, owing to the neglect of Brahmā, no deaths took place among men or beasts, while births went on as usual. As a result of such a great increase in the population, the earth sank down to a distance of seven thousand miles. When the earth appealed to Vishnu for help, he assumed the form of a boar and raised up the earth to its place with a single tusk. This deliverance is attributed to Brahmā in the earlier literature, *e.g.* in one of the two accounts, and presumably the older, that are recorded in the *Rāmāyana*. Brahmā's (or Prajāpati's) feats are in this way transferred to Vishnu.

(2) For Vishnu's appearance as a man-lion, see Legend XIX.

(3) In the *Rāmāyana* (i. 31) it is said that a demon called Bali had by the might of his asceticism secured control of the three worlds. The gods appealed to Vishnu to take the form of a dwarf and by stratagem get the better of Bali, who was so generous to suppliants that he granted the prayer of every one who came before him. According to their request, Vishnu appeared before Bali in the form of a dwarf, and made the apparently simple request that he be granted as much earth as he could cover in three steps. When the demon had acceded to his petition, the dwarf at once enlarged himself to so great a size that in three steps he traversed the whole expanse of earth and heaven. Bali was thus deprived of lordship over everything but the lower regions, to which he was immediately hurled. The germ of this legend appears in the *Rig-Veda* (i. 22), where we read : "Vishnu strode over this universe : in three places he planted his steps." Indian commentators explain that Vishnu is the Sun (*Aditya*), and that he plants one foot on the place of rising, another in the meridian sky, and the third on the hill of setting (see Muir, *O. S. T.*, vol. iv. pp. 63, 65). In the *Shatapatha Brāhmana*, i. 2, 5, the legend has begun to grow, and tells of one of the many battles between the demons (*Asuras*) and the gods, in which the latter had sustained defeat. It says that when the demons began to divide the earth among themselves the gods asked for a share. The demons replied that they would give as much as Vishnu, who was a dwarf, could lie on. Once they had got so much the celestials gradually recovered the earth.

Note to Legend VIII.

SONLESS MEN.—"Nothing is more noteworthy in comparing Hinduism with other religions than the elaborate nature of its funeral rites and the extraordinary importance attached to marriage with a view to providing

sons for the due performance of those rites." These
rites supply the departed spirit "with a kind of intermediate body, and were it not for this intermediate frame
—believed to be created by the offerings made during
funeral ceremonies—the spirit would remain . . . in the
condition of an impure and unquiet ghost wandering
about the earth, or in the air among demons and evil
spirits, and condemned itself to become an evil spirit"
(Monier Williams). A son is called *putra* because he
delivers (*trahyate*) his father from hell (*put*) by the ceremonies he alone is able to perform. Rāma, the incarnation of Vishnu, is made to quote an ancient saying :

> " A son is born his sire to free
> From *Put's* infernal pains.
> Hence saviour of his father he
> The name of *putra* gains."
> (Griffith's translation, p. 216.)

Note to Legend IX.

The WATER OBLATION forms an important part of the
ceremonies for the dead. Balls of rice or flour are also
offered.

GARUDA, the vehicle of Vishnu, on which that god always
appears riding, was a great bird. He was a son of Kashyapa, born to him by one of his numerous wives. He
was thus a grandson of Brahmā. His mother was a
daughter of one of the lords of creatures. He was a
virulent enemy of his half-brothers of the serpent race.

The reverence for the *Ganges* as a sacred stream is
shown in both the epics. In the *Rig-Veda* it is only
mentioned twice, and that quite casually. But the river
Saraswati (now disappeared) appears to have been to the
earlier Indians what the Ganges became to their descendants (Muir, *O. S. T.*, vol. v. p. 338).

Note to Legend X.

MANU.—The references to *Father Manu* in the *Rig-Veda*
are very numerous, and show that the authors of these
hymns looked to him as the progenitor of their race, or the

first *Manu*. But the legend in the *Shatapatha Brāhmana* presents him as the sole survivor of an earlier race. It will also be noticed that he and the wife, whom he secured by means of his sacrifices, became the parents of a new race of human beings, and not of gods, demons, beasts and men, as the epic declares.

Another point to be noted is that the *Fish* in the earlier story says nothing about himself; the later fish says that he is Brahmā. The followers of Vishnu were not content to allow this manifestation to Brahmā, and eventually claimed that the Fish was an incarnation of Vishnu.

FATHER MANU of the *Veda* and *Brāhmana* becomes Manu, the son of Vivasvat, or the Sun in the *Mahābhārata*; and this Manu is not the first, but the seventh Manu of Hindu chronology, which says that our universe will last for one thousand cycles of four ages—a period of 4320 million years—during which time there will exist or reign fourteen Manus, one succeeding the other. The *Rāmāyana* knows nothing of this vast chronology, but it exists in the *Mahābhārata* and in the *Purānas*, where it is set forth in great detail. The *Laws of Manu* sometimes claim that the first and sometimes the seventh or present Manu is their author.

It will also be observed that there is no mention of the *seven rishis* in the earlier legend.

NOTE TO LEGEND XI.

In view of this inordinate glorifying of the Brāhmin, it is only fair to add that he sometimes receives warnings against the dangers of pride, ignorance and greed, *e.g.*: "As an elephant made of wood, as an antelope made of leather, such is an unlearned Brāhmin; those three have nothing but the names. Let not a Brāhmin, even though in pain, speak words cutting others to the quick; let him not injure others in thought or deed; let him not utter speeches which make others afraid of him, since that will prevent him gaining heaven. A Brāhmin should always fear homage as if it were poison." He is also reminded that the receiving of gifts is dangerous, because through his accepting many presents "the divine light is soon

extinguished " (*Laws of Manu*, ii. 157, 161, 162, iv. 186).
In the *Mahābhārata* also, Yudhisthira declared that the
true Brāhmin was he in whom truthfulness, good conduct
and mercy were found, and that the Shūdra who possessed
these qualities was not a Shūdra but a Brāhmin, while the
Brāhmin who had them not was a Shūdra (iii. 180). But
both the *Laws* and the epic are remarkable for the variety
and the inconsistency of their teaching, as a further study
of this book will reveal.

THE GĀYATRĪ VERSE, also called Sāvitrī, is to be found
in the *Rig-Veda*, iii. 62. 10. It is as follows in English :
" Let us meditate on that excellent glory of the divine
vivifying sun (Savitar) ; may he enlighten our understanding." The Brāhmin who repeats this verse, the
sacred syllable *Om*, and the three words *Bhūr*, *Bhuvah*
and *Swar* (Earth, Atmosphere, Heaven), both morning and
evening, need do no more. He acquires as much merit
as if he had repeated the three Vedas. Any twice-born
man (that is, a member of any of the first three castes,
excluding the servile Shūdra) repeating them one thousand
times outside the village, will be freed from even a great
sin. They are the portal of the Veda and the gate leading
to Brahm. " Nothing surpasses the Gāyatrī verse " (*Laws
of Manu*, ii. 78–83).

YOGA.—The word *yoga* is interpreted to mean the act
of fixing or concentrating the mind in abstract meditation.
The repetition of the syllable *Om* is supposed to have
marvellous results in achieving this end, and emphasis is
laid on suppression of the breath, the adoption of certain
postures, the restraint of the senses, and fixing the eyes
intently and incessantly on the tip of the nose. Monier
Williams, from whom I quote, says that *yoga* appears to
be a contrivance for concentrating the mind with the
utmost intensity upon nothing in particular, and is a strange
compound of mental and bodily exercises. As taught by
its founder, it aims at union with the universal Spirit, but
in practice its methods, often of a distorted and exaggerated
character, have been employed by the Yogis, followers of
the god Shiva, in his more terrific aspect. (See *Indian
Wisdom*, p. 94.) The Yoga, which is commonly regarded

as a branch of the Sānkhya school, is scarcely worthy, says the same writer, of the name of a system of philosophy, but it always appears among India's *Six Systems of Philosophy*.

NOTE TO LEGEND XII.

This legend is taken from the *Vishnu Purāna*. As its name implies, it was written by the sectarian followers of that god, and they always seek to exalt their own particular deity at the expense of the others. But there are other *Purānas* which similarly sing the praises of Brahmā and Shiva. It is only the *Mahābhārata* which is tolerant enough to give room to all classes, and is prepared in succeeding chapters of the same book to emphasise the uniqueness and superiority of different gods.

But it will also be noted that the *Purāna* has developed, what already exists in the *Mahābhārata*, the declaration that the three gods, Brahmā the creator, Vishnu the preserver and Shiva the destroyer, are merely manifestations of Brahm the Supreme Soul of the universe. It is not, however, content with that, and insists on identifying with Brahm its own particular deity, who has just been said to be a manifestation of Brahm. But this is merely an introduction to the still more complete pantheism with which the legend ends.

The statement that the four castes sprang from Vishnu and not from Brahmā is another illustration of the way in which the sects appropriate to their own god attributes and works that had formerly belonged to other gods. (See Note III.)

NOTE TO LEGEND XIII.

"The dread of continued rebirth is the one haunting thought which colours the whole texture of Indian philosophy," says Monier Williams, and it is the burden of the common man as well, whose constant question is how shall I get rid of the *eighty-four*, or the eighty-four lakhs of births (8,400,000) through which each soul has to pass. But it is the deeds, the actions (*karma*) of his former life which are responsible for what each one is now. He comes not trailing clouds of glory, but burdened with his accumulated load of *karma*.

To their added sorrow, the characters in the epic were exposed to the most arbitrary and unjust cursings of those they happened to offend. But this also was explained as due to *karma* or Destiny. As other legends show, both Providence and Destiny are spoken of in ways difficult to reconcile either with one another or with *karma*.

NOTE TO LEGEND XIV.

The LUNAR RACE of kings claims descent from the moon god.

The NYMPHS OF HEAVEN were produced at the churning of the ocean (I.).

The GANDHARVAS, the offspring of Kashyapa according to the orthodox view, are also said to have originated from Brahmā's nose.

DIVIDED IT INTO THREE.—" The god of fire was sometimes held to possess a kind of triple essence in himself " (Monier Williams, p. 10); and the king was told to divide the fire into three, in accordance with the precepts of the Vedas.

PURURAVAS was a grandson of the moon. *Rig-Veda*, x. 95, consists of a dialogue, "sometimes almost unintelligible," between him and Urvasi. The legend also appears in the *Shatapatha Brāhmana*, xi. 5. 1, and the *Mahābhārata*, i. 75. Max Müller considers that the story is one of the myths of the Vedas which express the correlation of the dawn and the sun. But he also observes : " We must certainly admit that even in the Veda the poets . . . were ignorant of the original meaning of Urvasi and Pururavas. To them they were heroes, indefinite beings; men, yet not men; gods, yet not gods." (*Chips from a German Workshop*, vol. ii. p. 105).

URVASI.—When the pure-minded Arjuna went to heaven, he declined to associate with Urvasi, despite the fact that the god Indra wished him to do so. In her anger the nymph cursed him to become a eunuch (*M*. iii. 46).

NOTE TO LEGEND XV.

The *Purāna* from which this legend is taken says that this king was a great-grandson of Manu, the secondary creator of the present universe, and that during his absence in heaven twenty-seven revolutions of the four ages had passed away. Twenty-seven cycles of the four ages means more than one hundred million years. When the end of a cycle approaches, according to the *Mahābhārata*, the inhabitants grow more and more evil. Wicked kings like the Yavanas or Greeks secure sovereignty. In the fourth age even the Brāhmins abstain from sacrifice and the study of the Vedas : they desert the ascetic life of the forest, and are willing to eat anything. Shūdras (*i.e.* the fourth or servile caste) become prayerful, while the Brāhmins neglect the gods. Traders use false weights, and kings oppress their subjects : famine and disease cover the earth (*M.* iii. 188). See also the quotation at the head of this legend. When the fourth age has come to an end a new cycle begins.

The first age, called Krita, lasts	. 1,728,000 years.
The second age, called Tretā, lasts	. 1,296,000 ,,
The third age, called Dwāpara, lasts	. 864,000 ,,
The fourth age, called Kali, lasts	. 432,000 ,,
Total .	. 4,320,000 ,,

One thousand cycles of the four ages equals *a day of Brahmā*. At the end of a day of Brahmā the dissolution of the universe takes place. It is first consumed with fire, and then the fire is extinguished by torrents of water : gods and demons, beasts and men have all perished. Brahmā is left alone in the universe, and when he is thus left alone he falls asleep, and he remains asleep for what is called *a night of Brahmā*, which is equal in length to one of his days (*M.* iii. 188). Later legends say that it is Vishnu, not Brahmā, who thus falls asleep, and in saying so they identify him with Brahm, the supreme spirit ; and when the night of Brahmā has expired and Vishnu awakes, a lotus springs forth from Vishnu's navel.

Brahmā the creator emerges from the lotus, and, as the
agent of Vishnu, begins to create the universe and its
inhabitants, gods and demons, beasts and men, once more
(*R.* vii. 72 ; *M.* iii. 12).

Mārkandeya, the *rishi*, who was a friend of both Rāma
and Krishna, is said to have lived through many dissolutions of the universe.   During one of the nights of Brahmā
he spent some time in Vishnu's stomach, where he saw
gods and demons, beasts and men, rivers and mountains
and seas (*M.* iii. 188).   Vishnu is pictorially represented
as reclining during this period on the great serpent Shesha,
which is also a manifestation of himself.   The serpent
again rests on the waters with his many-headed hood
suspended over Vishnu, while the lotus springs from his
navel and the four-headed Brahmā is seen emerging
therefrom.   It is a very common picture in Indian homes.

NOTE TO LEGEND XVI.

The story of Shiva's intervention at the sacrifice of
Daksha is frequently referred to in the literature of India.
See also Legend XXVI., which probably contains the earlier
form of the legend.   The beginnings of it, however, appear
in the *Yajur-Veda*, and there we may suppose it is the
assertion of Rudra's superiority over the other Vedic
gods.   But as recorded in the epics we must see in it a
struggle between the worshippers of Vishnu and Shiva.
In a strongly sectarian work like the *Hari-vansa* such a
situation could not be tolerated, and there we read that
it is Vishnu and not Brahmā who intervenes, and much
more drastically.   According to that work, when the
sacrifice was destroyed and the gods fled in dismay,
Vishnu seized Shiva by the throat and compelled him to
desist and to acknowledge his master (Dowson).

The *Mahābhārata*, with its usual impartiality, finds
room for the exclusive praise of both deities.   In the
thirteenth book, for instance, Krishna, the incarnation of
Vishnu, says that the gods, including Brahmā and Indra,
find Shiva beyond their comprehension.   It was Shiva,
and Shiva alone, whom the gods worshipped.   In a previous

birth Krishna had worshipped Shiva for millions of years,
and Krishna himself declared that it did not matter what
sins a man committed—he might be the destroyer of the
whole universe and be stained with every sort of evil—
if he worshipped Shiva these sins would all be wiped away.
Despite the fact that no one was so dear to Shiva as
Krishna, Krishna had not been able to look at Shiva.
He received, however, a number of boons, one of which
was that he should have sixteen thousand wives; he was
made acquainted with Shiva's one thousand and eight
names, and told that Shiva was the original cause of all
things, the Supreme Soul of the universe. Some of these
names are as follows : " You are existent, you are non-
existent, you are eternal time, you are the soul of all
creatures, you have big nails, you have a big stomach,
you have a large nose, you cover infinite space, you have
bloody eyes ; you are attainable by knowledge alone,
you are the supreme phallic emblem, which is worshipped
by both gods and demons ; you are the greatest of the
gods and an object of veneration even to Vishnu " (*M.*
xiii. 14–18). On the other hand, a later chapter says that
Krishna, the incarnation of Vishnu, is the lord of the
universe, the god of gods, the infinite, the foremost of all
beings and the highest Brahm.

UMĀ, the wife of Shiva, because of a quarrel between
her husband and her father, cast herself into the sacrificial
fire and became the first Sati (Suttee). The word *Sati*
means the true or virtuous woman, and was applied to
those wives who mounted the funeral pyre of their dead
husbands. The more terrific forms of Shiva's consorts
are *Durgā* and *Kāli.* " Kāli is represented as a black
woman with four arms ; in one hand she has a sword, in
another the head of a giant she has slain, with the other
two she is encouraging her worshippers. For ear-rings she
has two dead bodies, and wears a necklace of skulls ; her
only clothing is a girdle made of dead men's skulls,
and her tongue protrudes from her mouth. Her eyes
are red as those of a drunkard, and her face and breasts
are smeared with blood " (Wilkins' *Hindu Mythology,*
p. 318). Rough-coloured drawings of Kāli, as thus

described, are sold in the bazaars and hung up in Hindu homes.

NOTE TO LEGEND XVII.

The legend not only shows the exalted rank of Brāhmins as greater even than the gods, but the power of asceticism. A very sorry tale, it was told to the lofty-minded monarch to show that even the gods had sometimes to go into exile and hide themselves, just as he had to do. The narrator adds that this story is of the same rank as the Veda in sanctity.

NOTE TO LEGEND XVIII.

EVERY HYMN THEY UTTERED ADDED TO INDRA'S STRENGTH.—Compare with this the statement in the *Shatapatha Brāhmana* (3. 1, 4. 3). "By means of the sacrifice the gods obtained that supreme authority which they now wield."

AGASTYA does not usually appear in the list of the seven *rishis*, who are supposed to be the mind-born sons of Brahmā. The lists given in the *Brāhmanas* differ from those given in the epics.

NOTE TO LEGEND XIX.

Vishnu's incarnations as the Tortoise (I.) and the Fish (X.) have been given already. His chief incarnations are spoken of as ten in number : (1) the Tortoise ; (2) the Fish ; (3) the Boar (see Note VII.) ; (4) the Man-Lion ; (5) the Dwarf, to circumvent the demon Bali, a grandson of the hero of this legend (Note VII.) ; (6) Parashurāma, to slay the warrior caste (*M*. iii. 117) ; (7) Rāma (XX.) ; (8) Krishna (XXIV.) ; (9) Buddha, to deceive the demons (XXVIII.) ; and (10) Kalki, which is yet to take place, to destroy the wicked at the close of the present evil age, and re-establish righteousness (*V. P.* iv. 24).

LEARN TO ADORE VISHNU.—This legend is taken from the *Purānas*, which are some centuries later than the *Rāmāyana* and the *Mahābhārata*. In the interval the doctrine of *bhakti*, already patent in the *Bhagavadgītā*, had

had time to develop. This doctrine taught the duty of devotion and faith towards the object of one's worship. Later centuries were to develop that idea still further, as in the *Rāmāyan of Tulsidās* (1532–1623 A.D.). Students of Hinduism, such as Professor Weber, think that the introduction of faith and devotion into the Hindu system is due to the influence of Christianity. Whether that be so or not, there is no doubt that the presence of these elements is the highest and most refining influence that exists in Hinduism to-day.

The *Vishnu Purāna* also elaborates, in a way that neither of the epic poems does, the view that Vishnu is not merely one of the Hindu triad (Brahmā, Vishnu and Shiva), but that he is the eternal spirit Brahm, with whom the individual spirit also must seek to be identified. The reader will not fail to contrast this lofty language with the gruesome narrative of how the man-lion tore to pieces the demon king.

SĀMA-VEDA is the third Veda, but it is almost entirely drawn from the *Rig-Veda*, the earliest of the four. It was specially arranged for musical purposes.

BRAHM IS MY NAME.—As this book is for the general reader, it has been thought best to read Brahm for the eternal Soul of the Universe, *i.e.* Brahma (final " a " short) to avoid confusion with Brahmā (final " a " long), the creator god. In the second part of this book the reader will obtain many illustrations of the central doctrine of philosophic Hinduism : " I am all things, all things are in me, Brahm is my name " ; the way of knowledge which leads to emancipation and saves from the burden of re-birth. Such a belief, however, does not abolish the gods. It merely recognises their temporary and subordinate nature. In the *Bhagavadgītā*, Krishna, while declaring himself to be the Supreme Spirit, says, " Those who worship the gods go to the gods, and my worshippers likewise go to me " (vii. 23, ix. 25), and " even the gods are always desiring to see this form of mine " (xi. 52).

Note to Legend XX.

RĀVANA SAW THE THREE WORLDS IN THE STOMACH OF VISHNU. — This is a very common conceit. In the *Bhagavadgītā*, when Arjuna was favoured with a vision of Krishna in his divine form, he cried out, " O god ! I see within thy body the gods, as also all the groups of various beings ; and the lord Brahmā seated on his lotus seat, and all the sages and celestial snakes " (xi. 15).

THE GOLDEN PHALLUS.—The *Padma Purāna* says that the employment of the male and female reproductive organs as the emblems of Shiva and his wife was due to a curse pronounced by the sage Bhrigu, when the god, owing to being immersed in pleasure, failed to grant him an interview (Wilkins' *Hindu Mythology*, p. 288).

GARUDA, the vehicle of Vishnu. See Note IX.

RĀVANA, great-grandson of Brahmā ; his grandfather was Pulastya, one of Brahmā's mind-born sons and one of the seven *rishis*. According to one narrative, Pulastya was the father of the demon race.

Note to Legend XXI.

DASHARATHA'S AGE.—Another version says he was sixty thousand years old.

AYODHYĀ, the capital of Koshala, the modern Oudh, in the United Provinces ; probably not far from the present Fyzabad.

THE WHITE UMBRELLA was the emblem of sovereignty.

THE THIRTY-THREE GODS.—See Note I.

THERE IS NO HEAVEN FOR A SONLESS MAN.—See Note VIII.

THE BUDDHIST AS A THIEF.—For Hinduism's attitude to Buddhism, see Legend XXVIII.

Note to Legend XXII.

The reader is referred to Legends XXX. and XXXIV. for other pictures of Indian womanhood, and also to Note B.

VĀLMĪKI, the author of the *Rāmāyana*, was, according

to i. 2, commanded by Brahmā to compose that work, with the promise that it would not contain a single untruth. By virtue of his *yoga* powers the poet was able to see the characters of his poem "laughing, talking and bearing themselves as in real life."

SĪTĀ'S SECOND REPUDIATION.—It is difficult to understand why the poet should attribute such base and callous conduct to his hero. Happily for Rāma's fame, there is reason for believing that a later and meaner hand is responsible for making this futile addition to the original poem. Tulsidās, in his work, ignores this second repudiation.

LAKSHMANA'S character is almost consistently of a high order. It is all the more wonderful that he should be represented as feeling comforted by this story. The duty of giving shelter to a suppliant is recognised as always binding on mortals. The sage who cursed Vishnu was Bhrigu, who cursed Shiva on another occasion. See Note XX.

NOTE TO LEGEND XXIII.

SHŪDRA.—The members of the fourth caste were not allowed to practise asceticism, to read or listen to the Vedas. The Brāhmin who explained the law to a Shūdra or dictated to him a penance, was told that he would go down with his pupil to the hell that had no bounds. His name had to be one expressive of contempt. It was no great matter to kill a Shūdra. The penance for killing him was the same as that appointed for killing a dog, a lizard or a crow. But no penance could expiate the killing of a Brāhmin (see *Laws of Manu*, i. 91, ii. 31, xi. 90 and xi. 132). The earlier books of the *Rāmāyana* do not indicate such contempt for the low caste, or even for the outcaste.

DURVĀSA.—We shall find in another legend (XXVII.) that this ill-natured *rishi* again interfered with equally disastrous results. Durvāsa's asceticism had apparently no effect on his moral character. Unfortunately, asceticism and morals were not often related. "Such an ascetic," says Hopkins, "has no ordinary rules of morality. In fact, his practices are most peculiar, for to seduce young women is one of his commonest occupations; and in his anger, to cause an injury to his foes is one of the ends for which he toils. The gods are nothing to him. They are puppets whom he makes shake and tremble at will. As portrayed in the epic in terms of common sense, the Muni (silent saint) is a morose and very vulgar-minded old man, who seeks to intimidate others by a show of miraculous power." Mr. Hopkins recognises, of course, that there were others of a different type, and it should be remembered that Vishvāmitra's asceticism did not prevail till he had conquered both anger and lust.

LAKSHMI, the goddess of prosperity, was supposed to have appeared in the form of Sītā.

OM (AUM).—Monier Williams suggests that the three letters AUM were originally the initial letters of the names of Fire, Wind and Sun, that is, Agni, Vāyu and Mitra. In later times they were taken to typify Brahmā, Vishnu and Shiva. "The syllable OM is the supreme Brahm and can never be destroyed" (*L. of M.* ii. 83, 84).

GĀYATRĪ VERSE.—See Note XI.

EVEN THE MOST DEGRADED.—See also the passage in the *Bhagavadgītā*. "Even those who are of sinful birth, women, members of the third caste and the fourth caste, likewise resorting to me, attain the supreme goal. What then need be said of holy Brāhmins and royal saints who are my devotees" (ix. 32).

IF THEY SEE ALL THINGS IN VISHNU.—The reader will not find such a pantheistic statement in the earlier books of the *Rāmāyana*.

NOTE TO LEGEND XXIV.

MUTTRA (Mathura), on the banks of the Jumna River. As the birthplace of Krishna, it is still a place of pilgrimage.

SEA OF MILK.—See Legend I.

NĀRADA, known as the monkey-faced or mischief-maker, because of the satisfaction he found in causing strife. He travelled constantly between earth and heaven. In a quarrel he had with the creator, Brahmā condemned him to a life of sensuality. In reply, he cursed Brahmā to commit the sin of incest and to be unworthy of the worship of men.

BALARĀMA.—See Legend XV. for the story of his bride. Cow DUNG is still reckoned as very holy.

THE SNAKE WAS MERELY FULFILLING THE LAW OF ITS BEING.—See *Bhagavadgītā* (xviii. 47), where it says : " One's duty though defective is better than another's duty well performed. Performing the duty prescribed by nature, one does not commit sin. One should not abandon a natural duty—though tainted with evil."

THE WIVES AND DAUGHTERS OF THE COWHERDS.—The best comment on these incidents is to quote from the *Prem Sāgar*, c. 34, which is the Hindi version of the tenth book of the *Bhāgavata Purāna*. "Then taking the cow-herdesses, Krishna went to the banks of the Jumna, entered the water, and having relieved fatigue and come out and satisfied the desire of all, he said, ' Now four gharis of the night remain, do you all go home.' . . . On hearing this remark . . . each went to her own home ; and no one of the families knew the secret that they had not been there." The listener to this statement interrogated the narrator as follows : " Why did Krishna dance and sport with the wives of others ? This, indeed, is the act of a libertine, who enjoys the wife of another." And the answer he received was, " Revere the actions of Hari, but do not give your mind to the doing of them."

NOTE TO LEGEND XXV.

BHĪMA.—In other parts of the epic he shows himself of a lower type than his brothers (xxxiv.). On Krishna's conduct here also, we have the *Mahābhārata's* own observation : " As to those acts of the gods and the ascetics, a pious man should never imitate them, or when he hears of them should never censure them " (xii. 292. 18). Unfortunately there have always been others who, like Bhīma, thought there could be no harm in copying the example of the gods. Krishna himself was of that opinion.

THE GODS HAD USED DECEIT.—See Legend I.

Note to Legend XXVI.

Sacrifice of Daksha.—See Legend XVI.

Bhaga, Savitar and Pushan were all Vedic deities.
It is to Savitar as the Sun that the Gāyatrī verse was
addressed. The story gives hints of the time when the
other Vedic gods were being pushed aside by the Rudra,
who ultimately became the great god Shiva.

Shiva.—See also Note XVI. When Krishna and Arjuna,
in the hope of obtaining Shiva's assistance in battle, paid
a visit to Shiva's heaven, Krishna sang his praises as the
creator of the universe and the highest Brahm, the source
of all. Shiva addressed Krishna and his companion as
the foremost of men, while Arjuna to his great amazement saw lying beside Shiva the offerings he had nightly
presented to Vishnu (*M*. vii. 80). After the battle a sort
of reconciliation of opposites was achieved when Krishna
said, " I am the soul of the worlds ; Rudra (Shiva) again
is my soul. It is for this that I always worship him. If
that god of gods be adored, then is Vishnu always adored.
If I do not worship him, nobody would worship my own
self " (*M*. xii. 342). Hopkins remarks that Brahmā never
had a strong sect to push his claims as the two other
deities had. But it is worth noting that both *R*. (vi. 106)
and *M*. (iii. 3) have hymns in praise of the Sun, which
not only say that he is all the other gods, who are duly
named, but assert that the other gods obtained their
lofty state as a reward of worshipping him.

Condemned his proposal as immoral.—Despite the
recognition of this fact, the sacrificer was able by the
power of his sacrifice to secure the assistance of the god
in the performance of a wicked deed. No legend shows
more clearly the divorce between religion and morals.

Note to Legend XXVII.

Yoga.—See Note XI.

Balarāma.—For his manifestation as Shesha, see
Legend XXIV. It is on Shesha that Vishnu reclines
during the intervals of creation. It was Shesha, or

Vasuki, whom the gods made use of at the churning of the ocean.

NĀRĀYANA.—This name was originally an epithet of Brahmā and was appropriated by Vishnu; so called because the waters (*nara*) were his first dwelling-place (*ayana*) (*L. of M.* i. 10).

SATI.—See Note XVI.

NOTE TO LEGEND XXVIII.

That demons as well as gods, bad men as well as good, read the Vedas and practised asceticism and other religious rites, is clear from both the epics and the *Purānas*.

JAINS.—This sect still exists in Western India.

BUDDHISTS.—For many centuries there have been no Buddhists in India. They still prevail in Burmah and Ceylon. The *Bhāgavata Purāna* cleverly brings in a reference to both heresies by saying: "Vishnu will become incarnate under the name of Buddha, the son of Jina, for the purpose of deluding the enemy of the gods." The *Skanda Purāna* also refers to the delusive instructions of Buddha, who spoke "with a low, sweet and affectionate voice" (Wilkins' *Mythology*, p. 230). It was the atheistic implications of the Buddha's teaching, "this world exists without support," which offended India as much as his criticism of the Vedas and his abuse of Brāhmins.

NOTE TO LEGEND XXIX.

SVAYAMVARA was the maiden's choice of her husband. This practice was not uncommon among the warrior caste at least.

VIDEHA was the country of Sītā, the wife of Rāma. It corresponds with Northern Bihār. Vaidishā is the modern Bhīlsa in Central India.

CHANGED INTO A DOG.—It is usually assumed that the soul spends long periods in heaven or hell between each life on earth.

THE PRINCESS CAUSED THE PEACOCK TO BE BATHED.— "The man who, after confessing his crime, . . . bathes at the close of a horse sacrifice is freed from guilt " (*L. of M*. xi. 83).

NOTE TO LEGEND XXXI.

WHEN HIS DAUGHTER REACHED PUBERTY.—This passage indicates that early marriage was not approved of. It is spoken of as the characteristic of the fourth or evil age, that girls of seven years of age give birth to children (*M*. iii. 188), while in *M*. i. 64, it is said that in the first or golden age marriage never took place till womanhood was reached. On the other hand, it is distinctly laid down as a law that a man of thirty should marry a girl of ten and a man of twenty-one a girl of seven (*M*. xiii. 44). *Manu* says that a father may give his daughter in marriage even before the proper age if the bridegroom is good-looking and worthy. He does not say what the proper age is, but some commentators say that the proper age is eight years (ix. 88).

NOTE TO LEGEND XXXII.

NALA NEGLECTED TO WASH HIS FEET.—See Diti's blunder, Legend II.

KALI-YUGA.—See Note XV. Time itself is personified in Legend XXIII. *Yuga* means " age."

NOTE TO LEGEND XXXIV.

FIVE BROTHERS HAD ONE WIFE.—The authors of the epic try to excuse the polyandry by saying that Draupadi on five separate occasions asked Shiva to give her a husband, and the god granted her prayer literally.

THE FATHER OF THE RACE.—Kashyapa. See Note I.

RIGHTEOUSNESS CARES FOR THE RIGHTEOUS.—Shortly before this incident Balarāma, the incarnation of Vishnu, said to Draupadi : " I do not find that the practice of virtue leads to any good, or that sinful practices cause any evil. The great-souled Yudhisthira wanders in the forest and his wicked cousins rule the earth."

THE CREATOR.—Commenting on this incident, Professor Hopkins remarks : " The theological position taken, the absence of Vishnu, the appeal to the creator as the highest power, takes one back to a former age." One of the words employed for God is Ishana, which means *master, lord*, an epithet of Shiva primarily, but also of Vishnu.

THE GREAT LAW-GIVER MANU.—In *L. of M.* vii. 205, we read that "all undertakings in this world depend both on the ordering of fate and human exertion."

NOTE TO LEGEND XXXVI.

EATING AFTER A HUSBAND.—This, the rule in ancient India, still prevails to-day.

RATNIDEVA used to kill twenty-one thousand cows on one night to feed his Brāhmin guests. His cooks, who numbered two hundred thousand, were so anxious there would not be enough of meat that they urged the guests to drink a lot of soup (*M.* vii. 67).

ANIMALS SACRIFICED GO TO HEAVEN.—See the scornful references to this by the *Chārvākas* (XXVIII.). In the *Rig-Veda*, i. 162, it is said that the horse when sacrificed goes to the gods. "No! here thou diest not; thou art not injured. By easy paths unto the gods thou goest."

STICK TO THE PRECEPTS AND PRACTICES OF YOUR OWN CASTE.—See quotation from *Bhagavadgītā* in Note XXIV.

REPENTANCE PURGES THE HEART.—There are so few references to repentance in this or any other Indian book that one would like to quote in full from the *Laws of Manu* (xi. 229, 231) the fine utterance: "In proportion as a man who has done wrong himself confesses it, even so far is he freed from his guilt as a snake is freed from its slough. In proportion as his heart loathes his evil deeds, even so far is his body freed from that guilt. He who has committed a sin and has repented, is freed from that sin, but he is purified only by the resolution of ceasing to sin and thinking, 'I will do so no more.'" In the *Mahābhārata*, xiii. 112. 4, we have a statement similar to that of the fowler. "A man who feels the pangs of repentance and sets his heart on meditation has not to suffer the consequences of his sin. A man becomes freed from his sins inasmuch as he repents of them."

IT IS VERY DIFFICULT FOR A MAN OF LOW BIRTH TO
ACQUIRE DIVINE MYSTERIES.—" Never give advice to a
Shūdra, and never explain the sacred law to him.   If you
do, you will go to hell " (*L. of M*. iv. 80, 81).

NOTE TO LEGEND XXXVII.

STRIKING A BRĀHMIN.—See heading to Legend III.

STRIKING A COW.—Strange to say, the *Laws of Manu*,
much of whose material is drawn from the same source
as the *Mahābhārata*, speaks of killing a cow as one of the
minor sins, and prescribes a penance of three months'
duration.   It includes bathing in the urine of cows, serving
and worshipping them (xi. 60, 109).

SANSKRIT.—From a number of references we infer that
at the time the epics were written the common people
did not speak Sanskrit, but dialects derived therefrom ;
Prākrits.

NOTE TO LEGEND XXXVIII.

The *Bhagavadgītā*, which has been introduced into the
Mahābhārata, is professedly the argument of the god
Krishna to persuade ARJUNA, one of the Pāndu princes,
to fight, when he also was reluctant to slay his fellow-
countrymen.

THE GODS MOST WORSHIPPED ARE ALL DESTROYERS AND
REMORSELESS.—In the *Rāmāyana*, Rāma says that people
in their ignorance pay no heed to Brahmā when he shows
himself compassionate, although he is the best of all the
gods (iii. 64).

LIBERATION AND ANNIHILATION.—In *M*. xii. 302,
Yudhisthira asked Bhīshma to say plainly if there was
consciousness in *liberation*.   If there was not, then he
thought that the religion of works was superior.   If consciousness disappeared with liberation, then the liberated
person was like a person sunk in dreamless slumber.
Bhīshma confessed that even learned people were stupefied
in answering this question.   He insisted, however, that
liberation and knowledge were best, presumably because

the soul would come back no more. " Freed from both merit and demerit, the individual soul, entering the Supreme Soul which is shorn of all attributes, . . . does not return " (verse 97).

NOTE TO LEGEND XXXIX.

THE VEDA SAYS WE ARE TO PERFORM ACTS, IT ALSO SAYS WE ARE TO REFRAIN FROM ACTS.—See *Bhagavadgītā*, v. 1, where Arjuna says, " O Krishna, you praise renunciation of actions and also the pursuit of them ; tell me determinately which one of these two is superior " ; and he gets no very distinct answer.

RELIGION OF HARMLESSNESS.—Ahinsā, or non-injury.

VASHAT.—An exclamation used in making an oblation to a deity with fire. For OM, see Note XI. In *R.* i. 65, Vishvāmitra says, " Let OMkār and Vashatkār crown me." They are both personified in *R.* vii. 122, and attend Rāma on his way to heaven in company with the four Vedas and the Gāyatrī verse.

THE SACRIFICER AND THE ANIMAL SACRIFICED GO TO HEAVEN TOGETHER.—See Legends XXVIII. and XXXVI.

PERFORMANCE OF ACTS ONLY SECURES A TEMPORARY REWARD.—When they have exhausted their stock of merit they return to this world. " Those who wish for objects of desire and resort to the ordinances of the three Vedas, obtain as the fruit going and coming " (*i.e.* transmigration or rebirth) (*Bhag.* ix. 20). " Kapila appears in this story as a teacher of unorthodox non-injury, and maintains to the end (so that his view is presented as really correct) that not the sacrifice of animals, but the sacrifice (worship) of knowledge is the best. Elsewhere also, we find the same antithesis between the old orthodoxy and the new science of thought which not only disregards Vedic ceremonies, but condemns them " (Hopkins, *The Great Epic of India*, p. 99). It will be remembered that to the disciples of *yoga* the ordinary heaven is little better than hell. It is at best a temporary state of happiness, and does not save from rebirth.

Note to Legend XL.

A CLOD OF EARTH, A STONE AND A PIECE OF GOLD ARE ALL THE SAME TO ME.—This is a common phrase; see *Bhag.* vi. 8, and Legend XLV.

THE TEACHING OF THE VEDAS.—The Vedas were appealed to on behalf of the most conflicting teaching. Growse, the translator of Tulsidās' *Rāmāyan*, says: "Though Tulsidās constantly appeals to the authority of the Vedas, it is clear that, like nine hundred and ninety-nine out of a thousand of the most educated of his countrymen at the present day, he had not the faintest idea of their contents" (p. 399).

FAITH.—*Shraddhā* is not the same as *bhakti*, devotion, though some writers are inclined to translate *bhakti* as faith. The birds said: "Those acts that injure others destroy faith, and faith being destroyed brings ruin on the destroyer. Only one person in the world, viz., he who has no faith, is unfit to make offerings to the gods. Want of faith is a great sin. Faith is a purifier of sins. The religion of abstention (from injury) is superior to all sacred things" (*M.* xii. 264).

Note to Legend XLI.

The Three Qualities or *gunas* are: goodness or purity; passion or activity; and darkness or ignorance; *sattva*, *rajas*, and *tamas*. According to the *Laws of Manu*, all existences are pervaded by the three qualities at all times. The character of each soul depends on which of these dominates the body, xii. 24-50. The Supreme Soul is quality-less, *nir-guna*.

Note to Legend XLIII.

BY THE GRACE OF THE CREATOR.—"This is an important passage," says Hume, "as being the first explicit statement of the doctrine of grace (*prasāda*). . . . This method of salvation is directly opposed to the general Upanishadic doctrine of salvation through knowledge" (p. 350).

NOTE TO LEGEND XLV.

DURVĀSA.—Here is Durvāsa once more ; see legends XXIII. and XXVII.

EVEN AT THE DISSOLUTION OF THE UNIVERSE THEY CONTINUE TO EXIST.—It is usually said that all creatures, *i.e.* gods, demons, men and beasts, perish at the dissolution of the universe except Brahmā, who lives for one hundred years—years whose days each constitute the duration of a universe.

NIRVĀNA.—" Blown out, gone out, put out, extinguished (as a fire), lost, disappeared, liberated from existence (literally having the fire of life extinguished) : dead, deceased, defunct, set (as a planet), calmed, quieted . . . dissolution, liberation, eternal bliss, emancipation from matter and reunion with the deity, union with the supreme spirit," etc. (see Monier Williams' *Dictionary*, p. 500).

NOTE TO LEGEND XLVI.

THERE WERE FIVE BROTHERS.—These are the five Pāndus referred to so often in previous legends.

BIBLIOGRAPHY.

Rāmāyana : translated into English verse. Ralph T. H. Griffith. (Luzac & Co., London.)

Rāmāyana : translated into English prose. Manmatha N. Dutt. 2 vols. (Calcutta.)

Mahābhārata : translated into English prose. Manmatha N. Dutt. 3 vols. (Calcutta.)

Mahābhārata : translated into Hindi. 18 vols. (Nawal Kishore Press, Lucknow.)

Upanishads, Thirteen Principal. Translation, R. E. Hume. New York. (Milford.)

Brāhmana, Aitareya. With English translation, Haug. 2 vols. (Trübner & Co.)

Brāhmana, Shatapatha. Translation, Eggeling. 5 vols. (S.B.E.) (Clarendon Press.)

Bhagavadgītā. Translation, Telang. (S.B.E.) (Clarendon Press.)

Laws of Manu. Translation, Bühler. (S.B.E.) (Clarendon Press.)

Prem Sāgar. Translation, Eastwick. (A. Constable & Co.)

Vishnu Purāna. Translation, H. H. Wilson. 5 vols. (Trübner & Co.)

Original Sanskrit Texts. With English translation, Muir. 5 vols. (Trübner & Co.)